*F R E U D: Political and Social Thought*

# FREUD

*Political and Social Thought*

*Paul Roazen*

Vintage Books
*A DIVISION OF RANDOM HOUSE / NEW YORK*

Copyright © 1968 by Paul Roazen

All rights reserved under International and Pan-American Copyright Conventions. Published in the United States by Alfred A. Knopf, Inc., New York, and simultaneously in Canada by Random House of Canada Limited, Toronto. Distributed by Random House, Inc., New York. Originally published by Alfred A. Knopf, Inc., in 1968.

*Grateful acknowledgment is made to the following persons and firms who have allowed the use of copyrighted material in this book:*

*To Basic Books, Inc., for quotations from* Collected Papers of Sigmund Freud, *edited by Ernest Jones, M.D.*

*To The Hogarth Press Ltd., Sigmund Freud Copyrights Ltd., and the Estate of Mr. James Strachey for quotations from* Standard Edition of the Complete Psychological Works of Sigmund Freud, *edited by James Strachey.*

*To Basic Books, Inc., The Hogarth Press Ltd., and Sigmund Freud Copyrights Ltd. for quotations from* The Letters of Sigmund Freud, 1873–1939, *edited by Ernst L. Freud.*

*To Basic Books, Inc., Mrs. Katherine Jones, and The Hogarth Press Ltd. for quotations from* The Life and Work of Sigmund Freud, *by Ernest Jones, M.D. (published in Great Britain as* Sigmund Freud: Life and Work)

*To Basic Books, Inc., The Hogarth Press Ltd., and Sigmund Freud Copyrights Ltd. for quotations from* The Origins of Psychoanalysis *by Sigmund Freud, edited by Maria Bonaparte, Anna Freud, and Ernst Kris.*

Library of Congress Catalog Card Number: 68-12670

Manufactured in the United States of America

Vintage Books Edition, September 1970

*For my Mother and Father*

*Preface*

Since the themes within this book tend to move in several directions at the same time, a few prefatory remarks might help the reader keep the general argument in focus. The title of the book combines those intellectual traditions in which I have grown up. By "Freud" I am referring to his own writings and those of the psychiatric community which can be traced directly to his inspiration. I cannot claim to have examined comprehensively all the new developments in the psychiatry of our time. It is my conviction, however, that the ideas of Freud and his pupils, and what they have to contribute to our understanding of human nature, are important enough in intellectual history to justify treatment as a self-sufficient unit. "Political and Social Thought" in academic life has come to mean a grab bag of moral and legal ideas, in addition to more strictly social and political concepts; it also has a heritage, however, of the most re-spected kind, which begins with the philosophic activities of Plato and Aristotle, and which has over the centuries tried to relate human needs to social life.

The multiple audience at which this book is directed might welcome a rough road map, so that readers with dif-

fering interests can know when they will encounter what
they can afford to skip. For the general reader and those
more specifically interested in Freud than in problems of
social science, the liveliest starting point is probably Chapter II. The Introduction discusses the methodological road-
blocks to applying psychoanalysis in the study of politics,
and should be of interest mainly to those with a professional commitment to political science. Chapter I provides
a general view of psychoanalytic concepts and their use
in the human sciences, and suggests some of the more
basic implications of Freud's postulation of unconscious mental processes for normative and empirical research. While
Chapter I is a schematic presentation of Freud's ideas, Chapter II presents them in their historical sequence and sociological context. I have not hesitated throughout to apply
Freud's theories to explain the development of his own
ideas.

The remaining chapters of the book examine Freud's
own applications of his concepts to social life and explore
some of the implications of his work for political and social thought. In the context of Freud's essays on religion,
Chapter III raises such problems as the justification for punishment, the nature of authority relationships, the possibilities for human spontaneity, and the existence of cultural
continuities. The last section of this chapter contains my
most sustained attempt at understanding Freud's mind and
character through the analysis of a text—*Moses and Monotheism*.

Using Freud's essays on war and social cohesion as the
main textual vehicles, Chapter IV focuses on the psychology
of aggression and the issues involved in limit-setting and
permissiveness. Recent advances in ego psychology make it
possible to extend the relevance of Freud's own contribu-

tions to social philosophy. Chapter V discusses some of the more normative aspects of Freud's notions, such as cultural reform, the problem of psychological health, and freedom as a moral value.

The Introduction and Chapters I through V were completed before the publication of the Freud-Bullitt study of Woodrow Wilson, so the Epilogue tries to bring together my previous analyses in order to make the oddity of that collaborative effort more comprehensible. Here too I found that an understanding of Freud's own psychology was crucial in illuminating some of the major causes of that book's limitations.

Much of the contemporary research which to a greater or less extent utilizes Freudian theory will not be discussed here, unless it raises major theoretical questions. While I have not examined anything like all the social and political research which has drawn on the Freudian tradition, I have tried to discuss the whole range of concepts involved in relating the Freudian view of man to society.

My own personal experience lies behind the conception of this book. As an undergraduate honors candidate specializing in political theory in the Harvard Government Department (1954–8), I was introduced to many exciting approaches to the study of politics. But it was at the University of Chicago, as a beginning graduate student in political science, that I first developed a working acquaintance with Freud's ideas and began to consider the significance of unconscious motives in human behavior for political philosophy. The next year (1959–60) I studied political theory at Oxford, and although this ancient tradition was carried on in a very elaborate way, depth psychology was not an acknowledged part of the curriculum. Since that time I have tried to work out some of the ways of using psychodynamic concepts in political theory. If parts of this book seem too elementary to some, I can only say that it attempts to fill a gap which, as a result of my education, I am convinced still exists widely within political science as a whole.

Many people have helped my work, but I will thank here only those who read this manuscript for me. Above all, Louis Hartz and Judith Shklar have sustained me, with their encouragement and criticism, during the years in which this book evolved. Other social scientists who have read it for me and to whom I am grateful include Suzanne Berger, David Greenstone, Bertha Heller, Alex Inkeles, Sanford Lakoff, Alan Ritter, John Rodman, and Michael Rogin. Among the psychoanalysts I am greatly indebted to the inspiration of Dr. Helene Deutsch; Dr. Elizabeth Rosenberg Zetzel has also made useful suggestions to me. I am deeply grateful to my wife, Deborah Heller Roazen, for all her patient editing.

I wish to thank the London Institute of Psychoanalysis for giving me permission to consult the Ernest Jones Archives. The Massachusetts Mental Health Center has been good enough to permit me to attend case conferences, and the Boston Psychoanalytic Institute's granting of guest privileges has enabled me to attend their meetings. The Harvard Government Department has been very generous in giving me research time. The Committee on Legal and Political Philosophy of the Social Science Research Council has helped this work by its fellowship support.

P. R.

*Cambridge, Massachusetts*
*May 1967*

# Contents

*F R E U D: Political and Social Thought*

*INTRODUCTION*

# Human Nature in Politics

## Psychology and Politics

Almost every college instructor in an introductory course in political science will point out that all political philosophies in the past have been based on theories of human nature. One could scarcely find a more recurrent problem in political theory than the concept of human nature, and yet at present very few political theorists focus on this issue. Still, it is hard to imagine how any of the humanistic sciences are going to be able to develop very far without a fairly systematic notion of human motivation. While there are a number of approaches to useful theoretical constructions of personality, many contemporaries have either implicitly or explicitly chosen the alternative of psychoanalysis. Whatever the inadequacies of psychoanalytic formulations, they at least have their roots in clinical work; that is, in the direct observation of human nature. As Freud once put it, "our theories are based on experience . . . and not just fabricated out of thin air or thought up over the writing desk."[1] It has been clear to many that psychoanalysis, as a working theory for clinicians, has valuable possibilities for political thought. Freud's postulation of unconscious mental processes ranks as a turning point in how human beings think about themselves.

At times Freud himself was boldly hopeful, if not a bit grandiose, about the future relevance of psychoanalysis for other fields.

As a "depth psychology," a theory of the mental unconscious, it can become indispensable to all the sciences which are concerned with the evolution of human civilization and its major institutions such as art, religion and the social order . . . I can assure you that the hypothesis of there being unconscious mental processes paves the way to a decisive new orientation in the world and in science.[2]

Students of politics have been intermittently aware of Freud's innovations in our understanding of human psychology. Walter Lippmann deserves the credit for being one of the first to seize upon the potential implications of psychoanalysis for political science. By the time that Lippmann's interests had begun to shift, Harold Lasswell in turn was using depth psychology in political studies.

And yet when one surveys the history of the relationship of psychoanalysis to the study of politics, it is easy to feel a sense of disappointment. Whatever insistence on psychodynamic theory there has been, the work has tended to be very

[1] S. Freud: *Psychoanalysis and Faith*, ed. H. Meng and E. Freud (New York: Basic Books; 1963), p. 27.

[2] *The Standard Edition of the Complete Psychological Works of Sigmund Freud*, ed. James Strachey (London: Hogarth Press; 1953–     ), Vol. 20, p. 248, and Vol. 15, p. 22. Hereafter this edition of Freud's works will be referred to simply as *Standard Edition*.

readily dissolved within academic political science. A psychoanalytically informed work such as *The Authoritarian Personality* has had little permanent professional impact; the study of personality theory is still of very marginal interest to political scientists. As a result, Freud has not yet become part of the conventional wisdom of academic political thinking. In a recent study of public opinion, a political scientist in the forefront of the discipline commented that "one of the troubles about Freudian psychology is that once a person begins to believe it, he can believe anything."[3] When one does find interest in psychology and politics, one wonders whether the necessary priorities have been properly established. Freud's concepts are at best treated as of equal status to those of his pupils, whose work would be inconceivable if read apart from the writings of their great teacher. Meanwhile Freud has remained throughout political science something of a spook.

Within social theory itself, taken in a very broad sense, there has been a vast, if vague, testimony of the relevance of psychoanalytic theory. David Riesman's concept of "other-direction," for example, is an amplification of the "marketing-orientation" of Erich Fromm. Many others, each in their individual way, have had their encounters with the work of Freud and his students. It is hard to imagine any contemporary social theorist with genuinely constructive interests not being influenced by Freud.

One reason for this pervasive, even if only partially self-conscious, use of psychoanalytic doctrine is the relative disenchantment with Marx. Due to the collapse of many of his hopes and the blasting of many of his predictions, Marx is not the figure in contemporary Western intellectual

[3] V. O. Key: *Public Opinion and American Democracy* (New York: Knopf; 1961), p. 293.

life that he was thirty years ago. While Freud is by no means a precise substitute, he has helped to fill the gap. Even though in any obvious sense Freud may not seem as socially relevant, certain aspects of his ideas make him equally attractive.

The systematic character of Freud's thought, for example, matches that of Marx; indeed, much of the disinclination to use Freud stems from the memory of unhappy experiences with Marx. Freud presented his findings in an integrated, internally consistent system. Throughout his life he tried to incorporate his fresh observations into increasingly encompassing theoretical form. And since his death there have been renewed attempts at systematization. As a theory increases in elegance, its intellectual attractiveness usually grows; while a series of new observations about human nature might be useful, interesting but not compelling, packaged as a vast system they become less resistible. Freud's thought is coherent enough to comprise a system, centering as it does on the unconscious, and at certain points it is abstract enough to attract speculative minds.

Not only has Freudian theory plugged the intellectual hole of Marxism, but it has also provided for some a similar basis for radical aspirations. It is possible to find in Freud not merely a substructure for one's ideas, a central intellectual core, but also a moral criticism of the *status quo*. Freud was throughout his work a caustic critic of Victorian sexual hypocrisy, arguing on behalf of individual self-fulfillment. In his essays on religion it is possible to see most explicitly the utopian strain in his thinking; in other respects, too, it has become a commonplace to see Freud as a child of the Enlightenment, relentlessly reasonable in the face of the irrational. "Freudian doctrine . . . from a historical perspective was but the logical continuation of the rationalistic tradition: to understand natural phenomena, including those of the mind, on the basis of scientific principles."[4]

If the decline of Marxism has been partially met by a wave of interest in psychoanalysis, the kind of work which uses psychoanalytic theory has been colored and distorted by this historical association. On the whole there has been an extravagant character to much of the social utilizations of psychoanalysis, which has no doubt contributed to the corresponding shyness of professional political scientists. In the hands of the insensitive, psychoanalytic principles become overblown, if not phony, in their social applications. There is the danger here not only of producing a second-rate sociology, but also of possibly underemploying the strictly psychological perspective that was Freud's. The character of some of Freud's own all-encompassing aims, especially in his later years, has also helped to obscure what one might think would be the obvious contribution he made for the study of political life—a psychological theory of the human personality.

A good part of the difficulty here, the failure to scale down what psychoanalysis can contribute as well as to exploit what it legitimately offers, can be traced to a split within the history of psychoanalytic thought itself. Even while Freud was alive, psychoanalysts were not too clear what the relation was between Freud's social thought and his clinical theories; but then one could count on there being some personal integration for Freud himself between these two strands in his work. Since his death, the situation has grown far more acute; as psychoanalysis became almost exclusively a medical specialty, Freud's social thought received almost no attention at all from psychoanalysts themselves. The re-

[4] Franz Alexander: *The Western Mind in Transition* (New York: Random House; 1960), p. 50.

sult is that today Freud's books on social matters have almost no meaning to professional psychoanalysts. On the other hand, this aspect of Freud's thought was continued by social theorists who had little concern for the clinical preoccupations which Freud himself took for granted.

The upshot of these two diverging trends of Freud's thought has been harmful for both groups. For example, the study of Freud's social thought can contribute to the larger understanding of Freud's mind and character, and therefore to our deeper comprehension of his psychology and its limitations. For while psychoanalytic principles, or at least some of them, have scientific status, everything that Freud wrote was in a sense self-revelatory and autobiographical. This can be seen most clearly where Freud is least objective; the piety among psychoanalysts has left his books on Leonardo and Moses, and now Woodrow Wilson, in an interpretive limbo. In all these cases Freud was using a historical figure as a projective screen for his self-understanding. It is hardly enough to point to the "mistakes" in these studies, "errors" that Freud committed which detract from their objective validity; it would be untrue to the spirit of Freud himself not to attempt to explain what conflicts might have motivated these "errors."

If psychoanalysis has lost in richness because it has become narrower than the legacy Freud bequeathed to history, political theory has sacrificed something by its one-sided treatment of his social thought. By relying only on Freud's social thought, apart from his clinical contributions, one would get a very strange view of psychoanalytic theory. In fact there is a rather hothouse quality about much of the recent interest in Freud's social thought; it is divorced not only from clinical psychoanalysis, but from the inner preoccupations of Freud in those social works. The alternative would be to reunite the social as well as the clinical strands in his work.

For a political theorist to study Freud's social works requires more than just a mechanical enterprise of a collaborative sort; all too often social scientists are apt to think that problems in self-education can be skipped by temporarily putting a practitioner of one discipline in the same room as the practitioner of another. The ideal would be to have these contrasting talents integrated, even if only partially, within the individuals themselves, so that in the future they can rely on expert authority when it proves relevant. But this strategy presupposes that the individuals are sufficiently knowledgeable to be able to spot ahead of time the type of problem for which outside help would be useful.

In this chapter and the next, problems of political research will be in the forefront; later on it will be evident that certain classical problems of moral theory can also be reinterpreted in the light of Freud's ideas. The purpose of such a study is to fulfill a traditional role of political theory: the clarification of conceptual issues that arise in the discussion of political life. Historical scholarship is necessary; it is hoped that it will be textual criticism with a purpose. The study of political theory too often becomes Talmudic; the breakdown in communications between the theorist and the fieldworker is well known and much lamented. Much of political theorizing has left us with a narrow conception of man, too lifeless for field work and too desiccated for adequate moral theory. Political theory should be studied not just as an academic exercise, but because it helps to enlarge one's imagination.

The job of the political theorist is pre-eminently conceptual: to think about how we think. To say that psychoanalysis opens some doors is not by any means to claim that it opens them all. Whether it be true that political thinkers have always been "manipulators of ideas rather than extenders of knowledge,"[5] this century certainly has been for political theory an era of adaptation and reconciliation. The time has come for a clarification of personality theory in the study of politics. Some might suggest that the successfully demonstrated use of an intellectual tool like psychoanalysis might well carry more conviction, and teach more lessons, than any such second-level discussion as this. The accumulation of psychoanalytically informed political studies, and the reformulation of moral theory wherever psychoanalysis proves relevant, might well end whatever skepticism still exists about this approach.

And yet, as was mentioned before, what has been done up to now along these lines has tended to get diffused within political science; the impact of psychoanalysis has been partially hidden, though substantial. There has of course been an invisible impact of Freud's ideas on the rest of intellectual life as well. Yet the psychoanalytic tenor of our day is one of those aspects of intellectual history which is as obvious as it is hard to document. The difficulty in objectifying the obvious is notorious; for that which we assume is compelling by its very elusiveness.

In the writing of intellectual history, as in life, there is a fine line between a deep truth and the shallowest cliché; that which is hard to see, precisely because it is so all important, rapidly becomes a commonplace once it has been fully noted. In terms of American intellectual history at least, the impact of Freud is paralleled only by that of Darwin a few generations back. The very intellectual air we breathe has been infused with Freud's categories of thought.

[5] John Plamenatz: *The English Utilitarians* (Oxford: Blackwell; 1958), p. 20.

What we are concerned with here is the more narrow and less intractable issue of the methodology of utilizing psychoanalysis in the study of politics. For despite the programmatic statements, despite the examples of the successful use of psychoanalytic theory, the whole enterprise seems in perpetual danger of petering out. If professional legitimization is still lacking, may it not be because research has gone ahead without conceptual clarification? The place of personality theory in political science is still an unsettled matter. In order to shift the focus to a more advanced level, at which theory of human psychology can most fruitfully be coordinated with political science, one must first acknowledge how much of our thinking is psychoanalytically informed. Undeniably a well-developed theory of human nature in politics would be useful for our political studies.

What follows here and in Chapter I may seem unduly limited and elementary; but the importance of these issues makes conceptualizing necessary. Our subsequent examination of the development of psychoanalytic theory, seen through Freud's social treatises, will be helpful. It is necessary to put in order the foundations for the use of psychoanalytic knowledge in political science, and this can be at least partly accomplished through historical research. Now historical work such as this is not intrinsically self-justifying; it can be defended, though, if it ultimately serves a liberating function. While Freud's social thought has a fragmentary character to it, it should be possible to elucidate what are the notions implicit in his other work which are relevant to political thinking. And it should be possible there, as well as anywhere else in the world Freud created, to spot what are—from the point of view of political theory —some of the defects in his constructions.

## 2   The Obstacles

Even if one were to take a much more optimistic view of
what has already been accomplished by applying psychoanalytic principles in political science, it is still arguable
that the methodological issues inevitably involved have not
been systematically discussed. Studying these problems
should ensure a more stable relationship between psychoanalysis and politics, even though methodological sophistication obviously cannot by itself ensure creativity.

Given the character of psychoanalytic concerns, it is appropriate to begin with the emotional complications which
inevitably must arise. Freud wrote about issues that touch
on the most intimate parts of our lives. No matter how we
manage to cope with some of our inner conflicts, none of
us can be too confident that whatever inner harmony we
maintain is based on the self-confidence of self-knowledge
rather than the defensiveness of self-deception. It should be
apparent that some of our difficulties in handling psychoanalytic concepts may stem from our own personal inadequacies rather than from their objective weaknesses.

In the course of psychoanalytic therapy, the patient's chief
difficulties in attaining the Socratic ideal of the examined
life are the main focus of the treatment. "Turn your eyes
inward, look into your own depths, learn first to know yourself! Then you will understand why you were bound to fall
ill; and perhaps, you will avoid falling ill in the future."[1]
As Freud wrote elsewhere in more technical language, "all
the forces which have caused the libido to regress will rise
up as 'resistances' against the work of analysis, in order to

---

[1] *Standard Edition*, Vol. 17, p. 143.

conserve the new state of things."[2] Obviously, a concept such as "resistance" can very easily be misused, especially in a polemical context. Yet the notion that we resist realizations which endanger our self-image is a crucial aspect of the psychoanalytic structure. This struggle to maintain our self-deceptions is almost as much an obstacle to an accurate handling of psychoanalytic propositions as it is a difficulty within treatment.

While we must be on our guard lest our own personalities blind us to certain aspects of the psychoanalytic system, our own inadequacies may lead instead to a different difficulty. Intellectual acceptance of psychoanalysis, instead of being frustrated, may in fact be motivated by our personal emotional complexes. Just as within psychoanalytic treatment intellectualized acceptance of Freud's teachings may be a substitute for the emotional experience of an analysis, so in intellectual life psychoanalysis may become a haven for the insecure, a fortress to be defended rather than a vehicle for understanding. Enthusiasm for the psychoanalytic system can lead to isolating analysis from the rest of our knowledge, and to defensively substituting analytic categories for all other intellectual perspectives.

Just as it is unfortunate in therapy to substitute a formalistic reliance on analytic treatment for genuine self-knowledge, so intellectually psychoanalysis can only be a tool for understanding, not an alternative to psychological empathy. One of Freud's early pupils touched on this issue in 1907:

. . . a depth psychologist too may be superficial and a surface psychologist may be deep. Such works as Herman Grimm's *Michelangelo*, or Dilthey's *Experience and Literature* are brilliant biographies, psychological studies, even though their authors have not used Freud's technique; and a mediocre mind working with

2 Ibid., Vol. 12, p. 102.

Freud's technique will certainly achieve less profound results. . . . The decisive factor, no doubt, is the mental capacity with which a task is approached. Freud's technique by itself does not make a person clever or profound. Its value is that it provides one who knows the psyche with a new and very fine, but also a very fragile, tool for exploring the unconscious. However, it cannot carry forward one who is a psychological botcher.[3]

Psychoanalytic concepts, then, are no substitute for mature intelligence. Emotionally it is as much a snare to latch onto Freud to relieve our insecurities, as it is regrettable to misunderstand him to maintain our self-deceptions. Only if we recognize the limits of the uses of psychoanalytic theory can we begin to exploit its full potentialities.

Magical expectations have also played their role among the emotional obstacles to integrating psychoanalysis and the study of politics. Analysts are familiar with patients who expect too great a therapeutic impact from analytic treatment. Magical beliefs interfere with the proper use of psychoanalytic theory as much as they do with clinical treatment itself. The terminology of psychoanalysis, alien as in one sense it still is, offers fertile territory for unrealistic hopes. There are never any single keys to the study of human lives, or if there are, psychoanalytic concepts can obscure as well as reveal them. Reality is likely to be so much richer than any of the niggardly labels psychoanalysis has given us, that one must be quite sure that there is a net interpretive gain in using a technical concept. A conceptualization can freeze our capacity for insight, as well as liberate our energies.

[3] Herman Nunberg and Ernst Federn, eds.: *Minutes of the Vienna Psychoanalytic Society* (New York: International Universities Press; 1962), Vol. I, p. 261.

When social scientists become disappointed in their hopes for applying psychoanalysis, they are wont, not surprisingly, to blame the analysts; it is they, with their arrogance and superciliousness, who have led us to expect more than we have been able to find. Psychiatric guesswork about Goldwater during the 1964 presidential election, for example, lends support to the view that psychoanalysts have made excessive claims as to how much they have learned about human nature.[4]

And yet the social scientists themselves have been prone to ask far too much from psychoanalysis. The suggestion,[5] for example, that public officials periodically be given psychiatric examinations for the prevention and detection of mental illness is based on a rather naïve understanding of the current state of clinical practice. Another example of such excessive expectations is revealed by an analyst's account of his interview with a group of social scientists studying the origins of Nazism:

I mentioned among other factors . . . the failure of German nineteenth century liberalism, and the subsequent success of Prussian militarism. . . . I also mentioned the impact of rapid industrialization upon a society still almost feudal. . . . I was then interrupted by my host . . . ; this was not what I had been expected to contribute. As a psychoanalyst I should point out how Nazism had developed from the German form of child rearing. I replied that I did not think that there was any such relationship; in fact, political opinion did not seem to me to be determined in

[4] For an excellent rebuttal to this use of psychiatric knowledge, cf. Heinz Kohut: "A Statement on the Use of Psychiatric Opinions in the Political Realm by the American Psychoanalytic Association," *Journal of the American Psychoanalytic Association*, Vol. 13, No. 2 (April 1965), pp. 450–1.

[5] Arnold A. Rogow: *James Forrestal* (New York: The Macmillan Co.; 1963).

early childhood at all. This view was not accepted and I was told that the way the German mother holds her baby must be different from that of mothers in democracies. When we parted, it was clear that my hosts felt that they had wasted their time.[6]

Yet however irrational we may be in turning psychoanalysis into a quasi-religious ideology for solving all our intellectual difficulties, I think there is a sense in which, in reality, psychoanalysis does lend itself to unbounded intellectual hopes. "Since societies are composed of human beings . . . all social behavior has a psychological component which can be isolated and described. . . ."[7] Freud presents us, after all, with a whole new world, that of the unconscious. One "learns a new language through the capacity to read . . . [one's] own unconscious."[8] Jung, for example, after first talking with Freud reports the feeling of having "caught a glimpse of a new, unknown country from which swarms of new ideas flew to meet me."[9]

Not, of course, that there were no perceptions of unconscious processes long before Freud described them; Dostoevsky and Nietzsche, among others, gave remarkable descriptions of most of the same things Freud later came upon. As Freud himself repeatedly acknowledged,

creative writers are valuable allies and their evidence is to be prized highly, for they are apt to know a whole host of things between heaven and earth of which our philosophy has not let us dream. In their knowledge of the mind they are far in advance

[6] Robert Waelder: *Basic Theory of Psychoanalysis* (New York: International Universities Press; 1960), pp. 53–4.

[7] Geoffrey Gorer: *Death, Grief and Mourning in Contemporary Britain* (London: The Cresset Press; 1965), p. viii.

[8] Sylvia Payne, in John D. Sutherland, ed.: *Psychoanalysis and Contemporary Thought* (New York: Grove Press; 1959), p. 12.

[9] C. G. Jung: *Memories, Dreams, Reflections* (London: Collins and Routledge & Kegan Paul; 1963), p. 158.

of us everyday people, for they draw upon sources which we have not yet opened up for science.[1]

There is a sense in which there is nothing new under the sun; for virtually all Freud's insights, one could compile abundant evidence of precursors and anticipations. What Freud has to offer, and what marks novelty in intellectual history, is a new framework. It is in the restructuring of ideas, many of which are ancient in themselves, that Freud's intellectual greatness lies.

But there is a further difference between Freud and his precursors. For Freud came upon these unconscious processes in a different way. An artist's vision "is its own justification and . . . [he] does not need to relate his vision so closely to the brute facts of the external world—and so he has no reason to alter it provided it continues to please him."[2] To see the difference in Freud's case, the extent to which psychoanalysis arose out of clinical material, one has to read his early work, written long before he made his theoretical discoveries. Of course the origin of psychoanalysis was intimately tied to the course of Freud's own self-analysis. Nevertheless, if one watches Freud as he comes upon the therapeutic uses of hypnotic suggestion and of the talking cure, as he abandons hypnosis for hand-pressing on the forehead, as he blunders into believing real the fantasies of childhood seduction, and as he moves into the clear light of the acceptance of the importance of psychological reality, in short if one follows Freud historically, one becomes keenly aware that this was no closet philosopher cooking up a theoretical system in his study.

The radical aspect of Freud lies precisely in the clinical

[1] *Standard Edition*, Vol. 9, p. 8.
[2] Anthony Storr: *The Integrity of the Personality* (London: Penguin Books; 1963), p. 13.

origins and usage of his theories. Freud does indeed present us with a new world—but not a "world" in the sense that Joyce and Dostoevsky each had their vision. For Freud claimed, and at least for the sake of the argument here we will accept Freud at his word, that his world was grounded in reality, perceived by scientific methods. It must always be remembered that while Freud had, especially in his later years, many philosophic aspirations, he was initially a psychologist, a doctor.

Our expectations, then, have been raised by the novelty of Freud's outlook, by its grounding in reality, as well as by its devotion to scientific method. Still, in order to avoid exaggerating our anticipations and precipitating consequent disappointments, it is well to remember the boundaries Freud at his most modest foresaw to the contribution of psychoanalysis: "Psychoanalysis has never claimed to provide a complete theory of human mentality in general, but only expected that what it offered should be applied to supplement and correct the knowledge acquired by other means."[3]

The causes for discouragement at the gap between the potential and the actual relationship of psychoanalysis to the study of politics are not confined to distortions imposed by emotional conflicts, but extend to more strictly intellectual spheres. For example, as I have already mentioned, there has been a characteristic myopia in the approach of political scientists to Freud's ideas: they have been almost exclusively interested in his philosophic speculations. Without in any way devaluating books like *Civilization and Its Discontents*, it should be pointed out that Freud felt that the substance of psychoanalysis was quite independent of such applications. "The degree to which these various layers

[3] *Standard Edition*, Vol. 14, p. 50.

in psychoanalytic writings are known to the outside world are in inverse relevance for psychoanalysis."[4] The heart of the psychoanalytic orientation lies elsewhere than in these late works. It is, at any rate, impossible to understand these late social and political speculations of Freud's without fitting them into the context of his theories of clinical psychoanalysis.

Outsiders like political scientists have in part been thrown off the track by the nature of some of the published material on Freud's work. Jones's biography of Freud lays heavy stress on the political aspects of the growth of psychoanalysis. As Erich Fromm has pointed out, "anyone reading these headings [in Vol. III of the Jones biography] would hardly doubt that the book deals with the history of a political or a religious movement, its growth and its schisms; that this is the history of a therapy, or a psychological theory, would be a most unexpected surprise."[5] We have also been misled about the character of Freud's mind by the selective choice of letters for publication. Letters written to the great names of the literary world were very readily publishable, while those written about the treatment of patients had to be withheld either for reasons of medical discretion or because they seemed much less easily understandable outside the context of the living clinical material itself.

The origins within psychoanalysis itself for the failure of many social scientists to understand the center of gravity of Freud's work, their inability to distinguish between his dicta and his central hypotheses, are much more fundamental.

[4] Robert Waelder: "Psychoanalysis, Scientific Method, and Philosophy," *Journal of the American Psychoanalytic Association*, Vol. 10, No. 3 (July 1962), p. 621.

[5] Erich Fromm: *Sigmund Freud's Mission* (New York: Harper & Bros.; 1959), p. 83.

The training institutes for psychoanalysts have, especially in America, become highly institutionalized as the years have passed. In Europe the training of psychoanalysts had the flavor of self-education; through an apprentice relationship to an experienced psychoanalyst, one received a private education, tailored to one's own talents and capacities.

In America, psychoanalytic training is more likely to be marred by a spirit of vocationalism. Psychoanalysis became quickly professionalized, along with almost every other occupation in America. Part of this organizational trend was stimulated by numerical pressures from the increased number of candidates who wanted psychoanalytic training. But in part at least it was an outgrowth of American over-emphasis on formal education. The result has been a much more bureaucratized approach to psychoanalytic education; at least one major psychoanalytic institute in America now has a program of written examinations.

It is arguable of course that this has resulted in much more competently trained psychotherapists. But it has also meant the stultification of efforts to use psychoanalytic principles in the social sciences. For a social scientist to enroll in an institute for psychoanalytic training invariably means he becomes a second-class citizen, since the organizations are devoted to training therapists; moreover, the seminars given by the institutes are unlikely to be of much use to his work. While the ideal for those interested in using psychoanalysis in one of the social sciences might seem to be formal training in both fields, the exigencies of a career in one of them would in any case be a partial deterrent. But given the character of the education the formal training institutes offer now, it is not at all surprising that there has been a haphazard quality to the bridges that have been built between psychoanalysis and the social sciences. A personal psychoanalysis can do a lot to orient the student in the problems of understanding this new field. But it is hard for anyone with a professional interest in the process of education to believe that the present institutional set-up, in America at least, is at all helpful to the research needs of social scientists.

It behooves any outsider to be very cautious about treading on technical psychoanalytic ground. But if it is presumptuous of us to maintain any pretenses about extending psychoanalytic theory itself, it is not unreasonable to exploit the intellectual advantages of the contemporary psychoanalytic state of affairs. Outsiders can appreciate those aspects of Freud's work which have been relatively neglected as psychoanalysis has become a medical specialty. Freud's hopes for psychoanalysis were certainly quite otherwise. And to the extent that Freud himself ranged beyond medical or therapeutic issues, laymen are peculiarly able to understand his speculations.

Laymen, however, are also especially liable to take the mistaken short cut of focusing solely on Freud's social thought, exclusive of the concerns of clinical psychoanalysis (as one can best understand them). It is only by keeping in mind Freud's clinical research that we can avoid the mistake of the metaphysicians searching for a new metaphysics. Political scientists have also contributed to this distortion by specifically taking Freud's essays on war, for example, or his *Group Psychology*—those essays most explicitly addressed to politics—and trying to build bridges immediately from Freud's politics to academic political science. The jump is much too abrupt.

An analogous fallacy of moving too directly from psychoanalysis to politics, neglecting the center of Freud's teachings, can be seen in the temptation to write biographies of political leaders who have had psychotic experiences. There can of course be no intrinsic objection to such studies, were it not for the possible implication that only such subjects would be safe ground for a psychoanalytically oriented writer. In principle there are certain universal human experiences which make anyone eligible for a biography written from a psychoanalytic viewpoint. We need the ability to use Freud's doctrines at the more subtle and tangential points of contact between psychoanalysis and politics.

If to start out by studying "psychotic" politicians, without first developing some general notions of the personality of politicians, seems to be putting the cart before the horse, there are still other pitfalls in this kind of biographical research. Whatever psychological hypotheses are advanced should be adequately cautious, given the fact that one is dealing with the material at a much greater distance than in the clinical context in which psychoanalytic theories usually operate. Furthermore, it is essential that the subjects of biographical investigation not be treated merely as case histories. It is possible to become so fascinated with interpreting problems of personality as to neglect to integrate this material with the actual achievements of the subject in question. After all, political figures matter to history not because of their psychic conflicts, but for what they managed to accomplish in spite of these problems. The investigation of the psychic level can only be justified insofar as it helps us to understand the nature and limitations of the accomplishments themselves.

That political scientists, then, may have anxieties about meshing psychoanalysis and politics would seem to be perfectly legitimate. Their most likely initial objection is a fundamental one: "Why Freud?" Granting the importance of a psychological theory, even a psychoanalytic one, why

pick Freud out of a welter of possible theorists? Now whatever the merits of the various psychoanalytic schools, in
terms of the history of ideas Freud's place is not just that
of one among equals. Freud was, after all, the first psychoanalyst, and all succeeding analysts are in a sense his pupils.
Freud altered the psychological map so radically that all
succeeding theorists, either as opponents or as supporters,
have been thinking with him in mind.

Much of the criticism of Freud is in one sense a testimony
to his greatness; the enduring need to come to terms with
him is an index of the contemporaneous quality of his ideas.
He not only has not become an irrelevant thinker, but the
publication of each new collection of his correspondence
reveals a new facet of his stature. As the evidence from his
pen continues to come in, it contributes to a world-wide
discussion of his significance.

As for his opponents, the wisest course at this stage
seems to me to avoid doctrinal haggling whenever possible.
The issues between, say, Freud and Adler, or Freud and
Jung, cannot be legitimately contested in the same old terms
in our time. There have been too many concessions from
within classical psychoanalysis to the various seceding
schools; by now it is hard not to believe that many of the
original quarrels were ordained not so much by enduring
intellectual considerations as by transitory difficulties and
intense personal differences. The issues were sometimes questions of loyalty, of personal power, of institutional preroga-
tives, or of pragmatic clinical tactics.

The history of these struggles has been so mythologized
that it is very difficult at this point to untangle what was
really going on between the contestants. On the one hand
certain labels have become stereotypes, for example Jung as
a "mystic." Whatever Jung's occult beliefs may have been,

he deserves recognition for his pioneering attempts to apply principles of the new depth psychology to more seriously disturbed patients than Freud himself would have thought accessible to psychological treatment. On the other hand, there has been so much silent incorporation within classical psychoanalysis, so much taking over of ideas from defeated opponents, that it is all too easy to read back into past "orthodox" doctrine what is in fact only accepted today. There is therefore the danger of reading into the old scriptures whatever one needs now to expound.

Our focusing on Freud, then, entails no animosity toward the contributions of Adler or Jung. Freud's rejection of these dissidents was often the expulsion of a part of his own ego, an attempt to master an unruly part of his own soul.[6] It is important to bear in mind, however, that Freud has remained as controversial now as when he was alive; either people are seduced or they are repelled, and it is very hard to maintain a semblance of objectivity toward his contribution.

It will be reasonable to re-enter these disputes only if they serve to highlight some permanent aspect of Freud's views. Sometimes it will be necessary to touch on various themes within revisionist movements to the extent that they involve either the history or validity of Freud's ideas. Still, for the purposes of political theory it is very possible to be misled by focusing too much on these splits, however interesting they may be to the intellectual historian. We must not lose sight of the evolving continuity in psychoanalysis, those areas of agreement that persist quietly underneath all the public controversies. Whatever one disagrees about in Freud's thinking, it is beyond dispute that he uncovered

---

[6] Fritz Wittels: *Sigmund Freud* (New York: Dodd, Mead & Co.; 1924), p. 233.

the world of the unconscious, the role of transference, the power of resistances, and at least some of the dynamics of the analytic situation. Although Freud did not map the geography of the mind to anything like a complete extent, the example he set as an observer of human nature has served as a model for others who, using his techniques, were able to revise some of his theories. The attitude of looking for meaning in mental life has enabled us to go beyond him. However difficult it may be to decide those questions that are in dispute, one still has to begin, at least, with Freud's own views. It is important for outsiders to be aware of the differences that do exist, but not to forget the unspoken circumference of common agreement which surrounds whatever issues are still in question.

It is this conceptualization—stemming basically from Freud, while incorporating some innovations of his dissident followers—which has dominated much of American psychiatry. If political scientists are to communicate with the psychiatric community, they need to be clear at the outset about some of the major conceptual lines. That Freud won against, say, Adler, Jung, or Rank, logically proves little about the validity of his initial ideas; a successful movement has a way of absorbing into itself some of the best ideas of the opposition. There is obviously more in psychiatry than can be found just in Freud's own works. But to argue that one must accept the limits of Freud's contribution is not to contradict the assertion that one must know it.

There are, of course, special problems when we focus on Freud's own thought. He was one of the great fighters in the modern world, and he could be as cruel to opponents as he was generous to supporters. When attacked, he would defend his earlier writings; he was not a man to admit readily inconsistencies in his own thought. Besides what-

ever limitations his personality or his education and background may have put upon his work, there is one special
quality to his mind which we should bear in mind lest it
needlessly put us off. Freud had a powerful sense of the
dramatic, and as a result some of his concepts (such as
castration anxiety or trauma) or his case names (the "Rat-
Man" or the "Wolf-Man") sound misleadingly ominous.
In studying Freud one must be aware of his tendency to
exaggerate histrionically.

Since Freud's death, there has been further theoretical
elaboration within psychoanalysis. Although it is always
very difficult to put out of mind recent conceptual discussions, much of this later work does seem to be mainly a
clean-up campaign; psychoanalytic theorists have been interested in clarification and consolidation. Relatively few
strictly analytic discoveries have been made. The emphasis,
in America at least, has been on developing a general human psychology, which has involved a reintroduction of
much of academic psychology. Attention has shifted from
emotions to cognition, making of psychoanalysis a more
comprehensive structure. Conceptually the situation is neater
now, yet it has perhaps less to offer to outsiders. Intellectual
formalism has followed the period of great psychological
discoveries.

There is a rather tame quality to contemporary psychoanalytic theorizing; the model of the human personality
which lies behind much of the recent work seems less passionate than Freud's own version, and more like what proverbial common sense would tell us. The minutiae of much
contemporary "ego psychology" is reminiscent of the "vulgar
conception of man as a creature divided into tidy compart-
ments—passion, will, reason, self-interest, and the like."[7]

[7] Albert Guérard: *André Gide* (New York: E. P. Dutton; 1963), p. 137.

Theoretical interest in unconscious motivations has declined.[8] The rationalistic trend in recent theorizing has focused on the ego's adaptations—which are often conscious—in coping with the outside world. There has been a corresponding decline in the more traditional concern with defenses against inner stresses, which are mainly unconscious.

It is as if the institutionalizing of training centers has ensured the recruitment of less eccentric analysts than characterized the early days of psychoanalysis, and that therefore analytic attention has shifted from apparently bizarre processes to more "normal" psychological problems. At the same time that unconscious processes may now be better understood in relation to external realities, and so more useful to the social sciences, there is the danger of incorporating a conscious psychology by elaborating ego processes.

Given the history of the relationship between psychoanalysis and political thinking, it would seem a mistake to start with very recent psychoanalytic theories, since the initial contribution of Freud himself has not been adequately absorbed by students of politics. There is the likelihood that the popularization of post-Freudian thought might inhibit our understanding of psychoanalytic material. Whatever the merits of contemporary ego psychology, it must be placed within the context of the development of psychoanalysis as a late phase; it would be a mistake for outsiders to come to it first, lest they miss Freud's most original ideas.

My intention then is to concentrate fairly centrally on Freud himself, as well as on the additions of some of his followers. It would be tempting to think that one had been able to capture the "true" Freud, that which is the "essence"

[8] Merton Gill: "The Present State of Psychoanalytic Theory," *Journal of Abnormal and Social Psychology*, Vol. 58 (1959), pp. 4, 6.

of his teachings. However, since any principle of selection from within the psychoanalytic literature would be arbitrary, it is best not to pretend to have snared "the mainstream" of psychoanalysis for political thought. It would be more realistic to admit that it is in principle impossible to exhaust all the possible implications of any great thinker. For the purposes of our thinking about politics, it seems most productive to focus first on what psychoanalysis has to teach us about the unconscious and its relation to the external world. The object of this study will not be to complete or fulfill Freud's own social thought, nor indeed to provide a definitive psychoanalytic social theory. My justification lies rather in the suggestiveness of Freud's theories. This is one of the occasions when it is fitting to point in one theoretical direction, and say, "Look there."

Aside from the anxieties which are bound to arise in political science from using Freud rather than any other theorist of personality, someone is bound to raise the issue of statistical controls and experimentation. Given the difficulties of measuring the material of psychoanalysis, combined with the apparently farfetched character of many of its propositions, a skeptic might well be led to fear that the upshot would be mere guesswork. It is even very difficult to get independent access to the same evidence, at least on some occasions. We must admit from the start that psychoanalysis accumulates its "data" by means of introspection and empathy. "It is a field devoted to the understanding of the most individual features of every person, a field in which differences are in the focus of interest, a field which shuns the statistical handling of human beings. . . ."[9] Even during Freud's pre-psychoanalytic work, "the rare fact, even the singular fact, always commanded respect, and impelled

[9] Alexander: *The Western Mind in Transition*, p. 122.

as much scientific thinking as the conspicuous, statistical sample based on impressive numbers."[1]

On examination the problem of statistical verification can be reduced. Statistics, after all, can only provide one kind of evidence. Clinical material is available, accumulated by investigators all over the world for over half a century, bearing on the central psychoanalytic propositions. Admittedly analytic material is difficult to reproduce under anything like laboratory conditions. Still, "science cannot ignore the most important processes of mental life merely because experimentation cannot yet accommodate them. On the other hand, some specific problems in psychoanalysis are amenable to experimentation. We can consider the theory of symbolization to have been experimentally proven. . . ."[2] One must remember the seriousness of purpose of these investigators, their respect for their patients, as well as the difficulties of having mental illness as a field of work. If psychoanalysis seems subjectivistic, that does not entail a fatal lack of discipline. We should remember that the "ultimate goal of all research is not objectivity, but truth."[3] Between the narrowness of statistical sophistication and the vagueness of mere impressionism it is possible to find a middle way.

There is one final source of discontent which can be allayed—the fear lest relating the two fields entail fusion rather than reciprocity. Of course political behavior can never be predicted from attitudes or psychological predispo-

[1] Siegfried Bernfeld: "Freud's Studies on Cocaine, 1884–87," *Journal of the American Psychoanalytic Association*, Vol. 1, No. 4 (October 1953), p. 606.

[2] Heinz Hartmann: "Concept Formation in Psychoanalysis," *Psychoanalytic Study of the Child*, ed. Ruth Eissler et al. (New York: International Universities Press; 1964), Vol 19, p. 28.

[3] Helene Deutsch: *The Psychology of Women* (New York: Grune & Stratton; 1944), Vol. I, p. xii.

sitions alone; there are always intervening historical or organizational structures which must be taken into account, in addition to the personality factor. For example, one can readily imagine some social forces, such as an economic depression, which may seem relatively independent of any personality theory. Yet the way in which people respond to a depression is a human problem, and to that extent opens the way for psychoanalytic theory. A social event has meaning as refracted through individual minds.[4] A depression which is tolerable in one context may be considered unacceptable under different conditions, and the difference in the way the same "objective" event is interpreted may be due to a different set of human expectations. (One need only think here of the effect of Keynesian thinking on our attitude toward business cycles.)

The possible gap between an external event like a depression and the way people view it reminds us that in political life there are forces independent of the men involved. One of the misleading appeals of personality theory for the liberal mind is the illusory notion that the psyche is the only source of limitation and failure, and that potentially the outside world can be made tractable if only one's inner self were under control. This kind of utopianism can lead to discounting the relevance of social forces, to believing, for example, that the limits to the presidency are simply set by the President's own personality. One could argue however that had Eisenhower been elected on the Democratic ticket, he would have been subjected to a very different set of pressures, and would therefore have made a very different President.

A focus on personality factors need not entail a version of

[4] Alex Inkeles: *What Is Sociology?* (Englewood Cliffs, N. J.: Prentice-Hall; 1964), p. 48.

the great-man theory of history. The good man, as Aristotle argued, is not the same as the good citizen. It is possible to describe many human qualities as psychologically mature, and yet not conclude that they underlie successful political leadership. As Speaker Rayburn is reported to have said of General Eisenhower in 1952: "No, won't do. Good man. Wrong profession."[5] Public virtues may be quite distinct from private virtues.

Political leadership, especially in America where the controversies tend to be less about rival ideas of how one ought to live and more about questions of loaves and fishes, may require an ability to manipulate people. Politicians are characteristically egoistic and nonintrospective. They do not tend to be soul-seekers or dreamers. They have of course a good deal of savvy; but their empathy is goal-directed, instrumental, and action-oriented. They have little interest in fantasying for its own sake. They have been rewarded for their abilities at externalizing—debating, arguing, verbalizing, convincing. For them to shift political positions, to move to the Right or the Left, should entail no more inner turmoil than for a lawyer to defend a new client or to invent a new ploy. Politicians seem exempt from many restraints of conscience that one might want to expect from them.

And yet this tendency of politicians to act out their problems rather than to internalize them is peculiarly adaptive in political life. The true politician must be able to fight hard for his position, without becoming too personally involved in it. He needs a talent for self-effacement. He must be able to maintain a distance from whatever he defends or proposes, if he is going to be able to compromise later to help reach a tolerable solution.

To function in institutional life, one must be able to make

[5] Richard E. Neustadt: *Presidential Power* (New York: Wiley; 1960), p. 194.

judgments on a fairly impersonal basis. Eisenhower, for example, sometimes erred in letting his personal feelings and ties interfere with objective considerations. His feelings of personal betrayal, toward both Eden after Suez and Faubus after Little Rock, might have been appropriate to normal personal relationships, but were out of place in the world of statecraft, and complicated the resolution of those crises. Principles of everyday personal behavior can interfere with the politician's role as a broker among competing groups.

But from a clinician's point of view, what is adaptive politically may look quite pathological under an analytic microscope. It is not a matter of politicians being infected with some elemental power drive. A politician has difficulty regulating his self-esteem within his own conscience, and therefore needs to verify his self-respect through external activities. In order to do this, he must sustain a wide gulf between his inner self and his behavioral life, which is why some politicians come to seem frighteningly empty as human beings. The ability to use people as things is part of the politician's great art as a mediator.

The public figure in the last decade or two who least fits this sketch of the American politician would be Adlai Stevenson, known by many as a Hamlet-like personality. Shortly after Stevenson's death, Eric Sevareid wrote that he was a "wonderful public figure, but he was essentially a private person."[6] If success in American politics requires the externalization of one's self and the acceptance of one's identity as defined by one's political position, then it is no accident that Stevenson's life was politically less successful than it might have been otherwise. Of course a figure like Lincoln would contradict the notion that one needs this

[6] Eric Sevareid: "The Final Troubled Hours of Stevenson," *Look* (November 30, 1965), p. 86.

sort of nonintrospective personality in order to function successfully in American politics; and yet the ability to sustain a rich inner life while still functioning as a politician is that rare talent that makes for true greatness in American public life. Strictly political talents alone will never be enough to earn Lincoln's kind of greatness; one has to be able to call upon inner, nonpolitical resources as well.

A biography of a man like Nixon, for example, might require on the face of it little psychological subtlety. On a deeper level, of course, it might be interesting to discover the roots of a calculatedly self-interested character structure. Reality motives here seem so clear, though, that the psychological determinants appear of less immediate help in explaining his career. The task of writing a biography of a man like Trotsky, however, would require psychological skill simply on the face of it, to cope with his artistic capacities. Such a task would obviously demand "a syndrome of . . . qualities such as psychological-mindness, empathy with others, self-awareness—a proclivity to seek out and enjoy the subjective and personal in human affairs."[7]

The distinction between a talent for inner realities and an understanding of external political life suggests a further reason why the prospects for using psychoanalysis in political science are not rosier than they are. For the abilities that make one sensitive to inner realities are likely to make one obtuse to external ones, and *vice versa*. Even within one's own life there are periods when one is especially sensitive to emotional nuances, and other times when one is expertly attuned to external power relations. Proverbially this is one of the lines which psychologically separates women from men; we need only think how difficult it is for most women

---

[7] Myron R. Sharaf and Daniel J. Levinson: "The Quest for Omnipotence in Professional Training," *Psychiatry*, Vol. 27 (1964), p. 138.

to understand straightforward political issues, and how insensitive to emotional shadings men can be. Although of course one must be cautious about what may be culturally determined in these sexually distinct traits, there does seem in our society to be a difference between the intuitiveness of feminine understanding and the logic of masculine control.

If so much of political life seems explicable, at least on the surface, in reaction to reality factors of power, prestige, and the like, it is no wonder that political scientists have found conscious psychologies adequate for their needs. Yet just as in each of us there is always something of a manipulating politician, so also do we each have inner selves, regardless of the degrees to which we externalize them. The failure to develop an inner life is as much a psychological fact as any other.

Forrestal's life illustrates this principle as graphically as one could want. As the Reverend Davies, who knew him, said after his suicide:

Very few tragedies indeed do not have a personal and intimate side to them and it is not often that a man takes his own life if the inner fortress of his personal happiness is still secure. For this gives him a place of refuge: a life within a life, from the joy of which his strength is renewed and he finds fortitude. But in the case we are considering, devotion to the public service had been substituted for the forlorn hope of personal happiness.[8]

In Forrestal's case, it would seem that the normal politician's gap between the inner and the outer became so great as to smash the inner citadel completely. Exceptional though his life was, it does suggest the way in which the separation between public and private can be a special way of relieving inner tensions; people externalize after all for inner mo-

8 Rogow: *James Forrestal*, p. 43.

tives. While some of us like to associate the psychological with the private, an extreme example like that of Forrestal's illustrates the way in which the public and the psychological can also become inextricably associated.

The difficulty of understanding the private life as well as the public, added to the other obstacles to using psycho-analytic formulations in political science, may go far in explaining the pervading discontent with what has been accomplished up to now. The fundamental mistake of those interested in using Freud to increase our understanding of politics has been their neglect of the methodological considerations involved. The fact that these issues have had to be faced here is an index of the relatively backward state of the use of psychoanalysis in the study of politics, as opposed to its use in other disciplines. Legitimate anxieties have gone unassuaged, expectations have run riot, the emotional issues have been unexamined, and Freud's social works have not been adequately placed within psychoanalysis as a whole. By being too direct in applying psychoanalysis, without first clarifying the nature of psychoanalytic propositions and their limitations, social scientists have missed the full potential significance of psychoanalysis for the study of politics.

private
public } politician

*CHAPTER I*

# Psychoanalysis and the Study of Politics

## The Discipline

If one were to construct a spectrum of the social sciences on the basis of the attention that each discipline has paid to a psychoanalytic view of personality factors, the range would run from economics, where the impact of Freud would be close to zero, to cultural anthropology, where psychoanalysis has made its most notable contribution. Political science would fall toward the middle of the spectrum, but probably rather nearer to economics than to cultural anthropology. Although anthropology is not now moving in the direction of culture and personality, the thoroughgoing penetration of psychoanalytic concepts in the past has left a residue of sophistication in these matters which is unsurpassed within the social sciences.

Freud himself made the initial psychoanalytic contributions to anthropology, but they were scarcely of a kind to encourage anthropologists to be receptive to the rest of his ideas. Freud's anthropological views ran directly counter to the mainstream of the profession as it has developed in this century. For example, Freud equated the customs of living nonliterate peoples with the early ancestors of man. He also spoke of the "primal horde" as if it were a historical fact, being unwilling to claim merely that it was a psychological truth. To make matters worse, Freud tenaciously held to the belief in the inheritance of acquired characteristics; the guilt over the slaying of the primal father was transmitted, Freud held, genetically. The whole tone of Freud's anthropological speculations was bound to annoy any anthropologist; he repeatedly spoke of nonliterate cultures as "primitive" and "child-like," phrases bound to offend those who had fought to emancipate anthropology from nineteenth-century ethnocentrism. Finally, Freud's whole argument was grounded on secondary sources. Of course at the time Freud wrote *Totem and Taboo* (1912–13) there was hardly a better authority than Frazer, but as the commitment of anthropologists to field research became settled, Freud's arguments seemed invalid on methodological grounds alone.

Nor was Freud particularly adaptable in the anthropological positions that he adopted; despite the criticism that was levelled at *Totem and Taboo*, Freud reiterated his theses to the end of his life. It is remarkable that despite the bad footing on which anthropology and psychoanalysis began, the relationship has developed to an extent unsurpassed in any other field.[1] Now that the intellectual battles are over, and much of the protests of the anthropologically oriented revisionists like Clara Thompson and Karen Horney have

[1] Weston La Barre: "The Influence of Freud on Anthropology," *The American Imago*, Vol. 15, No. 3 (Fall 1958), pp. 275–328.

been accepted, it is possible to view the relationship of anthropology to psychoanalysis in historical perspective.

Anthropologists, in contrast to political scientists, were
scarcely tempted to move directly from Freud's own applications to the discipline in question. "Those aspects [of
Freud's work] which they find most useful are not the
specifically anthropogical ones but rather those dealing with
individual development."[2] Weston La Barre has maintained
that for understanding religion in nonliterate societies,
"no anthropologist is competent to study such subjects unless he is also psychoanalytically sophisticated."[3] Further,
"most modern anthropologists are now aware of the projective significance of folklore and mythology."[4]

One major explanation for the anthropological use of
analytic theories can surely be found in the intimate nature
of the fieldworker's involvement with his subjects of observation. As Clyde Kluckhohn has pointed out, both psychiatrists and anthropologists "operate with procedures that
are essentially 'clinical.' "[5] Anthropologists during their field
work are confronted with a range of apparently bizarre material which has required the use of an apparently bizarre
theory, psychoanalysis, to explain it. In field research, moreover, one inevitably makes use of one's own personality.

[2] J. A. C. Brown: *Freud, and the Post-Freudians* (Baltimore: Penguin Books;
1961), p. 108.

[3] Weston La Barre: "Psychoanalysis in Anthropology," in *Psychoanalysis and
Social Process*, ed. Jules H. Masserman (New York: Grune & Stratton; 1961),
p. 11.

[4] George Devereux and Weston La Barre: "Art and Mythology," in *Studying
Personality Cross-culturally*, ed. Bert Kaplan (New York: Harper & Row; 1961),
p. 392.

[5] Clyde Kluckhohn: "The Impact of Freud on Anthropology," in *Freud and
Contemporary Culture*, ed. Iago Galdston (New York: International Universities Press; 1957), p. 70.

Since what the fieldworker finds out is very much influenced by the limitations of his own personality, he becomes aware that his personality constitutes a valuable research instrument. It therefore becomes harder for him not to be aware of the importance of the variable of personality theory in general.

Within political science, no strong tradition of field work has ever developed. With the recent interest in problems of developing nations, more people than before are becoming involved in field work. But even here, the researchers usually spend considerably less time in the field, study many more societies, and in general become much less involved in the material than would be expected among anthropologists. In contrast to anthropology, there is a characteristic distance about much of the research in political science. There are many research projects in which the head of the project sends out graduate students to do interviewing for him. People analyze American state election returns without being intimately acquainted with the states in question. And social survey work relies on statistics, keeping at a distance from the living material. Political scientists like to deal with reality in large aggregates, rather than on a face-to-face basis. Samuel Lubell's work on American politics would be the exception that proves the rule.

To some extent of course this situation is inevitable. The student of Russian politics cannot expect to be able to penetrate into the proceedings of the inner circles of the Soviet Communist Party. Yet the model of Kremlinology has become too central to political science. It seems as if by maintaining aloofness from one's material one hopes in a magical way to control political reality. In this connection, it is well to remember how on a presidential election eve, and in forecasting, newscasters and the rest of us "give" state X to candidate Y. All of us share, in some measure at least, this particular attraction to the study of politics.

For the anthropologist, on the other hand, his involvement in field work helps to objectify parts of his own personality, revealing buried layers of his self. The very fact that he is confronted with human material in an alien culture makes it easier for him to reach self-awareness; within his native culture his own personality would be threatened by the same insights. Research in an alien culture provides the fieldworker with enough emotional detachment to overcome a good deal of his resistance to psychoanalytic theories, combined with sufficiently intimate contact with primary human emotions.

A decisive factor in the relationship of psychoanalysis and anthropology was the historical accident that Freud appeared on the scene after the thesis of cultural relativity had begun to wear thin. "Anthropologists now see that we have been so successful in establishing the relativity of cultures as to risk throwing out the baby with the bath: the universal similarities of all mankind. Understandably, then, there is now a strong movement back to the search for essential human nature."[6] Margaret Mead and others have begun to look for the universals underlying all cultures. Anthropologists have a tradition of challenging us "to think more deeply about what is specifically human about human society."[7] Hence there has been a sound foundation for a confluence between anthropology and psychoanalysis.

[6] Weston La Barre: *The Human Animal* (Chicago: Phoenix Books; 1961), p. xiii.

[7] Edmund Leach: "Claude Lévi-Strauss," *New Left Review*, No. 34 (November–December 1965), p. 26.

All human infants, regardless of culture, know the psychological experience of helplessness and dependency. Situations making for competition for the affection of one or both parents, for sibling rivalry, can be to some extent channeled this way or that way by a culture but they cannot be eliminated, given the universality of family life.[8]

By this point we can see that anthropologists have been preoccupied with problems quite traditional in the history of political theory. The interest in cultural uniformities, the quest for that which is humanly universal, links up with the whole tradition of natural law and natural rights. If natural law thinking has survived the well-known logical onslaughts upon it, whether by Hume or Bentham,[9] surely in part this has been because the natural law advocates have been addressing themselves to an enduring perplexity: what are those basic human needs which underlie any culture, and under what circumstances has man been intolerably distorted from his deepest aspirations? "Our political notions," Sir Isaiah Berlin has written, "are part of our conception of what it is to be human. . . ."[1] This then was the "kernel of truth in the old a priori Natural Law doctrines."[2]

One difficulty with this tendency within the tradition of natural law, dating at least as far back as Ulpian, was an excessively rationalistic approach. Grotius, for example, ticked off the minimal qualities of a human being, the inalienable properties of a man. While human needs were

---

[8] Clyde Kluckhohn and William Morgan: "Some Notes on Navaho Dreams," in *Psychoanalysis and Culture*, ed. George Wilbur and Warner Muensterberger (New York: International Universities Press; 1951), pp. 120–1.

[9] Bentham called natural law thinking "nonsense on stilts."

[1] Sir Isaiah Berlin: "Does Political Theory Still Exist?" in *Philosophy, Politics and Society*, 2nd Series, ed. Peter Laslett and W. G. Runciman (Oxford: Blackwell; 1962), p. 22.

[2] Ibid., p. 27.

implicit in the concept of natural rights, still natural law "notions about human nature were lifeless and abstract."[3] The place of the individual has been prominent within political thought, especially within the liberal tradition; generally, however, thinkers such as Locke and Mill have discussed a theory of education for children, and have then gone on to discuss adult life as if the child did not still persist in all of us.

With the growth of cultural anthropology and psychoanalytic theory, our understanding of human uniformities has been broadened by cultural space and deepened by psychological understanding. Margaret Mead, for example, considers as universal the existence of a category of murder, incest rules, and private property.[4] Clyde Kluckhohn was in fairly close agreement:

Every culture has a concept of murder, distinguishing this from execution, killing in war, and other "justifiable homicides." The notions of incest and other regulations upon sexual behavior, of prohibitions upon untruth under defined circumstances, of restitution and reciprocity, of mutual obligations between parents and children—these and many other moral concepts are altogether universal.[5]

Does this sound so very different from many of the natural law thinkers of old? Their moral maxims were in part expressions of their sense of the existence of basic human needs.

There is a danger of course in this universalistic quest, one which has beset the natural law tradition for centuries.

[3] Franz Alexander: *Our Age of Unreason*, rev. ed. (New York: Lippincott; 1951), p. 35.

[4] Margaret Mead: "Some Anthropological Considerations Concerning Natural Law," *Natural Law Forum*, No. 6 (1961), pp. 52–3.

[5] Clyde Kluckhohn: "Ethical Relativity: Sic et Non," in *Culture and Behavior*, ed. Richard Kluckhohn (New York: The Free Press of Glencoe; 1962), p. 276.

It is logically improper to deduce moral precepts from uniform customs; a moral *ought* cannot be logically entailed by a factual *is*. The use of natural law frequently invited confusion of the *ought* and the *is*, offering the "mental luxury of certainty, of feeling that what ought to be must be. . . ."[6] It is possible, though, to be clear about the logical status of one's principles, and yet retain the Enlightenment interest in accepting human urges and shaping them to their finest expression.

These are, of course, old chestnuts; but one of the promises of psychoanalysis is that it offers the means for reviving some classical questions in the history of political theory. Sir Isaiah Berlin has described the nature of political theory in a way which points toward the relevancy of Freud. Political theory is concerned with

such questions as what is specifically human and what is not, and why; whether specific categories . . . are indispensable to understanding what men are; and so, inevitably, with the source, scope and validity of certain human goals . . . who will deny that political problems, e.g., about what men and groups can or should be or do, depend logically and directly on what man's nature is taken to be?[7]

Berlin's view of the nature of political theory has a long intellectual pedigree. Some theorists have been explicit about the relation between man and politics; Plato, John of Salisbury, and Hobbes thought of political life as in some sense man "writ large." Other thinkers have been more or less unaware of the extent to which they assumed rather than explored the nature of man. Even those theorists who were the most value-oriented, who set out boldly to construct the

---

[6] Judith N. Shklar: *Legalism* (Cambridge: Harvard University Press; 1962), p. 78.

[7] Berlin: "Does Political Theory Still Exist?" pp. 47, 28.

good civil society, were unable to avoid the problem of the nature of the human beings they were dealing with.

Moreover, one of the traditional tasks of political theory was to isolate those human needs which were not being satisfied, those social groups whose human possibilities were being denied.

The study of politics is the study of people; the dead, discarded philosophies . . . are those which rest on no observation or no imaginative projection, into actual conditions of life, actual needs and feelings . . . they are irrelevant, unless they bring to the surface some force of motive or of need so far left out of account . . . the concept of human nature really has been enlarged, and there are now fewer forgotten men, and forgotten needs, both in the writing of history and in the discussion of contemporary problems.[8]

It is not only on grounds of human happiness that political theory needs this broadened understanding of human needs. For the sake of political stability one must be aware of potential sources of trouble, where the shoe no longer fits. The difficulty lies in having the sensibility to perceive pain, even if unexpressed.

It is ironic that psychoanalysis, which has made us so aware of the subjective origins of our ideas that it has helped to deter political theorizing by undermining our self-confidence,[9] should at a later time contribute to the revival of traditional modes of political thought. That it should do so in conjunction with cultural anthropology is even more surprising, since one of the platitudes of our time is that Malinowski established that the oedipal constellation was

---

[8] Stuart Hampshire: "Human Nature in Politics," *The Listener*, Vol. 50, No. 1292 (December 3, 1953), p. 948.

[9] Judith N. Shklar: *After Utopia* (Princeton, N. J.: Princeton University Press; 1957), p. 271.

peculiar to Western European society; in a matriarchal family setting, the hostile impulses of the boy were focused on the mother's brother rather than the father, and the positive feelings were mainly directed toward the sister rather than the mother.

No one could deny that Malinowski enriched our understanding of the oedipal complex; but in general, cultural anthropologists have defined that nuclear conflict too narrowly, neglecting the variety of forms in which basic human needs can be patterned. According to psychoanalytic doctrine, the universality of the Oedipus complex is simply derived from the nature of human childhood. As Fenichel has said, "the human infant is biologically more helpless than other mammalian children. He needs care and love. Therefore, he will always ask for love from the nursing and protecting adults around him and develop hate and jealousy of persons who take this love away from him."[1] Another psychoanalytic theorist maintained that the oedipal complex refers to the "intensity of love and hate, of yearning and jealousy, of fury and fear that rages within the child."[2] The oedipal complex represents a variety of conflicting emotions: it is "not a matter only of feelings of hate and rivalry towards one parent and love towards the other, but feelings of love and the sense of guilt also enter in connection with the rival parent."[3]

There is no theoretical necessity for the love to be directed toward the biological mother or the hate to be focused on the natural father; that would only be the case in family

[1] Otto Fenichel: *The Psychoanalytic Theory of Neurosis* (New York: W. W. Norton; 1945), p. 97.

[2] Charles Brenner: *An Elementary Textbook of Psychoanalysis* (New York: Doubleday Anchor Books; 1957), p. 119.

[3] Melanie Klein: "Our Adult World and its Roots in Infancy" (London: Tavistock Publications; 1959), p. 7.

life as we have so far known it in the West. If the nuclear family is universal, then the "same conditions for the rise of the typical Oedipus complex exist in every individual and generation."[4] If, on the other hand, "the institution of the family were to change, the pattern of the oedipus complex would necessarily change also."[5] It is possible then for the "form taken by the complex . . . [to vary] from culture to culture."[6]

What Malinowski and others like him have tended to do is to "draw conclusions from observed to underlying motivation and neglect . . . to take into account that in different environments similar impulses may find different expressions."[7] The way one culture expresses an emotion may be very misleading to an observer from another society. Alexander once expressed a psychoanalytic position on instinctual uniformity and societal differences thus:

The instinctual drives, the aspirations and the conflicts of western man today appear not much different from what we can reconstruct from Greek, Roman or medieval literature. . . . In the deep unconscious all men are akin; individuality is formed nearer the surface. Ego-psychology permits us to recognize and estimate those features of personality which are molded by the cultural environment and are superimposed upon a more or less uniform biological and emotional substratum.[8]

The whole argument between Malinowski and the early psychoanalysts tended to focus mistakenly on the question

[4] La Barre: "The Influence of Freud on Anthropology," p. 290.

[5] Fenichel: *The Psychoanalytic Theory of Neurosis*, p. 97.

[6] Brown: *Freud and The Post-Freudians*, p. 191.

[7] Heinz Hartmann, Ernst Kris, and Rudolf Loewenstein: "Some Psychoanalytic Comments on 'Culture and Personality,' " *Psychoanalysis and Culture*, p. 28.

[8] Alexander: *The Western Mind in Transition*, p. 193; Alexander: *Our Age of Unreason*, p. 7.

of the universality of the Oedipus complex, instead of on the problem of "what is the possible range within which culture can utilize and elaborate the instinctively given human potentialities, and what are the psychologically given limits of this range?"[9] This restatement would mean that an instinctivistic psychology need not entail a denial of the plasticity of human nature. Plamenatz, for example, has argued that "to say anything is 'human nature' is only another way of saying that it cannot be changed."[1] The instinctual drives that Freud was concerned with are capable of a variety of gratifications. And it is culture which is primarily responsible for the various patterns that we see.

Once again the confluence of cultural anthropology and psychoanalysis has revived an issue familiar in the history of political theory; the postulation of primary human needs and universal human experiences does not foreclose the issue of cultural patterns of gratification. What has stymied the revival of this issue within political science, along with others raised by Freud's theories, has not been the much-discussed question of increased academic specialization so much as an inadequate understanding of the ways of applying psychoanalysis in the social sciences. For a variety of reasons cultural anthropology was peculiarly well situated to respond to Freud's teachings. By accepting the challenge of a new theory of human nature, it is possible to alter our thinking not only about the more normative issues within political theory, but also about research problems within political science.

[9] Anne Parsons: "Is the Oedipus Complex Universal? The Jones-Malinowski Debate Revisited and A South Italian Nuclear Complex," *The Psychoanalytic Study of Society*, ed. Warner Muensterberger and Sidney Axelrod (New York: International Universities Press; 1964), Vol. III, p. 326.

[1] Plamenatz: *The English Utilitarians*, p. 187.

## 2   The Unconscious

Whatever the results of a psychoanalytically informed political science turn out to be, they need not involve any cook-
book formulas for "applying" psychoanalysis in a rigidly
direct fashion. Our hope must be to change the way we
think about problems, or, perhaps more likely, to revive
some neglected ways of thinking through the fresh slant
provided by a new set of labels. We have seen how some of
the implications of Freud point toward traditional concerns of the political theorist; it is time now to show more
systematically how Freud can affect our attitude to empirical
political reality. It is here that we can begin to gauge the
failure, to date, to use psychoanalysis to understand politics;
otherwise the limitations of political behavioralism would
have been made more apparent by now. That psychoanalysis has not yet altered our attitude toward election statistics,
interviewing, and the other techniques of contemporary
political science, is in part due to the neglect of Freud's
more strictly technical writings. For Freud has a viewpoint
to contribute which is far more sweeping, and yet more
concrete, than anything that can be found in the psychoanalytic texts political scientists usually consult.

Freud's basic orientation has often been missed. His central achievement, the discovery of the unconscious, cuts
across all aspects of psychoanalysis. Freud arrived at this
concept in the course of his clinical work. Early in his medical career he had watched a demonstration of a post-hypnotic command by Bernheim at Nancy.

Bernheim had told a man . . .(under hypnosis) that he would
open an umbrella and walk around the room with it on awaken-
ing—which the man did, and then attempted to explain it

rationally; he just wanted to see if the umbrella was intact. When Bernheim insisted however that that was not the real reason, the man slowly and with difficulty said he was doing it upon command. . . .[1]

Freud was to return again and again to this phenomenon of post-hypnotic suggestion. If a man could be compelled, by psychological means, to perform an act without any awareness of the cause, and to rationalize a reason for what he did, then clearly there must be mental processes which are hidden. The concept of the unconscious was needed "in order to explain the discontinuity of manifest behavior."[2] It is difficult to express what Freud meant by the unconscious. Mrs. Riviere has put the feeling of becoming aware of an unconscious process in this way: "In my analysis he [Freud] one day made some interpretation, and I responded to it by an objection. He then said: 'It is *unconscious*.' I was over-whelmed then by the realization that I knew nothing about it—I knew nothing about it."[3]

Freud once defined the unconscious as "a psychical process . . . whose existence we are obliged to assume—for some such reason as that we infer it from its effects—, but of which we know nothing."[4] Freud's reason for employing the concept was a pragmatic one. It was in this sense that he felt that his ideas were part of science: "Any one who sets out to investigate the same region of phenomena and employs the same method will find himself compelled to take up the same position, however philosophers may ex-postulate."[5]

[1] Joseph Wortis: *Fragments of an Analysis with Freud* (New York: Charter Books; 1963), pp. 159–60.

[2] Brown: *Freud and the Post-Freudians*, p. 5.

[3] Sutherland, ed.: *Psychoanalysis and Contemporary Thought*, p. 149.

[4] *Standard Edition*, Vol. 22, p. 70.

[5] Ibid., Vol. 7, p. 113.

In his case history of Dora, Freud expressed just that outlook on unconscious processes which is his great achievement.

There is as a rule a great deal of symbolism . . . in life, but as a rule we pass it by without heeding it. When I set myself the task of bringing to light what human beings keep hidden within them, not by the compelling power of hypnosis, but by observing what they say and what they show, I thought the task was a harder one than it really is. He that has eyes to see and ears to hear may convince himself that no mortal can keep a secret. If his lips are silent, he chatters with his fingertips; betrayal oozes out of him at every pore. And thus the task of making conscious the most hidden recesses of the mind is one which it is quite possible to accomplish.[6]

It should be apparent that this is not a matter of listening to a sinner confess: "In Confession the sinner tells what he knows; in analysis the neurotic has to tell more."[7]

The psychoanalytic process involves a number of techniques, one of which is of interest to the human sciences. It is a basic principle of psychoanalytic understanding that "the order in which things come to mind also helps to establish the relationship that links them unconsciously."[8] As Freud put it, "when in analysis two things are brought out one immediately after the other, as though in one breath, we have to interpret this proximity as a connection of thought."[9] Aside from whatever other techniques Freud developed, or whatever content of the unconscious he postulated, it is the indirectness of the psychoanalytic outlook

---

[6] Ibid., pp. 77–8.

[7] Ibid., Vol. 20, p. 189.

[8] Ernst van den Haag: *Passion and Social Constraint* (New York: Stein & Day; 1963), p. 27.

[9] *Standard Edition,* Vol. 17, p. 153.

which is of potential interest to political scientists. "If his lips are silent, he chatters with his fingertips. . . ."

During other historical periods, men have repeatedly tried to express this same aspect of human experience. In Puritan New England, when the categories of thought were theological, the concept of God served as an expression of man's conviction of the reality of what we now call the unconscious. According to Perry Miller's account,

the Puritan . . . could never banish entirely from his mind the sense of something mysterious and terrible, of something that leaped when least expected, something that upset all regulations and defied all logic, something behind appearances that could not be tamed and brought to heel by men. . . . The essence of Calvinism and the essence of Puritanism is the hidden God, the unknowable, the unpredictable.[1]

If one wonders how people got along before Freud and the concept of the unconscious, the most obvious answer is that religious systems tried to explain the same phenomena. It is no wonder that a theologian like Luther was also a great psychologist; religious beliefs were a form of collective mastery of the unknown. But whereas Freud's system aims at focusing on the individual the responsibility for understanding his own feelings, religions have tended to project these feelings onto external figures. As Erikson has written about Luther, "what we today explain as meaningful slips, he simply called the devil's work."[2] Freud himself was aware of the way in which his psychology was to replace earlier attempts to handle the same material:

[1] Perry Miller: *Errand into the Wilderness* (Cambridge: Harvard University Press; 1956), pp. 94, 93.

[2] Erik Erikson: *Young Man Luther* (New York: W. W. Norton; 1958), p. 249.

A large part of the mythological view of the world, which extends a long way into the most modern religions, *is nothing but
psychology projected into the external world*. The obscure recognition . . . of psychical factors and relations in the unconscious
is mirrored . . . in the construction of a *supernatural reality*,
which is destined to be changed back once more by science into
the *psychology of the unconscious*.[3]

There have, of course, been many stages in this movement from religion to psychoanalysis. In American history,
for example, after two centuries the Puritan conception of
God had been divorced from theology, while still retaining
very much the same meaning. According to Matthiessen's
account of the American transcendentalists, they thought
that "reality could be caught only tangentially, and con-
veyed obliquely." Emerson stated that "everything in the
universe goes by indirection"; "we learn nothing rightly
until we learn the symbolic character of life."[4] What had
happened in the course of two centuries was that a conviction about the nature of the reality of the supernatural world
had been transformed into a feeling about the character of
the natural world. In our own time it has been above all
the artists who have insisted that life displays itself most
revealingly just when it does so most fleetingly.

There is, then, truth to the notion that there is nothing
new under the sun; everything about human nature has
probably been known always. Our customary criticisms of
the crudeness of past knowledge are really a reflection of

---

[3] *Standard Edition*, Vol. 6, pp. 258–9. Italics in the original.

[4] F. O. Matthiessen: *American Renaissance* (New York: Oxford University
Press; 1941), pp. 57–8. Matthiessen discusses Emerson's conviction "that the
only way in which his mind could gain knowledge from experience was not
by worrying it with analysis, but by unquestioning immersion in the flow of
every day, thus penetrating the mystery by living it." Ibid., p. 57. This attitude
is parallel to Freud's recommendation to analysts of evenly hovering attention.

our own inadequacies. If an old system of thought like Puritanism or transcendentalism seems humanly preposterous, a good corrective to our sense of self-importance can be a reminder of the difficulties in human communication. For just as each individual expresses himself in his own emotional language, so each age has its own way of communicating those human insights which it is tempting to think we have discovered for the first time.

One task of intellectual history is to restore the broken links between one age and its predecessors. An empathic knowledge of the past not only reminds us how little we know for ourselves in an articulated way; it also enables us to see exactly what was living in old systems of thought. A definition of a "new" system of thought would be one which helps to revive in an organized way the aspirations, as well as the pains, of peoples distant in time or space.

In the instance of Freud, he needed to combine the knowledge of the artist and the scientist in order to achieve his central contribution. "Very often it is the poet who senses the hidden and unspoken, the general and far-reaching."[5] Yet about his own artistic capacities, Freud was sometimes apologetic. In writing one of his earliest case histories, he paused to comment: "It still strikes me myself as strange that the case histories I write should read like short stories and that, as one might say, they lack the serious stamp of science."[6] A glance at the ideal of a novelist like Henry James suggests the extent to which Freud's intuitive gifts were those of the creative artist:

The power to guess the unseen from the seen, to trace the implication of things, to judge the whole piece by the pattern, the

[5] Kurt Eissler: "Mankind at Its Best," *Journal of the American Psychoanalytic Association*, Vol. 12, No. 1 (January 1964), p. 212.

[6] *Standard Edition*, Vol. 2, p. 160.

condition of feeling life in general so completely that you are well on your way to knowing any particular corner of it—this cluster of gifts may almost be said to constitute experience.[7]

Like James, Freud held that everything we do is in a sense an expression of ourselves; every slip, every stammer, every symptom points to verbally unexpressed emotions. And sometimes we conceal more when we speak than when we are silent. Our bodies speak when our tongues fail us.

It will be apparent, then, that to an analytically inclined observer, the concept of "behavior" is more complex than we generally assume. In fact the more obvious behavior often reveals little or nothing of what lies behind it.

One may be a conservative out of fear or superb courage. A radical may be such because he is so secure in his fundamental psychic organization as to have no fear for the future, or, on the contrary, his courage may be merely the fantasied rebound from fear of the only too well known.[8]

Behavioral reality can hide latent meanings; the quality of an act, the texture of an experience, all that comprises what we have come to know as psychic reality is left out of a merely behavioral account.

Of course it might be possible to extend the meaning of the concept of "behavior" in such a way as to embrace more fully the facts as we know them. Nevertheless, there must remain at bottom a difference between acts and motives, between behavior directly and indirectly perceptible, between that which is knowingly or unwittingly revealed. Psychoanalysis is concerned above all with the "gap between word and deed, the emotional tone that belies the overt

[7] *The Portable Henry James,* ed. M. D. Zabel (New York: Viking; 1951), p. 402.

[8] Edward Sapir: *Culture, Language, and Personality* (Berkeley, Calif.: University of California Press; 1960), p. 160.

ideal allegiance, the apparently careless phrase or gesture betraying an unrecognized intention. . . ."[9] This is perhaps that aspect of experience that Little Hans, the child subject of one of Freud's most beautiful case histories, was referring to when he said to his father one day that "wanting's not doing, and doing's not wanting."[1]

In part this outlook was an expression once more of Freud's artistic gifts; for it has been traditionally the novelists and poets who have had a feel for the "sensibility with which the outer world is appreciated and felt."[2] People do "move in their own envelope of consciousness, isolated and undivined."[3] The insistence on the importance of the inwardness of experience runs throughout psychoanalysis. Glover, for example, remarks that the "ideal approach to any important problem is from within outwards."[4] Psychoanalysis is above all interested in the texture of experience, in the qualities of life, in the way things are done.

Historians, too, the recorders of past realities, have at their best been in Freud's sense natural psychologists. "The historian's primary need is the knowledge that is like knowledge of someone's character or face, not like knowledge of facts."[5] To make this point, Sir Lewis Namier invokes the poet-novelist George Meredith, who

calls it an ironical habit of mind to believe that the wishes of men are expressed by their utterances. . . . To treat them [political

[9] H. Stuart Hughes: "History and Psychoanalysis," in *History as Art and as Science* (New York: Harper & Row; 1964), p. 50.

[1] *Standard Edition*, Vol. 10, p. 31.

[2] Leon Edel: *The Modern Psychological Novel* (New York: Doubleday Anchor Books; 1959), p. 133.

[3] Ibid., p. 91.

[4] Edward Glover: "War and Pacifism," *Character and Personality*, Vol. 4, No. 4 (June 1936), p. 312.

[5] Sir Isaiah Berlin: "History and Theory: The Concept of Scientific History," *History and Theory*, Vol. 1, No. 1 (1960), p. 75.

ideas] as the offspring of pure reason would be to assign to them a parentage about as mythological as that of Pallas Athene. What matters most is the underlying emotions, the music, to which ideas are a mere libretto, often of very inferior quality; and once the emotions have ebbed, the ideas established high and dry, become doctrine, or at best innocuous clichés.[6]

The most memorable accounts of the history of ideas manage to pierce the smokescreen which, for one motive or another, each of us needs to defend his deepest feelings. As Nietzsche once said, "philosophic systems have one point which is entirely irrefutable, a personal mood or color; one can use them to get the picture of the philosopher. . . ."[7]

The gulf between "doing" and "wanting," between action and motives, between external and internal reality, is of importance for understanding not only the history of ideas, but all of political life. The penumbra surrounding political issues is vital to an understanding of what is at stake in any conflict, and it is the absence of that crucial shadowland which we feel most keenly when we study the politics of another culture or another period.

"Doing" by itself, even electoral returns, tells us a lot less than the full reality. One must also understand how people perceived the election, what their psychic needs and expectations were. This is, after all, why intellectual history is so important. Richard Hofstadter has recently stressed the importance of the symbolic aspects of politics.

To the present generation of historical and political writers it has become increasingly clear that people not only seek their interests but also express and even in a measure define themselves

[6] Sir Lewis Namier: "Human Nature in Politics," *The Listener,* Vol. 50, No. 1295 (December 24, 1953), p. 1078.

[7] Quoted in Walter Kaufmann: *Nietzsche* (Princeton, N. J.: Princeton University Press; 1950), p. 58.

in politics; that political life acts as a sounding board for identities, values, fears, and aspirations. . . . I have no interest in denying the reality, or even the primacy, of the problems of money and power, but only in helping to define their reality by turning attention to the human context in which they arise and in which they have to be settled.[8]

Academic political science as a whole has been too concerned with brute data and has been afraid to deal with the more elusive question of qualities of experience, or at least to acknowledge so doing. In part this is due to a justified fear of vague impressionism. But it also fits a peculiarly American attitude to reality. "In the American metaphysic, reality is always material reality, hard, resistant, unformed, impenetrable, and unpleasant. And that mind is alone felt to be trustworthy which most resembles this reality by most nearly reproducing the sensations it affords."[9] It is as if there were a fixed quantity of this "objectivist" spirit in American intellectual life. Earlier in this century, the exponents of scientific history expressed this impulse. Carl Becker's critique of the use of historical facts needs to be turned nowadays upon the behavioralist use of data. "While we speak of historical facts as if they were pebbles to be gathered in a cup, there is in truth no unit fact in history . . . to set forth historical facts is not comparable to dumping a barrow of bricks."[1] Becker insisted on the importance of the "inner psychic dimension of history, in contrast to the positivists' external and atomistic treatment of the past."[2]

[8] Richard Hofstadter: *The Paranoid Style in American Politics* (New York: Knopf; 1965), pp. ix–x.

[9] Lionel Trilling: *The Liberal Imagination* (New York: Doubleday Anchor Books; 1957), pp. 10–11.

[1] Quoted in Cushing Strout: *The Pragmatic Revolt in American History* (New Haven, Conn.: Yale University Press; 1958), pp. 34–5.

[2] Ibid., p. 65.

It is no accident that in America we find this persistent inclination to focus on the externals of behavior. It is in large part an ideological consequence of a liberal society. Historically it has been one of the tasks of liberalism to defend the distinction between a man's mind and his actions, his intentions and his deeds; otherwise there seemed a danger of the individual not being able to defend himself against state action. Hence the well-known maxim from English law that "the thought of man is not tryable; the Devil alone knows the thought of man." To judge the soul of a man, instead of his actions, seemed to open the way to tyranny. This division between inner and outer states also played its part in the history of the rise of religious toleration; the "Render unto Caesar" line of thought figured prominently, for example, in John Locke.

All the life and power of true religion consist in the inward and full persuasion of the mind; and faith is not faith without believing . . . all the power of civil authority relates only to men's civil interests, is confined to the care of the things of this world, and hath nothing to do with the world to come . . . men cannot be forced to be saved whether they will or no.[3]

This characteristic attitude can be traced throughout liberal legal theory. It was one reason for Justice Holmes's insistence on external standards in criminal liability, since morals concern the "actual internal state of the individual's mind, what he actually intends."[4] The same liberal attitude that strove to separate law from morality was also at work in the old opposition of liberal legal theory to equity. To exclaim, as Thoreau did of John Brown, that "the method

[3] John Locke: *Treatise of Civil Government and A Letter Concerning Toleration* (New York: Appleton-Century-Crofts; 1937), pp. 173, 175, 192.

[4] Quoted in Morton White: *Social Thought in America* (Boston: Beacon Press; 1957), p. 68.

is nothing, the spirit is all,"[5] is to depart from liberalism's characteristic reliance on procedural justice. Traditionally it has been the political reactionaries who have sat in judgment on men's hearts.[6] Concentration on inner sinfulness, for example, can lead to political authoritarianism, as it certainly did for the Inquisitions.

But this liberal norm of confining the state's interest to external behavior rather than inner feelings has too often influenced political science in its empirical research. Margaret Mead has noted a similar tendency in American society, commenting on the "one-dimensional public language, a language oriented to the description of external aspects of behavior, weak in overtones."[7] Liberalism has contributed to our blindness to expressiveness, which in a sense was the crux of John Stuart Mill's criticism of Bentham.

What has happened time and time again is that political scientists profess to be dubious about understanding motives, are skeptical about psychoanalytic theory, and then proceed, in an undercover way, to infer a rationalistic set of motives from political behavior. Perhaps the point can be made plausible by referring to an explanation of voting behavioralists. The notion that cross-pressured voters tend to abstain from voting is widely accepted.[8] Yet if one considers that notion from a psychoanalytic point of view, it quickly becomes an unlikely account of reality. What they would have us believe is that mental conflict about how to vote produces withdrawal from voting; yet we know that

[5] C. Vann Woodward: *The Burden of Southern History* (Baton Rouge, La.: Louisiana State University Press; 1960), p. 56.

[6] Shklar: *Legalism*, p. 43.

[7] Margaret Mead: *And Keep Your Powder Dry* (New York: William Morrow; 1942), p. 89.

[8] B. R. Berelson, P. F. Lazarsfeld, and W. N. McPhee: *Voting* (Chicago: The University of Chicago Press; 1954). But cf. Robert E. Lane: *Political Life* (New York: The Free Press of Glencoe; 1965), p. 116.

mental conflict can in principle produce just about any kind
of behavior, from abstention to hyperinvolvement.

It is on the face of it strange to insist that there is only
one behavioral outcome of a psychic conflict. One could
point to men caught between the claims of a traditional
society and the attractions of modernization who have responded to these "cross-pressures" with revolutionary political action. What the voting behavioralists have done is to
describe their material in an excessively elliptical way. What
they can be taken to mean is that in a very special type of
conflict situation, voters tend to display an exceptional behavioral reaction.

It is not nit-picking to insist on a more elaborate expression of the psychology of voting behavior. What the original
notion of cross-pressured voters tends to overlook is that the
state of being cross-pressured is not extraordinary; all of us
suffer from cross pressures, in one area of our lives or another. In American history, white Southerners have openly
displayed their inner conflicts over the treatment of the
Negroes. That the Southerners were not wholly racist, but
that underneath their behavior were elements of a Jeffer-
sonian conscience, was misunderstood by Eisenhower; the
tragedy of his Administration was the wasted opportunity
for racial justice. The extent to which Southern political
leaders were politicians as well as racists can be seen in the
ease with which some of them adjusted to the increased
voting power of Negroes. It was not that they abandoned
former convictions, but that the new electoral realities mobilized different elements in their set of beliefs. For it is
psychologically quite usual for a person's convictions to be
in conflict with each other.

Behavioralists have difficulty in handling the problem of
how much one counts one pressure against another, with

how much emotional importance one invests any one influence. If they are too concerned with behavioral "doing," they have difficulties rendering an accurate account of experience as a whole. Fred Greenstein concluded from his study of the development of children's knowledge and preferences in politics that "the significance of children's choices of exemplars becomes fully clear only when we have reasonably comprehensive data on the meaning of the choice to the child. . . . We need not only inventories of responses, but also knowledge of the meanings of responses."[9]

What any behavioralistic account must necessarily underplay is what Little Hans meant by "wanting." A considerable portion of life consists of intentions, fantasies, and the expressive gestures which reveal them; and according to Freud those of which we are unaware become all the more important in determining what we are like and what we do. No one could get through life without at least a partial understanding of the role of these emotions. As Freud put it, "everyone possesses in his own unconscious an instrument with which he can interpret the utterances of the unconscious in other people."[1] And yet it is remarkable how little we seem to admit intellectually the importance of such unconscious factors.

In our daily life we all know that a gesture, an inflection, a nuance of phrase, may show a latent meaning which is the opposite of the patent one. In our working life, however, we fear to rely on such "human" knowledge because of the difficulties of proof, of standardization, and of validation.[2]

---

[9] Fred I. Greenstein: *Children and Politics* (New Haven, Conn.: Yale University Press; 1965), p. 151.

[1] *Standard Edition*, Vol. 12, p. 320.

[2] David Riesman: *Individualism Reconsidered* (New York: The Free Press of Glencoe; 1954), p. 507.

Acknowledging unconscious mental processes can set limits on the research techniques of political science. The use of questionnaires should be reconsidered; if people do not know themselves, if they deceive themselves about what they think, then consciously expressed opinions and attitudes have to be interpreted with subtlety. So psychoanalysis becomes applicable precisely where behavioralism's short-comings begin to show up. In doing research on the response of some college students to the death of President Kennedy, Fred Greenstein commented that survey research would probably be unable to bring to light ambivalent responses to Mrs. Kennedy, and that many of the statements that did appear in his interviews "certainly would not have emerged from structured questionnaires."[3]

The conflict between the approach of the techniques of social survey research and psychoanalytic theory exists within some political science projects themselves. For many people who have used psychiatric knowledge in political science have done so without reconsidering whether their techniques are at odds with the theoretical structure they intend to implement. There is a widespread reluctance to acknowledge the subjectivist character of psychological knowledge, and a corresponding tendency to attempt to render psychological insights prematurely scientific by social survey techniques. That psychological understanding is first of all a question of the sensitivity of the finger tips has yet to be conceded.

It should of course be acknowledged that for certain purposes, like predicting voting behavior, the newest devices

---

[3] Fred I. Greenstein: "Young Men and the Death of a Young President," in *Children and the Death of a President*, ed. Martha Wolfenstein and Gilbert Kliman (New York: Doubleday & Co.; 1965), p. 173.

of polling may be excellent on theoretical grounds alone. If one wants to know, today, what the voters will be doing tomorrow, then survey research is quite appropriate. One can even go further in a nonpsychological direction: in a world of limited resources, analyses at a gross level, focusing on power considerations and conscious ideas, may be more economical in terms of expenditure of effort and predictive success than a more thorough study which includes unconscious personality factors, ideology, attitudes, and the like. One must surely insist that it is possible to learn things in politics in quite unclinical ways.

There is in fact, especially among psychologists, a danger of neglecting reality factors and objective considerations. As Erikson has pointed out,

when a devotional denial of the face, and a systematic mistrust of all surface are used as tools in a man's work-life, they can lead to an almost obsessional preoccupation with "the unconscious," a dogmatic emphasis on inner processes as the only true essence of things human, and an over-estimation of verbal meanings in human life. . . .[4]

When dealing with the unknown, one must reckon with the danger of magical thinking. The inevitable interplay between external and internal forces must always be remembered.

According to psychoanalysis, the human mind is structured at various levels, and the deepest layers are not always operative. If it were not for the "surface," after all, many more of us would commit crimes. One can be superficial in overemphasizing the unconscious as well as in neglecting it. Not everything in a human being is always in

[4] Erikson: *Young Man Luther*, p. 152.

operation. But psychoanalysis can still remind us that we live at more than one level at any given time. And for certain purposes in studying politics, for example to understand the political tradition of a nation, depth analysis may be quite essential.

The approach of depth psychology is designed to focus on the "way in which human beings in a specific situation subjectively experience themselves."[5] This approach to behavior, with its stress on inner psychic reality, is used within clinical psychoanalysis itself. "The psychoanalytic interest is not so much in what a man does as why he does it and how he feels about having done or not done it."[6] For diagnostic purposes, for example, Anna Freud thinks that "the manifest behavior of the child is very seldom ground for correct judgment."[7] The same psychic conflicts can sometimes be expressed by a shifting variety of manifest expressions. Yet the relation between overt behavioral symptoms and underlying conflicts has guidelines.[8]

If all this seems difficult, it is only because of the nature of the unconscious itself. Normal logic applies only to external or shared reality; "mental life is the arena and battleground for mutually opposing purposes . . . it consists of contradictions and pairs of contraries. Proof of the existence of a particular purpose is no argument against the existence of an opposite one: there is room for both."[9]

[5] Peter L. Berger: "Toward a Sociological Understanding of Psychoanalysis," *Social Research*, Vol. 32, No. 1 (Spring 1965), p. 33.

[6] Alex Inkeles, in *Psychoanalysis, Scientific Method, and Philosophy*, ed. Sidney Hook (New York: Grove Press; 1960), p. 126.

[7] A. Freud: *Psychoanalysis for Teachers and Parents* (Boston: Beacon Press; 1935), p. 109.

[8] A. Freud: "Four Contributions to the Psychoanalytic Study of the Child," *Bulletin of the Philadelphia Association for Psychoanalysis*, Vol. 11 (1961), p. 82.

[9] *Standard Edition*, Vol. 15, pp. 76–7.

The unconscious is first and last a topsy-turvy world, the bearer of our infantile past. "Psychoanalytic research . . . has no other end in view than to throw light on things by tracing what is manifest back to what is hidden."[1]

Not only in diagnosis, but in treatment as well, we find this psychoanalytic outlook on behavior. Analysts are insistent on aiming at "structural" psychological changes in patients instead of symptomatic changes: "the relief of the symptom is not the primary concern of the analyst, but the change of the psychic reality underlying a symptom is."[2] "The mere change of behavior *per se* is no criterion for the evaluation of a psychiatric treatment. . . ."[3] Analysts are not interested merely in adjustment, which is the focus of physical techniques of personality change.

The metrazol treated patient achieves his social adjustment at the expense of specifically human qualities which make the human being genuinely different from all other species. He acts like a termite in the social structure, rather than like a human being with his doubts, his sinful propensities, his hopes and disappointments.[4]

Precisely because of its preoccupation with motivation, because it is interested in psychic reality as well as external behavior, psychoanalysis can help to show the inadequacies of behavioralism. Freud has expanded our conception of the humanly plausible.

[1] Ibid., Vol. II, p. 187.

[2] Kurt Eissler: "The Chicago Institute of Psychoanalysis and the Sixth Period of the Development of Psychoanalytic Technique," *The Journal of General Psychology*, Vol. 42, First Half (January 1950), p. 118.

[3] Kurt Eissler: "Schizophrenia: Structural Analysis and Metrazol Treatment," *Psychiatry*, Vol. 6, No. 1 (1943), p. 81.

[4] Ibid.

## 3   Metapsychology

What the clinician does may be artistic and in a sense inexplicable, but political scientists need to be able to rely on some formulated scientific propositions. In order to extract these hypotheses, we must turn to the theoretical work which underlies clinical psychoanalytic practice. If we could not point to any agreed body of theory, we would have only the example of clinicians in action, which is hardly superior to the example of an intuitive historian like Arthur Schlesinger, Jr. at work. If psychoanalysis is to be of use to political studies, it must present a theoretical structure which eases communication among practitioners and enhances the awareness of outsiders.

While the theory of psychoanalysis is still not very well coordinated with what goes on in clinical practice, it is generally agreed that Freud looked on the self from four distinct points of view: (1) the topographical, (2) the dynamic, (3) the economic, and (4) the structural. Peculiar though this terminology may seem at first, it does manage to sum up some of Freud's chief theoretical orientations. By introducing these concepts at this point we not only obtain a schematic summary of Freud's conception of human nature, but also lay the background for later discussion.

By the topographical point of view, Freud meant the concepts conscious, preconscious, and unconscious. The distinction between conscious and preconscious is largely between that which one is already aware of and that which can come into awareness without resistances or outside help. The preconscious therefore approximates to what William James called the "fringes of consciousness." The unconscious is of course that which is forcibly kept from awareness by inner blocks. A thought may pass through the pre-conscious from the unconscious to consciousness. It needs to be stressed that any psychic structure or mental act can be looked at from the topographical point of view; large parts of the ego (the resistances) and superego (the need for punishment) are unconscious. The topographical stand-point, in other words, points to the degree of accessibility of emotions and thoughts.

By the dynamic point of view Freud meant the variety of mental forces, the conflicts between them, and the com-promises that are worked out; this includes, then, the vari-ous drives and the ego's defenses against them. It was this perspective which brought psychiatry out of its purely de-scriptive phase before psychoanalysis. The opposing forces embodied in a defense not only ward off anxiety from within, but also can function adaptively in relation to the outside world. From this standpoint, "any element of personality can become a defense mechanism: intelligence as well as stupidity, flight into reality as well as flight from reality."[1] Defenses can either postpone the gratification of instincts, or function more radically to avoid certain human relations entirely, in order to preclude losses or frustrations. It is these defenses which keep us ignorant of our motives and feelings.

A famous saying of Nietzsche's, for example, illustrates the mechanism of repression: " 'I did this,' says my Memory. 'I cannot have done this,' says my Pride and remains in-exorable. In the end—Memory yields."[2] By contrasting the concept of repression with that of the unconscious, we can see the distinction between the topographical and dynamic points of view:

[1] Helene Deutsch: *The Psychology of Women*, Vol. I, p. 23.
[2] Quoted in *Standard Edition*, Vol. 10, p. 184.

"Unconscious" is a purely descriptive term, one that is indefinite in some respects and, as we might say, static. "Repressed" is a dynamic expression which takes account of the interplay of mental forces. . . . The mark of something repressed is precisely that in spite of its intensity it is unable to enter consciousness.[3]

Repression is of course only one of the possible defense mechanisms; there are other methods, short of direct fulfillment, for handling the drives as well. To identify, for example, means to treat an external quality or person as though it were internal. As we shall see later, identifications with past political leaders and ideals can help explain social cohesion and cultural continuities. To project, on the other hand, means to treat an internal state as though it were in the external world. For example, people have for centuries negatively projected onto minorities, like Jews, their own disguised fears and impulses (inferiority, lasciviousness, greediness, etc.). Negroes in America have served a similar psychological function for objectifying a slightly different set of anxieties. Paradoxically people have also projected onto these groups their own unrealistic aspirations (the Jew's magical intelligence, the Negro's infinite patience and understanding). For our purposes here it will be sufficient to note that in addition to these defenses, the mind also has available such devices as reaction-formation, displacement, isolation, and so on.

The mechanism of sublimation is perhaps best illustrated by an anecdote of Heine's, retold by Freud at one of the private meetings at his apartment in Vienna:

One early summer morning many years ago, the inhabitants of a small German university town . . . made the horrifying discovery that all the dogs which had been running loose during

[3] Ibid., Vol. 9, p. 48.

the night in a certain part of the city had lost their tails. They learned that the medical students had attended a drinking bout that night and that when they left the party one young man had had the highly humorous inspiration to cut off the tails of the dogs. Later he became one of the most famous surgeons in the world.[4]

The problem of distinguishing between a neurotic defense and a genuine sublimation is a difficult one. Disregarding here the remote origins of the activities in question, they can be considered sublimations to the extent that they contribute to the growth of the ego and its adaptation to reality. Art, for example, disciplines impulses without negating them: "It liberates energies and is not parasitical on them. . . ."[5]

One defense mechanism which has obvious interest for political scientists is our capacity for rationalization. This psychological term was originally coined by Ernest Jones; he defined it as a "false explanation that has a plausible ring of rationality."[6] All of us are perfectly familiar with rationalization in political life; it approximates Marx's view of ideology, although the psychoanalytic view sees the motive in the individual's more strictly personal need for self-deception. Rationalization, like the other defense mechanisms, is part of the dynamic viewpoint in that it is a concept developed to handle the phenomena of psychic forces; in this case, an impulse is unconsciously unacceptable to our self-image until dressed in the cloak of a more acceptable motive.

Freud's economic viewpoint concerned the energies of

---

[4] Helene Deutsch: "Some Psychoanalytic Observations on Surgery," *Psychosomatic Medicine*, Vol. 4, No. 1 (January 1942), p. 115.

[5] Devereux: "Art and Mythology," p. 381.

[6] Ernest Jones: "Rationalization in Everyday Life," in *An Outline of Psychoanalysis*, ed. J. S. van Teslaar (New York: Modern Library; 1924), p. 104.

psychic life, the quantitative aspect of human psychology. This perspective points to the proportional strength of mental forces, and is especially relevant to the way Freud thought about the problem of normality. In principle there was no qualitative difference between normal and abnormal; all the most bizarre psychic mechanisms could be found in the dreams of normal people or in the slips of everyday life. The line could be drawn, however, on the basis of the relative strength of these mechanisms, the weight they had in daily life. The metaphor of quantities in psychic life also played a role in Freud's discussion of the pleasure principle. Unpleasure corresponded to the increase in the quantity of mental excitation, and pleasure to a diminution of excitation; it was the task of the mental apparatus as a whole to keep down the total level of excitation. Two of Freud's well-known concepts are economic. "Cathexis" refers to the mind's investment of psychic energy, "an accumulation of psychic energy in any one part of the psychic apparatus."[7] "Trauma" is also an economic concept, "referring not principally to the content of the experience but to its intensity. Trauma is overstimulation, whether from overgratifying or overfrustrating experiences; it involves not just what occurs externally but the dovetailing of external events and inner psychic organization."[8]

Certain familiar phenomena are explicable along economic lines. For example, certain early conflicts—dormant during the latency period—may become intensified during adolescence or menopause; these are periods of intensified instinctual urges, and hence the mental apparatus is sub-

[7] Richard Sterba: *Introduction to the Psychoanalytic Theory of Libido* (New York: Nervous and Mental Disease Monographs; 1942), p. 37.

[8] Heinz Kohut and Philip Seitz: "Concepts and Theories of Psychoanalysis," in *Concepts of Personality*, ed. Joseph M. Wepman and Ralph Heine (Chicago: Aldine Publishing Co.; 1963), p. 127.

jected to increased strains and fresh resolutions of old conflicts. Certain familial objects (father, mother, siblings) can be more or less cathected with emotional feeling; in other words, their emotional importance for the individual may increase or decrease at certain stages of the life cycle.

While the economic point of view was one of Freud's earliest notions, the structural point of view was formulated only in the 1920's.[9] Freud's ability to dramatize his concepts visually was never better illustrated than in the concepts of id, ego, and superego. The id is the repository of instinctual strivings; it is the oldest past of the mind and is entirely unconscious. Freud thought that the ego gradually separated off from the id: "In the id there are no conflicts; contradictions and antitheses persist side by side in it unconcernedly, and are often adjusted by the formation of compromises. . . . The ego is an organization characterized by a very remarkable trend towards unification, towards synthesis."[1] In a famous early image, Freud compared the ego in its relation to the id to "a man on horseback, who has to hold in check the superior strength of the horse; with this difference, that the rider tries to do so with his own strength while the ego uses borrowed forces."[2]

The ego can be described apart from the id, as more than a mediator between the wishes of the drives and the realities of the external world. As it has been conceived in recent years, "there are independent, or better, relatively independent ego interests and autonomous ego functions,

[9] It is not certain that Freud himself would have considered the structural point of view as part of his metapsychology; but since his death this perspective has been so widely shared as the basis of so much work among his pupils that it is now accepted as a legitimate part of psychoanalytic metapsychology, even if only implicitly within Freud's own writings.

[1] *Standard Edition*, Vol. 20, p. 196.

[2] Ibid., Vol. 19, p. 25.

which may be, but not necessarily, a part of mental conflict."[3] In other words, the ego can be described as a psychic
organization; it is a structure defined by its functions. From
the economic point of view, it derives its energy cathexis
from sublimated psychic energy: "the energy of instinctual
drives . . . [can] be sublimated or neutralized; desexualized
or de-aggressivized energy contributes the motor power for
the complex functions of the ego."[4] The ego consists not
only of all those defense mechanisms outlined under the
dynamic point of view, but also of perception, motility,
memory, etc. Not only can the ego as a psychic unit conflict with other parts of the mental apparatus, but it is possible for ego functions to conflict with each other.

As for the superego, there have been changes in the usage
of this concept. Earlier, there was a tendency to restrict its
meaning to the unconscious conscience or the sense of guilt,
labelling the conscious demands of conscience the "ego-
ideal." Nowadays, it is customary to distinguish between
superego and ego-ideal, not on the grounds of consciousness, but rather as to whether they stand for the restrictive
(superego) or aspirational (ego-ideal) aspects of conscience.

The harshness of the superego, in the sense of the restrictive aspect of conscience, is as much a consequence of the
child's projection of his own aggressions as it is a result
of actual parental standards: "the original severity of the
superego does not—or does not so much—represent the
severity which one [the child] has experienced from it [the
parental object], or which one attributes to it; it represents
rather one's own aggressiveness towards it."[5] There was

---

[3] Ernst Kris: "The Development of Ego Psychology," *Samiksa*, Vol. 5. No. 3
(1951), pp. 160–1.

[4] Ibid., p. 160.

[5] *Standard Edition*, Vol. 21, pp. 129–30.

even a period in the history of psychoanalysis when the aim of psychoanalytic treatment was described in terms of the dissolution of the superego; the superego's harshness is in excess of any rational standards, since it "originates in the id drives, and one of the functions of the superego, self-punishment, regresses frequently to its instinctual origin, thus often bringing about the sexualization of the punitive function."[6] The concept of the superego, and its importance within the psychic apparatus, supports Freud's claim that it was no part of his "intention to dispute the noble endeavors of human nature":

. . . I am exhibiting to you not only the evil dream-wishes which are censored but also the censorship, which suppresses them and makes them unrecognizable . . . human nature has a far greater extent, both for good and for evil, than it thinks it has—i.e. than its ego is aware of through conscious perception.[7]

These structural concepts of id, ego, and superego are all broadly familiar to us now. Just because of this familiarity, though, it should be emphasized again that the structural orientation is only one of several available; any thought or feeling or action can be looked at from each of these four standpoints. The structural point of view, despite the attractiveness of its imagery, must be recognized as a late formulation of Freud's; psychoanalysis can live as a system of thought without it. One of the distinctive advantages of the structural point of view is that it allows for the crystallization of psychic energies and forces into structures; otherwise it might become difficult to see why an individual, beset by mental conflicts, would not fail to cohere and disappear

[6] Rudolf M. Loewenstein: "A Special Form of Self-Punishment," *The Psychoanalytic Quarterly*, Vol. 14 (1945), p. 52.

[7] *Standard Edition*, Vol. 15, pp. 146–7; ibid., Vol. 19, p. 52.

psychologically into a puff of smoke.[8] "Forces and energies cannot exist in a structural vacuum; they must operate on masses arranged in particular organizations."[9]

Taken together, these four points of view (topographical, dynamic, economic, and structural) comprise what Freud considered his "metapsychology." "The 'meta' in the term points to a theory going 'beyond' the investigation of conscious phenomena."[1] Conviction in the explanation of an act becomes stronger the more these viewpoints converge in any one direction. It must be remembered that any such metaphyschological "ideas are not the foundation of science, upon which everything rests: that foundation is observation alone. They are not the bottom but the top of the whole structure, and they can be replaced and discarded without damaging it."[2]

To present psychoanalytic theory in this way is bound to be misleading in that it does not show how various layers were added or why many shifts were made. But at least this summary of Freud's ideas should demonstrate the extent to which he viewed man as ineluctably at odds with himself. Ernst Kris once defined the subject matter of psychoanalysis as "human behavior viewed as conflict."[3] Psychoanalysis, at least as Freud left it, becomes "less relevant in conflict-free areas."[4]

---

[8] Merton Gill: "Psychoanalysis and Exploratory Psychotherapy," *Journal of the American Psychoanalytic Association*, Vol. 11, No. 4 (October 1954), p. 791.

[9] Robert R. Holt: "Two Influences on Freud's Scientific Thought," in *The Study of Lives*, ed. Robert W. White (New York: Atherton Press; 1963), p. 374.

[1] Heinz Hartmann, in *Psychoanalysis, Scientific Method, and Philosophy*, p. 13.

[2] *Standard Edition*, Vol. 14, p. 77; cf. also Vol. 20, pp. 32–3.

[3] Ernst Kris: "The Nature of Psychoanalytic Propositions and Their Validation," in *Freedom and Experience*, ed. Sidney Hook and M. R. Konwitz (New York: Cornell University Press; 1947), p. 241.

[4] Robert Waelder: *Psychoanalytic Avenues to Art* (New York: International Universities Press; 1965), p. 11.

This account of some of Freud's central ideas is merely intended to set the stage by way of clarification for some of the later discussion. Psychoanalytic theory described apart from clinical material or social problems must necessarily seem dry as dust. But an outline cannot do more than clear some of the underbrush of misunderstanding. Another tack will be to examine some aspects of the history of psychoanalysis, adding a vertical look at the past to the horizontal understanding of logic. In this way we can avoid some of the artificialities of introducing Freud through the intricacies of either libido theory or ego psychology. By using psychoanalytic concepts to understand the origins of Freud's ideas, it may prove possible not only to give depth to our knowledge of Freud's thought, but also to establish more securely the relevance of psychoanalysis to political and social thought.

*CHAPTER 11*

# The Significance of a Theory

## The Origins

In order to avoid one more false start in utilizing psychoanalytic theory, it is helpful to have in mind an outline of
the growth and development of Freud's ideas. For no matter how much theorists prefer concepts arranged in tidy
little boxes, if we look at all closely at the birth of any scientific idea we are bound to see how much confusion there
really is. The groping and stumbling of a man like Freud
can teach us almost as much about the quality of his mind
as the substance of his scientific findings themselves.

Freud's crisis in the summer of 1897 is not only a central
turning point in the history of his ideas, but can also illustrate many of his most characteristic modes of thinking.
It was then that Freud abandoned his seduction theory; up
to that point he had believed that the source of the neuroses
of his patients could be traced to their sexual seduction as

children. Even Freud's own father was incriminated in such acts, on the basis of some symptoms in Freud's brother and his sisters.[1] When Freud interpreted a dream as containing a sexual wish toward his own eldest daughter, he wrote to his close friend Fliess that "the dream of course fulfils my wish to pin down a father as the originator of neurosis and put an end to my persistent doubts."[2]

Exactly what transformed the doubts he harbored into a conviction that he had been wrong has never been made quite clear. It has been suggested that Freud's self-analysis, which began at about this time, was responsible for his change of mind.[3] But it is as reasonable to suppose that his realization that he had been mistaken, and that he had helped to mislead his patients—at least partially out of an unsettled grudge against his own father—had, by itself, been enough of a jolt to accelerate his historic self-analysis.

The truest test of character is not the mistakes one makes, but what one can do with them. While it was years before Freud publicly discussed his abandonment of the seduction theory, and even then he never discussed the role of his unresolved problem with his own father, inwardly he began at this point to reconstruct his conceptions. His solution lay in treating the tales of his patients as fantasies instead of realities. Rather than holding that children were seduced

[1] Ernest Jones: *The Life and Work of Sigmund Freud* (London: Hogarth Press; 1954) (cited hereafter as *Sigmund Freud*), Vol. 1, 2nd edn., p. 254; S. Freud: *The Origins of Psychoanalysis*, ed. Marie Bonaparte, Anna Freud, and Ernst Kris (London: Imago; 1954), p. 219. Parts of this story, and many aspects of Freud's feelings during this whole period, have been suppressed in the volume of Freud's letters to Fliess. For a fuller version of the seduction theory, cf. *Standard Edition*, Vol. I, p. 259, where Freud writes that "in every case the father, *not excluding my own*, had to be blamed as a pervert." The clause italicized here was censored in the original publication of this letter to Fliess.

[2] Freud: *The Origins of Psychoanalysis*, p. 206.

[3] Ibid., p. 216.

into sexuality, Freud discovered that they <u>were themselves sexual beings</u>. Their tales of seduction were simply expressions of infantile desires, of which they were unconscious; these longings were mobilized in the therapeutic relationship, since the patient transferred to the therapist, as the surrogate for parental figures, all those infantile feelings which have since come to be labelled the oedipal complex.

We can learn much about Freud's mind by examining this experience. It was decisive for the future of his work in that for the first time psychic reality played a central role in how he thought about his patients; it was no longer a question of traumas being inflicted on helpless innocents, but of the ways in which people are responsible for their own nightmares. Yet this decisive moment in the history of psychotherapy was reached in almost complete solitude. Most of what we know about this period is derived from Freud's letters to his friend Fliess. But even he seems to have been oblivious to Freud's discovery. In October 1897 Freud sent a now famous letter to Fliess:

Only one idea of general value has occurred to me. I have found love of the mother and jealousy of the father in my own case too, and now believe it to be a general phenomenon of early childhood. . . . If that is the case, the gripping power of *Oedipus Rex*, in spite of all the rational objections to the inexorable fate that the story presupposes, becomes intelligible . . . the Greek myth seizes on a compulsion which everyone recognizes because he has felt traces of it in himself. Every member of the audience was once a budding Oedipus in phantasy, and this dream-fulfillment played out in reality causes everyone to recoil in horror, with the full measure of repression which separates his infantile from his present state. The idea has passed through my head that the same thing may lie at the root of *Hamlet*.[4]

----

[4] Ibid., pp. 223-4.

Fliess seems to have been unresponsive to Freud's newest formulations. "You have said nothing about my interpretation of *Oedipus Rex* and *Hamlet*,"[5] Freud lamented several letters later.

Although Freud did have a tendency to pose romantically in his letters, so that one must beware of exaggerating the loneliness of his great discoveries, he does seem to have been working in a void at this time. Later he felt both bitterness and pride about the heroic solitude of his discoveries: "what personal pleasure is to be derived from analysis I obtained during the time when I was alone. . . . An incurable breach must have come into existence at that time between me and other men."[6] This stance fitted an image of himself that he had communicated years before to his future wife: "I have often felt as though I had inherited all the defiance and all the passions with which our ancestors defended their Temple and would gladly sacrifice my life for one great moment in history."[7] He was always truculent about his work, for example even over-using the word "sexual" rather than a blander one like "erotic." "I like to avoid concessions to faintheartedness. One can never tell where that road may lead one; one gives way first in words, and then little by little in substance too . . . he who knows how to wait need make no concessions."[8] Freud communicated to his disciples this spirit of fighting against a world of enemies:

There is a way to represent one's cause and in doing so to treat the audience in such a cool and condescending manner that they are bound to notice one is not doing it to please them. The

5 Ibid., p. 229.
6 Freud: *Psychoanalysis and Faith*, p. 79.
7 S. Freud: *Letters*, ed. Ernst Freud (London: Hogarth Press; 1961), p. 215.
8 *Standard Edition*, Vol. 18, p. 91.

principle should always be not to make concessions to those
who do not have anything to give but who have everything to
gain from us. We can wait until they are begging on their knees
even if it takes a very long time.[9]

Given this kind of determination, it was no surprise if in
Vienna Freud was "appraised and opposed as an obstinate
and difficult intellectual hermit."[1] The distance between
Freud and his city was not just a matter of its hostility to
some of his ideas; his aloofness was also an expression of
his own desire to be left alone. He believed that "great de-
cisions in the realm of thought and momentous discoveries
and solutions of problems are only possible to an individual
working in solitude."[2]

Freud persisted in his self-isolation even among his followers. Lou Andreas-Salomé, with her usual psychological
skill, saw this at the psychoanalytic meetings she attended
in Vienna: Freud, she wrote, "enters the class with the appearance of moving to the side. There is in this gesture a
will to solitude, a concealment of himself within his own
purposes, which by his preference would be no concern of
his school or his public."[3] The records of the *Minutes* of
the Vienna Psychoanalytic Society give the impression of
Freud going very much his own way, standing alone in
a maelstrom of ideas with an inner center of preoccupation. He will often move into a chaotic discussion to bring
it into focus. But nowhere do we find a genuine give and
take between Freud and his pupils.

It is not that Freud did not use some of his students' ideas;

[9] S. Freud: "Letters to Ernst Simmel," *Journal of the American Psychoanalytic Association*, Vol. 12, No. 1 (January 1964), pp. 102–3.

[1] Stefan Zweig: *The World of Yesterday* (London: Cassell; 1953), pp. 419–20.

[2] *Standard Edition*, Vol. 18, p. 83.

[3] Lou Andreas-Salomé: *The Freud Journal*, ed. Stanley Leavy (New York:
Basic Books; 1964), p. 46.

but he was only able to do so when his own intellectual position was in need of them. Sometimes the formulations of his students needed to be only a hairbreadth away from his own for these ideas to appear foreign or even unintelligible to him. Freud cautioned his students about this particular aspect of his thinking:

It is not easy for me to feel my way into another person's thinking; as a whole I have to wait until I have found a connection with it in my own devious ways. So if you want to hold back a new idea every time until I can agree with it, it runs the risk of aging considerably in the meantime . . . it is never easy for me to follow a new train of thought that somehow does not go my own way or to which my way has not yet led me.[4]

Intellectual isolation, however, reinforced Freud's self-analysis. Although the method of introspection was hardly novel, Freud had one advantage over other soul-searchers— his patients. Through the struggle to understand the souls of his patients he found himself able to master his own inner conflicts. "I can only analyse myself with objectively acquired knowledge (as if I were a stranger); self-analysis is really impossible, otherwise there would be no illness."[5] By being able to objectify parts of himself in the course of his therapeutic efforts, Freud was able to relieve his own inner resistances to self-knowledge.

This method of self-understanding presupposed an extraordinary degree of self-detachment on Freud's part. He had to come into contact with some of the most disturbing elements of his own personality, and for that very reason he had to be able to maintain a tremendous distance from these feelings and memories if he was not to be swamped

[4] Quoted in Jessie Taft: *Otto Rank* (New York: Julian Press; 1958), pp. 87 and 107.

[5] Freud: *The Origins of Psychoanalysis*, pp. 234–5.

by his own undercurrents. Another therapist, Breuer for example, would have taken the intense feelings of his patients toward him as a personal matter, and would have fled in the face of the emotions that had been stirred up by the treatment. Freud, however, was able to treat the irrational affection and hatred of his patients as an impersonal matter, as feelings they would transfer from their past onto any outsider intervening in their emotional life. Marie Bonaparte used to tell an anecdote about Freud which illustrates this detachment. She once, while photographing him in his study, told Freud that he was a great man. "I am not a great man; I made a great discovery."[6] This ability to distinguish his own importance from that of his discovery was part of the same attitude that made possible his special kind of self-analysis.

No matter how clear Freud's style, how elegant his theoretical constructions, or how objectively scientific his findings, everything that he wrote about came from within his own emotional matrix. Although sometimes, as in the original seduction theory, Freud's own biases interfered with his work in a rather gross way, the peculiarly personal origin of his discoveries was also the chief source of their depth. Freud had the self-confidence to be unafraid of basing his theories on his own experience. By articulating that insight, by generalizing that plunge within himself, Freud was able to connect, however obliquely, with the experience of others. But by basing his system on his self-knowledge, he constantly exposed himself to the rejection of the less fearless.

Freud was not, it should be pointed out, as isolated as the history of psychoanalysis might lead one to expect. His ideas grew up in a cultural milieu that had many similari-

6 Rudolf Loewenstein: *Freud: Man and Scientist* (New York: International Universities Press; 1951), p. 17.

ties to his ideas. In those years Viennese intellectual life was a veritable Renaissance; in music, philosophy, mathematics, and economics there were new developments. What is more, there was a cultural unity within this intellectual elite, much of it composed of emancipated Jews. A man could shuttle from one field to another, and leaders in one area were aware of innovations in another.

What is remarkable in the case of Freud is not that he was influenced in any simple-minded way by Viennese intellectual life, but the extent to which he emerged with a unique intellectual system out of a cultural background shared in common with others. The extent to which Freud's early followers were all educated men is striking. The *Minutes* of the Vienna Society demonstrate that they all thought effortlessly in terms of broad cultural issues. The present-day editors of the *Minutes* by contrast are almost apologetic about how much time was spent on psychobiographies ("pathographies") of historical figures.[7] (The effort of Erikson and his students to apply psychoanalysis to biographical material is in a sense a return to the original preoccupations of Freud and his circle.) Yet it was no doubt automatic on the part of Freud and his followers to try to integrate their new way of thinking into their cultural heritage.

The relation of early psychoanalysis to its cultural background should not be confused, as it often is, with the influence of books. In 1895 Freud wrote to Fliess that "I am alone with my mind, in which so much is stirring. . . . I do not want to read, because it stirs up too many thoughts and stints me of the satisfaction of discovery."[8] And in 1898 Freud complained again to Fliess: "reading is a terrible in-

[7] Herman Nunberg: "Introduction," *Minutes of the Vienna Psychoanalytic Society*, Vol. I, p. xxviii.

[8] Freud: *The Origins of Psychoanalysis*, p. 126.

fliction imposed upon all who write. In the process everything of one's own drains away."[9] Many years later Freud
felt that "I owe the chance of making a discovery to my
not being well-read."[1] Intellectual historians, when writing
about the genesis of ideas, often speak in terms of the influence of one book upon another; they project their own
scholarly habits onto their objects of study, imputing a
specious bookishness where genuine theoretical creativity is
at work.

For example, parallels are often, and quite rightly, drawn
between Nietzsche's thought and Freud's. In fact the Vienna
Psychoanalytic Society spent a meeting in 1908 discussing
Nietzsche. At that time Freud maintained that his "occasional attempts at reading it [Nietzsche's work] were
smothered by an excess of interest."[2] In his *On the History
of the Psychoanalytic Movement* he said that "in later years
I have denied myself the very great pleasure of reading the
works of Nietzsche, with the deliberate object of not being
hampered in working out the impressions received in psychoanalysis by any sort of anticipatory ideas."[3] Freud reiterated this same theme in his *Autobiography*: "Nietzsche,
another philosopher whose guesses and intuitions often
agree in the most astonishing way with the laborious findings of psychoanalysis, was for a long time avoided by me
on that very account: I was less concerned with the question of priority than with keeping my mind unembar-
rassed."[4]

Besides whatever role Nietzsche may have played in
Freud's mind as a rival in psychological understanding,

[9] Ibid., p. 270.
[1] *Standard Edition*, Vol. 14, p. 15.
[2] *Minutes of the Vienna Psychoanalytic Society*, Vol. I, p. 359.
[3] *Standard Edition*, Vol. 14, pp. 15–16.
[4] Ibid., Vol. 20, p. 60.

Freud's view of Nietzsche's work casts light not merely on his own intellectual course, but—like his lonely self-discovery and his broad cultural background—on the creative act of theorizing. To have hunted up his precursors, whether Nietzsche or Dostoevsky or Schopenhauer, would have blunted the edge of his mind. Having made his own initial discovery, Freud spent the rest of his life spinning out its implications; protecting his autonomy was essential to his continued development. As Thomas Mann recognized,

Freud went his hard way quite alone, quite independent in his character as physician and natural scientist, unsupported by the encouragement which our literature might have given him, without the benefit of personal contact therewith. Perhaps it must always be so; the driving power of his work has undoubtedly been the greater for the lack.[5]

In Nietzsche's case, Freud had far more useful sources of information than books. In his youth, his friend Paneth wrote him about his (Paneth's) personal contact with Nietzsche. And later Lou Andreas-Salomé, once courted by Nietzsche and one of his early expositors, became a follower of Freud's. A living person is often a far more valuable source than a book. A book lies static and finished, it cannot be twisted into one's own line of thought; it can rarely have the force to jar one out of a preconceived line of reasoning. But from a person like Lou Andreas-Salomé Freud could demand answers to whatever questions about Nietzsche's ideas he might pose.

One mark of the original theorist is his willingness to pluck from others what he needs for his own system. In this way he can feed off other thinkers without impairing

[5] Thomas Mann: "Freud's Position in the History of Modern Thought," *Criterion*, Vol. 12 (1933), p. 567.

the integrity of his own preoccupations. This presupposes, of course, that the original insights are of a very high quality. Yet if they go really deep, despite their precursors, their life depends on their independent development. Eclecticism could only smother Freud's system. "The history of science does not support the notion that the way to make progress is to be eclectic and leave nothing out . . . commitment is more important than inclusiveness both in teaching and research, provided the commitment is not merely an inherited one . . . science thrives on sins of omission."[6]

Freud's intolerance of distraction, this insistence on letting his mind follow its own course, presupposed that essential drivenness which is so essential to creative theorizing. Freud was, as Alfred Kazin has put it, a "plunger."[7] "A man like me," Freud wrote to Fliess, "cannot live without a hobby-horse, a consuming passion. . . . I have found my tyrant and in his service I know no limits. My tyrant is psychology. . . ."[8] Once again to Fliess Freud revealed part of his inner identity: "I am not really a man of science, not an observer, not an experimenter, and not a thinker, I am nothing but by temperament a *conquistador*—an adventurer, if you want to translate the word—with the curiosity, the boldness, and the tenacity that belongs to that type of being."[9]

Freud was obsessed with fixed ideas; he was a reductionist, as his critics have so often charged. What they have not appreciated is that this attitude was the necessary consequence of the solitude of his discoveries, as well as a source

[6] David Riesman: *Constraint and Variety in American Education* (New York: Doubleday Anchor Books; 1958), pp. 113–14.

[7] Alfred Kazin, in Benjamin Nelson, ed.: *Freud and the Twentieth Century* (New York: Meridian Books; 1957), p. 18.

[8] Freud: *The Origins of Psychoanalysis*, p. 119.

[9] Jones: *Sigmund Freud*, Vol. I, p. 382.

for his whole creativity. In an age which has seen the political consequence of "terrible simplifiers," it is more difficult to appreciate the intellectual virtues of stubbornness. A century ago it was almost a commonplace. John Stuart Mill wrote that "one-eyed men like Bentham might see what men with normal vision would not. . . . Almost all rich veins of original and striking speculation have been opened by systematic half-thinkers."[1]

Much of the criticism of Freud's case histories has failed to remember this issue; each case was written not with the intention of exhausting the clinical realities, but in order to establish particular theoretical principles. Kris has made a similar point about Freud's *Interpretation of Dreams*: "Freud did not intend to offer a 'complete' analysis of his dreams, but used each example only for definite purposes. . . ."[2] There is after all an infinite amount to be said about human beings and their psychology.

Freud was not a comprehensive thinker; as he said in a letter to Groddeck, "*I have a special talent for being satisfied with a fragment.*"[3] And he advised his pupils to make their findings in a similar way, to "have one's ideas exclusively focused on one central interest."[4] Freud found that he had to "blind myself artificially in order to focus all the light on one dark spot. . . ."[5] To Putnam he admitted that "I must have needed this one-sidedness in order to see what remains hidden from others."[6] As he once wrote about one of his notions to Fliess, "if it had been sought for by anyone

---

[1] John Stuart Mill: "Bentham," in *Essays on Politics and Culture*, ed. Gertrude Himmelfarb (New York: Doubleday Anchor Books; 1963), p. 96.

[2] Freud: *The Origins of Psychoanalysis*, p. 35.

[3] Italics in orginal. Quoted in Carl and Sylvia Grossman: *The Wild Analyst* (New York: Braziller; 1965), p. 16.

[4] Hanns Sachs: *Freud* (London: Imago; 1945), p. 69.

[5] Freud: *Letters*, p. 318.

[6] Ibid., pp. 313–14.

less obstinately wedded to the idea, it would have been overlooked."[7] Freud's approach was almost that of the artist, disproportioning reality in order to heighten our perception of certain aspects of it. The narrowness of his mind, and his tenacity in developing his insights, were the concomitants for his discoveries. "Nothing is true in psychoanalysis," Adorno once said wisely, "but the exaggerations."

Our view of Freud's mind is clouded by the political events of our time. On both the Right and the Left we have been frightened by seeing the dangers of political fanaticism. We all share in part Orwell's disgust at "all the smelly little orthodoxies" which have contended for our souls. Hence we wince when Freud tells openly of his prejudices and how his commitment to them helped him in his work: "I am bound to say that it is sometimes most useful to have prejudices."[8] In the face of totalitarian politics, skepticism has become a very agreeable intellectual position. Commitments have come to seem treacherous.

One can grant the dangers of certain true believers to the existence of democratic societies, and yet restrict the implications of this threat for the life of the mind. Intellectually we are now imperiled less by dogmatism than by a vague yet pernicious spirit of "general education." One cannot arrive at a creative truth by conscientiously adding together political, economic, social, etc., explanations of a given event. There is more to the truth than the sum of all the available factors. Systematic exaggeration can be at least as productive. If the fool would persist in his folly, as the poet has it, he would soon become wise. In intellectual life, "when the effects of their actions need not be considered, even

[7] Freud: *The Origins of Psychoanalysis*, p. 81.
[8] *Standard Edition*, Vol. 11, p. 29.

fanatics are less annoying than the skeptics who, whatever else they may doubt are always sure of their own wisdom. And it is the religious who search their hearts."[9]

But in the current climate of opinion, tunnel vision arouses fears of a bloodbath. This is especially true for political scientists; politics matters so much to them that they have acquired a particular horror of any system that smacks of ideology. The result has been a fear of monistic explanations, and a flourishing of a kind of pluralism; often the upshot is an unimaginative college examination mentality. Presented with any system of thought, we all can "discuss critically." Skepticism of this sort comes easily nowadays; it more often represents timidity than emotional balance.

To theorize one must abstract; and abstraction involves oversimplification. Nevertheless, there are special virtues to an organized set of propositions. While the core notions in any system may be banal, the structured integration of concepts can provide an intellectual dynamism all its own. There was in fact such an inner momentum in the development of Freud's ideas. It should be possible to profit from the use of a concept here, or a sentence there. These offshoots from the psychoanalytic system are capable of setting off a chain of associations, by virtue of their derivation from the main body of thought.

There is something heroic about the ability to make, and profit by, such a commitment. Yet the very ability to see the heroism implies the degree of detachment which a broader outlook has given us. Psychoanalysis cannot offer us the "whole truth," but merely a disciplined articulation of a perspective. As Freud said, "psychoanalysis is certainly

[9] Plamenatz: *The English Utilitarians*, p. 45.

quite particularly one-sided, as being the science of the mental unconscious."[1] There are in life few sufficient conditions for any events. No explanations or suggestions will be offered here in a totalistic spirit, but rather with an air of systematic partiality.

We have nothing more nor less than a perspective whose legitimacy is proved by its fruitfulness, but which must be supplemented by other perspectives to be complete. . . . Science dissects reality only in order to observe it better by virtue of a play of converging searchlights whose beams continually intermingle and interpenetrate each other.[2]

Different perspectives, based on the study of different conceptually defined variables, are capable of checking one another. "They are not additive but complementary insights, susceptible of being unified on a higher level of abstraction, roughly in the sense in which one apple and one pear make two fruits."[3]

## 2  The Movement

The application of psychoanalytic concepts requires a familiarity not only with certain aspects of Freud's intellectual biography, but also with the whole growth of the psychoanalytic movement. In order to understand the substance of Freud's contribution, one must give due attention to his relationship with his pupils. It is these students of Freud, whether or not they remained devoted to his own formulations, who have been leaders in psychoanalytic thinking since the death of the master.

[1] *Standard Edition*, Vol. 20, p. 231.
[2] Marc Bloch: *The Historian's Craft* (New York: Knopf; 1954), p. 150.
[3] George Devereux, in *Science and Psychoanalysis*, ed. Jules H. Masserman (New York: Grune & Stratton; 1958), Vol. 1, p. 82.

Freud's critics, and especially his alienated pupils, have often accused him of being, like Marx, doctrinaire. Ernest Jones has treated this problem of Freud's intolerance in a deadpan way; he totals up the number of controversies that were Freud's fault, then sets against them those fights attributable to the emotional resistances of backsliding pupils, and concludes rather woodenly that since the latter exceeds the former Freud was tolerant about his ideas. It is undoubtably true that on certain issues Freud could permit contradiction. Friendship did not always fall before an ideological altar; his relationships with Binswanger and Pfister attest to his ability to countenance divergences.

To some extent people need the image of an angry father figure, one who can simultaneously be hated for his severity and admired for his strength. Any major figure in psychoanalysis is bound to attract intense emotional transferences; this is of course especially true in the case of the founder of psychoanalysis, and has produced some legendary versions of his personality. Yet the circle around Freud did have from a very early point in time the air of a royal court; and it is evident that Freud thought of himself as a monarch reigning over an "empire."[1] His territory included the inward realm of the previously unknown unconscious processes as well as the outward domain of followers scattering all over the world. His pupils needed to find a monarch in Freud as much as he had to consider himself one. In a novel about Goethe Thomas Mann has captured the spirit of the circle around a genius:

He dominated the room, simply because everybody took the key from him; he tyrannized over the company, not so much because he was a tyrant as because the others submitted to him

[1] Ludwig Binswanger: *Sigmund Freud* (New York: Grune & Stratton; 1957), p. 31.

and positively forced him into the role. So then he played the part; he ruled them, rapped on his table, ordered this and that. . . .[2]

It would be easy for the reader to go astray here. One must keep in mind the degree of personal involvement that went with being a pupil of Freud's. Public and private life, scientific research and personal therapy became so intertwined that it is hard sometimes to see why the whole group did not degenerate into a mere sect. From the pupils' point of view, Freud was their model and ego-ideal. They came to him with Godlike expectations of what he would be able to do for them. And in fact many of them did their most productive work when they were closest to him. The group around Freud illustrates an aspect of the psychology of learning. There must be an emotional component in the pupil-teacher relationship to provide the energy for the learning process; and yet that emotional element inevitably distorts one's perception of the truth. One needs heroes, and yet having them inevitably blinds one. So the relationship with Freud could cripple as well as liberate.

On his own part Freud had a very great need of this loyal audience. His relationship to his pupils was similar to his need for patients during his self-analysis. "His pupils were to be above all passive understanding listeners . . . projection objects through whom he reviewed—sometimes to correct or to retract them—his own ideas."[3]

Freud's design in the promotion of these gatherings [of students] was to have his own thoughts passed through the filter of other trained intelligences. It did not matter if the intelligences were mediocre. Indeed, he had little desire that these associates should

[2] Thomas Mann: *The Beloved Returns: Lotte In Weimar* (New York: Knopf; 1940), pp. 132–3.

[3] Helene Deutsch: "Freud and His Pupils," *Psychoanalytic Quarterly*, Vol. 9, No. 1 (1940), pp. 188–9.

be persons of strong individuality, that they should be critical
and ambitious collaborators. The realm of psychoanalysis was
his idea and his will, and he welcomed anyone who accepted his
views. What he wanted was to look into a kaleidoscope lined
with mirrors that would multiply the images he introduced into
it.[4]

Freud's writing style reflects his manner of working; its
directness indicates the origin of his ideas in his own emotional matrix, and the Socratic dialogue of much of his
narrative reflects that the issues have already been tested
out in contact with others.

It is true of course that one must be cautious when generalizing about Freud's relationships with his pupils, since
at different periods of his life the situation could be very
different. In general, however, "he came to regard these
men . . . as his spiritual sons who would insure his scientific immortality in the same way that his real sons would
provide for his spiritual immortality."[5] He could be very
difficult if they tried to rival him in conceptual originality.
As one of his "deviating" pupils put it so well in the 1920's,
"he is so much opposed to his pupils coining independent
ideas that he prefers to give them a superfluity from his
own mint."[6] He could be very touchy over issues of priority,
who thought of which idea first; he had difficulties accepting anything at second hand, and had to think everything out for himself.

All the difficulties of working with Freud should not
mislead one into thinking that he was personally disputa-
tious. He had the characteristic urbanity of a charmer in
the great Viennese tradition. "He was a kind, a benevolent,

4 Wittels: *Sigmund Freud*, p. 134.
5 Helen Walker Puner: *Freud* (New York: Howell, Soskin; 1947), pp. 152–3.
6 Wittels: *Sigmund Freud*, p. 131.

a good man, but he was kind without softness, benevolent without compassion, and good without mercy."[7] In his relation to his movement, he had always to guard against lapses into either mysticism on the one hand or scholasticism on the other. As one of Freud's early followers wrote of those Wednesday evening meetings recorded in the *Minutes*, "there was an atmosphere of the foundation of a religion in that room. . . . Freud's pupils . . . were his apostles. . . . Good hearted and considerate though he was in private life, Freud was hard and relentless in the presentation of his ideas."[8]

As we have already argued, for the sake of his intellectual system Freud had to be intolerant; great theorists, and this applies to Bentham or Veblen as well as to Marx, cannot retain their theoretical creativity and be eclectic at the same time. At some point any theorist must close down on intellectual options, must insist on certain tenets which are to be the substructure of his further exploration. In 1922 Freud outlined "the corner-stones of psychoanalytic theory":

The assumption that there are unconscious mental processes, the recognition of the theory of resistance and repression, the appreciation of the importance of sexuality and of the Oedipus complex—these constitute the principal subject matter of psychoanalysis and the foundations of its theory. No one who cannot accept them all should count himself a psychoanalyst.[9]

Freud was entitled as a theorist to decide which aspects of his work were essential to further exploration. The existence of a system of thought which was capable of having "corner-stones" made it possible for disciples to assemble

---

[7] Puner: *Freud*, p. 253.

[8] Max Graf: "Reminiscences of Professor Sigmund Freud," *Psychoanalytic Quarterly*, Vol. 11, No. 4 (1942), pp. 471–2.

[9] *Standard Edition*, Vol. 18, p. 247.

around Freud. The capacity to have disciples says much about the systematic character of a man's mind.

To demand of a thinker that he be boldly original as well as intellectually passive is asking to have one's cake and eat it too. Whether, however, his pupils are entitled to the same dogmatism is another question. As a historian of religion has noted, "beliefs seldom become doubts; they become ritual."[1] We are bound to be critical if Freud's system has operated merely as a "combined protective shield and sorting mechanism for the extraordinary rush of emotions released by the psychoanalytic process."[2] Still, toward these pupils as well we must allow some of the leeway of any theoretical structure. Since their insights are derived from an internally consistent system, they can hardly be criticized for holding onto the system that is their source of productivity. Nevertheless, the originator has paid a higher price for his system; his followers are after all followers, and hence they cannot expect the same wide tolerance for their consistency.

One ought not to forget also the costs these people paid in becoming disciples of Freud in the early days, regardless of the present-day success of the psychoanalytic movement. Graf, for example, reported that "in those days when one mentioned Freud's name in a Viennese gathering, everyone would begin to laugh, as if someone had told a joke."[3] Franz Alexander made a sacrifice which was a common experience for his generation: "To turn to psychoanalysis meant to give up every idea of an academic career. . . . In 1921 the decision to become a psychoanalyst placed a physi-

[1] Herbert Schneider: *The Puritan Mind* (Ann Arbor, Mich.: University of Michigan Press; 1958), p. 98.

[2] Robert J. Lifton: *Thought Reform and the Psychology of Totalism* (New York: W. W. Norton; 1963), p. 448.

[3] Graf: "Reminiscences of Professor Sigmund Freud," p. 469.

cian outside the medical fraternity."[4] Nor was Freud un-
appreciative; indeed he rather gloried in the isolation of his
movement. Speaking in 1915 of prospective psychoanalysts,
Freud said: "as things stand at present, such a choice of
profession would ruin any chance . . . of success at a University. . . ."[5] As Glover has reminisced,

it is essential to realize in what dark ages the science of psychoanalysis was born. Otherwise we cannot hope to understand the
quality and character of its earliest supporters. Attacked on two
sides, facing not only the hostility of the external world but the
more insidious influence of their own resistance, they must have
sustained themselves on something more refreshing than the
mere iconoclastic joys of assaulting current conventions.[6]

Especially after World War I, students came to Freud
from all over the world. If they were exiles from their native lands, they were, as a compensation, members of an
international movement. This is an aspect of the history of
psychoanalysis which has been neglected by Freud's "cul-
turalist" critics. Freud's patients also were not restricted to
Central Europe; and the disciples who have expounded his
teachings represent a number of different national traditions.

The international character of the psychoanalytic movement only highlights the extraordinary nature of the success
of Freud's doctrines in one country in particular—the United
States. This is true medically as well as among the general public. The contrast between the reception of Freud's
ideas in America and elsewhere existed from the very be-

[4] Alexander: *The Western Mind in Transition*, pp. 55, 81.
[5] *Standard Edition*, Vol. 15, p. 16.
[6] Edward Glover: "Eder as Psychoanalyst," in *David Eder*, ed. J. B. Hobman
(London: Gollancz; 1945), p. 93.

ginning. In 1909, "at a time when the two leading clinics in Germany, linguistically identical with and adjacent to Austria, had ignored Freud's work, at Ward's Island [N.Y.] the dynamic psychology of psychoanalysis was being used day in and day out to clarify the psychiatric syndromes of committed patients."[7] Of course in America too Freud's early followers were initially ridiculed. But in time psychoanalysis became integrated within the medical profession, achieving a respectability unequaled anywhere else in the world.

There is a well-known irony in the ease and extent of Freud's American triumph. For he had the utmost disdain and contempt for American life. "America," he joked, "is a mistake; a gigantic mistake, but a mistake."[8] He denied "hating" America; he merely "regretted" it.[9] His reasons for his difficulties in adjusting to American customs on his trip in 1909 ranged from the absence of public toilets, the quality of the water and the food, to the more common complaints about America—the manners, the sexual hypocrisy, the general lack of culture, the brash wealth. He justified his hatred for America with such a shifting variety of reasons that one can be sure only of the existence of the antipathy. Like Marx in his distaste for Russia, Freud detested the country which chose him as its prophet.

Regarding the development of the psychoanalytic movement, as well as the future of psychoanalytic theory, Freud thought that the Americans would be too quick to unite

[7] Clarence P. Oberndorf: *A History of Psychoanalysis in America* (New York: Grune & Stratton; 1953), p. 81.

[8] Ernest Jones: *Sigmund Freud*, Vol. II (New York: Basic Books; 1955), p. 60.

[9] Max Eastman: "Differing with Sigmund Freud," in *Einstein, Trotsky, Hemingway, Freud, and Other Great Companions* (New York: Collier Books; 1962), p. 129.

psychoanalysis to medical psychiatry. "The essence of his comment" to Martin Peck, shortly before Freud's death, "was that in America medical application of psychoanalysis was the rule, and contributions to its structure were the exception."[1] Hanns Sachs, one of Freud's disciples, reflected that

a point was reached where the scientific movement and the organization were bound to drift apart . . . the scientific trends in psychoanalysis have been separated and are bound to become still more divorced from the organization which, by its inherent law, becomes progressively more conservative, directed towards practical aims and a self-preservative purpose.[2]

The history of the psychoanalytic movement illustrates Michels's "iron law of oligarchy," which states that reform movements become bureaucratized and hierarchical, at odds with the spirit which created them. Even before Freud's death, it had become apparent that there was a conflict between creative genius and organizational needs; Freud's willingness to have foreign students trained in Vienna, whatever the wishes of home psychoanalytic societies, rendered him a menace to a bureaucratizing movement.

All Freud's fears about the future of psychoanalysis were focused on the symbol of America. He was shocked by the tendency to commercialize and sensationalize his ideas; and he was convinced that Americans lacked any intellectual creativity; "the contributions to our science from that vast country are exiguous and provide little that is new."[3] Ferenczi once contrasted the European and the American reactions to Freud's teachings:

[1] Martin Peck: "A Brief Visit with Freud," *Psychoanalytic Quarterly*, Vol. 9, No. 2 (1940), p. 206.

[2] Hanns Sachs: "The Prospects of Psychoanalysis," *International Journal of Psychoanalysis*, Vol. 20 (1939), pp. 462–3.

[3] *Standard Edition*, Vol. 21, p. 254.

In Europe it has become customary for people to appropriate a large part of Freud's life work, to dish it up in a new form and with a new terminology, and to publish it as their own original work. . . . On the other hand, it seems as though in America . . . people are much readier than we are in Europe to accept the watered-down and attenuated view of certain of Freud's former disciples.[4]

Hence Freud worried lest the American reception of his ideas be intellectually not muscular enough; "the ancient centres of culture, where the greatest resistance has been displayed, must be the scene of the decisive struggle over psychoanalysis."[5]

The American tendency, as Freud saw it, was to "shorten study and preparation and to proceed as fast as possible to practical application."[6] Freud had seen, first with Jung and later with Rank, the way America seemed to seduce his followers into abandoning parts of the psychoanalytic edifice. Freud's distrust of the American response to his ideas was buttressed by the American failure to welcome lay analysts.

He used the term "medical fixation" for the American scene, and regretted the alliance between psychiatry and psychoanalysis . . . there was implicit in this [American] argument a false assumption that the validity of psychoanalytic findings and theories was definitely established, while actually they were still in their beginning, and needed a great deal of development and repeated verification and confirmation.[7]

While American analysts were failing to produce work of fundamental importance, they were also, by opposing lay

---

[4] Sandor Ferenczi: *Final Contributions to the Problems and Methods of Psychoanalysis* (London: Hogarth Press; 1955), p. 42.

[5] *Standard Edition,* Vol. 14, p. 32.

[6] Ibid., Vol. 21, p. 255.

[7] Peck: "A Brief Visit with Freud," pp. 205–6.

analysis, undermining one of the sources of future contributions to psychoanalytic doctrine. The way Freud could per-
sonalize any dispute is illustrated by a couple of sentences
in a letter to Jelliffe: "I feel very hurt by the behavior of
American analysts in the matter of Lay-Analysis. They, it
seems, are not very fond of me."[8]

Freud's forebodings about what America would do to his
ideas have been in some measure fulfilled. The very size of
America precluded psychoanalysis from remaining under
European control, encapsulated from the rest of society. Despite the origins of psychoanalysis in Freud's theorizing,
"generally, psychoanalysts in America have turned in their
practice and scientific discussions to the concrete and the
utilitarian."[9] Just as in other areas of American life, for example in political thought, there has been a lack of theorizing, so within psychoanalysis pragmatism has triumphed.
For American analysts, "theory . . . was an aid to practical,
useful purposes and not an aim in itself . . . they were more
tolerant toward individual opinions and convictions . . .
perhaps less sophisticated in abstract thought, less dedicated
to search for truth for its own sake, but . . . bent on action, development, and organization."[1] The Americans have
also tended to contribute an emphasis on behavioral changes
in therapeutic treatment, rather than to retain Freud's own
insistence on structural changes in personality.

The history of the psychoanalytic movement, especially
since Freud's death, illustrates in reverse the truth behind
the origins of Freud's achievements in his theoretical capacities. Torn by inner divisions, rejected by the outside world,

[8] Quoted in Franz Alexander, Samuel Eisenstein, and Martin Grotjahn, eds.:
*Psychoanalytic Pioneers* (New York: Basic Books; 1966), p. 227.

[9] Oberndorf: *A History of Psychoanalysis in America*, p. 2.

[1] Alexander: *Western Mind in Transition*, pp. 90–1.

Freud was driven to achieve a balance between his clinical material and his theoretical principles. His students indeed went into exile when they went to Freud. The sacrifice they made was sufficient emotional incentive to ensure that they would make the venture intellectually worth while; and in fact it is the case that since Freud's death the psychoanalytic movement has been in large measure living off the ideas of a comparatively few immediate pupils of Freud. The Americans had much less need to produce any theoretical work. They could be content with institutionalizing Freud's ideas in medical practice. Since the battles they fought were not as costly a sacrifice as for the original disciples of Freud, they had correspondingly less incentive for intellectual creativity.

## 3  Society and Philosophy

Before turning to the explicit examination of Freud's own social works, further preliminary understanding of his whole contribution is necessary if we are to guard against the many false starts in utilizing psychoanalytic theory. One central conflict in Freud's work is of special importance here—the tension between the seer and the practical investigator, between the artist and the scientist. There is no doubt that Freud himself was aware of the attractions of these different enterprises; one of the main themes in his study of Leonardo was precisely this inner division in his work.

As Freud grew older, he tended to allow himself more leeway in the direction of speculation, always done a bit in the spirit of a holiday mood. In 1924 he noted that since 1920, "I have given free reign to the inclination, which I

kept down for so long, to speculation. . . ."[1] By 1935 Freud
was in a position to evaluate the work of his last years in
relation to his earlier phases:

a significant change has come about . . . interests which I had
acquired in the later part of my life have receded, while the older
and original ones become prominent once more. . . . [Since 1923]
I have made no further decisive contributions to psychoanalysis.
. . . My interests, after making a lifelong *détour* through the
natural sciences, medicine and psychotherapy, returned to the
cultural problems which had fascinated me long before, when I
was a youth scarcely old enough for thinking.[2]

The change that Freud saw in his own work was pin-
pointed at the year 1923; that was the year when he had
his first cancer, which began all the suffering that har-
rowed the rest of his life. Although Freud had always
shown elements of the social philosopher, and although
even before 1923 there was a discernible shift in his work
toward speculative rather than clinical concerns, the specter
of his own death accelerated this trend. The human being
in Freud began to die. He became less the healer and psychologist as he approached the end of his life, and more
the seer. It was as if by appealing to society through social
theory he could somehow stave off his own personal disintegration.

But Freud never blinded himself to the value of what he
was doing. As he is reported to have said, "I have allowed
myself to leave the pure empyrean of psychology, and I re-
gret it."[3] He had noticed his talents drying up as early as
1914. In a letter to Abraham he commented that "my way
of working was different years ago. I used to wait until an

[1] *Standard Edition*, Vol. 20, p. 57.

[2] Ibid., pp. 71–2.

[3] Personal communication from Dr. Helene Deutsch.

idea came to me. Now I go half-way to meet it, though I don't know whether I find it any the quicker."[4] Freud's early books were ones of exploration and discovery, while the later texts tend to dramatize positions he already held without carrying them much further. Although Freud reformulated a number of ideas before his death in 1939, this kind of conceptualizing had an abstract, almost formalistic quality to it, quite unlike his earlier clinical writings. His last case history was published in 1920.

Freud's own estimate of those of his works best known to social scientists was at times deprecatory to an extreme. For example, after completing the first draft of *Civilization and Its Discontents* Freud wrote to Lou Andreas-Salomé:

It deals with civilization, sense of guilt, happiness, and similar exalted subjects, and strikes me, no doubt rightly, as quite superfluous in contrast to earlier works which always sprang from some inner necessity. But what else can I do? One cannot smoke and play cards all day; I am no longer much good at walking, and most of what I read doesn't interest me any more. I wrote, and in doing so the time passed quite pleasantly. While engaged in this work I have discovered the most banal truths.[5]

Of *Future of an Illusion* Freud spoke very movingly to René Laforgue: "This is my worst book! . . . It isn't a book of Freud. . . . It's the book of an old man! . . . Besides Freud is dead now, and believe me, the genuine Freud was really a great man. I am particularly sorry for you that you didn't know him better. . . . The punch is lost."[6]

If Freud was harsh about his own efforts at political, re-

[4] Quoted in Jones: *Sigmund Freud*, Vol. I, p. 379.

[5] Freud, *Letters*, pp. 389–90.

[6] Quoted in Maryse Choisy: *Sigmund Freud* (New York: Citadel Press; 1963), p. 84.

ligious, and cultural abstractions, this was only a reflection of his own distrust of metaphysics of any kind. In writing to a German scholar in 1927, Freud remarked of metaphysics that "I not only have no talent for it but no respect for it, either. In secret—one cannot say such things aloud—I believe that one day metaphysics will be condemned as a nuisance, as an abuse of thinking, as a survival from the period of the religious *Weltanschauung*. I know well to what an extent this way of thinking estranges me from German cultural life."[7] According to the *Minutes* of the Vienna Psychoanalytic Society, in 1907 Freud remarked that "in metaphysics . . . we are dealing with a projection of so-called endopsychic perceptions."[8] Its "abstract nature" was "so unpleasant to him, that he has renounced the study of philosophy."[9] Freud is reported to have said many times that he "heartily abhorred philosophy."[1] "Even when I have moved away from observation, I have carefully avoided any contact with philosophy proper."[2] Late in his life Freud considered all such philosophical speculation as pathological: "the moment one inquires about the sense or value of life one is sick, since objectively neither of them has any existence. In doing so one is only admitting a surplus of unsatisfied libido. . . ."[3]

As for ethics, Freud considered that they were self-evident. To Pfister he wrote that "ethics are remote from me. . . . I do not break my head much about good and evil.

[7] Freud, *Letters*, p. 375.
[8] *Minutes of the Vienna Psychoanalytic Society*, Vol. I, p. 149.
[9] Ibid., p. 359.
[1] Letter of Siegfried Bernfeld to Ernest Jones, June 19, 1951 (Jones Archives).
[2] *Standard Edition*, Vol. 20, p. 59.
[3] Ernest Jones: *Sigmund Freud, Vol. III* (New York: Basic Books; 1957), p. 465.

. . . If we are to talk of ethics, I subscribe to a high ideal from which most of the human beings I have come across depart most lamentably."[4] Ethics, Freud held, are "not based on an external world order but on the inescapable exigencies of human cohabitation."[5] As he put it in *Moses and Monotheism*, "what seems to us so grandiose about ethics, so mysterious and, in a mystical fashion, so self-evident, owes these characteristics to its connection with religion, its origin from the will of the father."[6] He was quite sure at any rate that it was "unreasonable to expect science to produce a system of ethics. . . ."[7]

This dislike of such abstractions was rooted in a deep skepticism that metaphysics could be anything but a projective system, having only a casual contact with reality, and in a self-direction about morality which left no room for constructive moral preoccupations. Freud's devaluation of intellectual questions which are in principle unverifiable, including sometimes his own contributions in those areas, was also partially an attempt to emancipate himself from a climate of opinion that denied scientific standing to psychological investigations. Holt reminds us that "the psychology to which Freud was exposed in the university was largely that of Brentano and was a branch of philosophy on an equal footing with epistemology, metaphysics, and ethics."[8]

The outer fear that his work might be confused with untestable flights of imagination was buttressed by the inner fear of some of his strongest intellectual impulses. Freud read very little philosophy, just because of his own natural

4 Freud: *Psychoanalysis and Faith*, pp. 61–2.
5 Ibid., p. 129.
6 *Standard Edition*, Vol. 23, p. 122.
7 Freud: *Psychoanalysis and Faith*, p. 123.
8 Holt, in *The Study of Lives*, pp. 377–8.

talent for it. "As a young man I felt a strong attraction towards speculation and ruthlessly checked it."[9] Of course his self-distrust here was part of a generally self-critical attitude to his own work. His condemnation of his own speculative tendencies may be an expression of his austere intellectual standards; or his self-deprecation may have been a way of handling fantasied criticism from the outside world, by doing it first so to speak.

The only way of resolving the problem of Freud's attitude to his social works is to admit that he was deeply divided about them. He wrote the essays, they mattered very much to his whole way of thinking; he frequently classed *Totem and Taboo* among his favorite books. And yet he felt apart from these works in a way which had not been true of his earlier clinical works. Freud's self-image included scientific interests, especially medical ones, along with these philosophic inclinations: "as if driven by a unique force from within he stood to the last as a non-philosophical philosopher, denying his interest in philosophy and yet yearning for solutions, digging into the depth of the mysteries of life to which he would deny the privilege of being mysterious."[1] Freud's life work was in a sense an attempt to keep some sort of balance between these conflicting interests. At best it was a tenuous balance, and the inner instability repeatedly drove him to fresh attempts at resolving this conflict.

In the light of Freud's negative views on philosophy, it might seem remarkable to find him writing in 1896 to Fliess that "I secretly nurse the hope of arriving by the same

    [9] Jones: *Sigmund Freud*, Vol. I, p. 32.
    [1] Gregory Zilboorg: "Review of Vol. III of Jones's *Freud*," *Psychoanalytic Quarterly*, Vol. 27, No. 2 (1958), p. 261.

route [medicine] at my own original objective, philosophy.
For that was my original ambition, before I knew what I
was intended to do in the world."[2] Later that year Freud
wrote that "when I was young the only thing I longed for
was philosophic knowledge, and now that I am going over
from medicine to psychology I am in the process of obtaining it. I have become a therapist against my will. . . ."[3]
Jones recalled "as far back as 1910 his expressing his wish
with a sigh that he could retire from medical practice and
devote himself to the unraveling of cultural and historical
problems—ultimately the great problem of how man came
to be what he is."[4] Freud was not exaggerating the strength
of his impulse toward philosophical speculation, nor its
emergence in his old age as a "phase of regressive development"[5] in his intellectual life.

As a young man Freud considered studying law and then
becoming a politician, on the model of an admired older
friend. As he wrote to his fiancée in 1880, "Philosophy,
which I have always pictured as my goal and refuge in
old age, gains every day in attraction, as do human affairs
altogether or any cause to which I could give my devotion
at all costs, but the fear of the supreme uncertainty of all
political and local matters keeps me from that sphere."[6]
Despite his ultimate choice of medicine as a career, "neither
at that time, nor indeed in my later life, did I feel any particular predilection for the career of a doctor. I was moved,
rather, by a sort of curiosity, which was, however, directed

[2] Freud: *The Origins of Psychoanalysis*, p. 141.

[3] Ibid., p. 162.

[4] Jones: *Sigmund Freud*, Vol. I, p. 30.

[5] *Standard Edition*, Vol. 20, p. 72.

[6] Quoted in Zilboorg: "Review of Vol. III of Jones' *Freud*," p. 261.

more towards human concerns than towards natural objects. . . ."[7] Later he wrote that

after forty-one years of medical activity, my self-knowledge tells
me that I have never really been a doctor in the proper sense. I became a doctor through being compelled to deviate from my
original purpose; and the triumph of my life lies in my having,
after a long and roundabout journey, found my way back to
my earliest path. I have no knowledge of having had any craving
in my early childhood to help suffering humanity. My innate
sadistic disposition was not a very strong one, so that I had no
need to develop this one of its derivatives.[8]

The tension we have pointed out, his conflicting estimate
of his social thought, and his divided view of the importance of philosophy, while comprehensible, remains ultimately irreconcilable. Freud seems to have been unsure
whether his last works were a "regressive phase of development" or the "triumph" of his life. From his youth, when
he rejected law for medicine, to his maturity, when he
created a social metaphysics while despising philosophy, this
inner gulf remained unbridged. Freud the scientist, the
doctor, the healer of souls, the social critic, the philosopher
—the lines between the divisions are narrow, each enterprise slightly apart from the next.

A subtle stance must be maintained in the course of genuinely creative work between excessive self-preoccupation and
sophisticated self-awareness. It is possible to overrefine one's
categories, to objectify one's approach until one should
abandon it. In Freud's case he was aware of what he was
doing, and yet was not so preoccupied with methodology
as to stifle the ambiguous movement of intellectual creation.
There is a point beyond which self-knowledge can begin to

---

[7] *Standard Edition,* Vol. 20, p. 8.
[8] Ibid., p. 253.

cripple; and there was in the development of Freud's ideas a lurking danger of prematurely stifling the momentum of his thought. As he is reported to have remarked of the Viennese logical positivists, "those critics who limit their studies to methodological investigations remind me of people who are always polishing their glasses instead of putting them on and seeing with them."[9] Or, as Gide observed, "the literary creator who seeks himself runs a great risk—the risk of finding himself."

From then onwards he writes coldly, deliberately, in keeping with the self he has found. He imitates himself. . . . His great dread is no longer insincerity, but inconsistency. The true artist is never but half-conscious of himself when creating. He does not know exactly who he is. He learns to know himself only through his creation, in it, and after it.[1]

It should come as no surprise, then, that the conflicts between the multiple layers of Freud's mind did not lead him to any explicit attempt to integrate an internally consistent system, that the exponent of self-knowledge was in this respect unable fully to come to terms with himself; we have in fact a reliable index of the intensity of the diverging tendencies. Given some of the postulates of psychoanalytic theory, this failure on Freud's part is understandable; for conflict is not only an inevitable part of human existence, but can also be the very incentive for creativity. "The creative person seems to have greater problems and greater potentialities of individuation and identity."[2] Freud's failure ever to resolve his conflicting views of what he had to contribute

[9] Theodor Reik: *From Thirty Years with Freud* (New York: Farrar & Rinehart; 1940), p. 138.

[1] André Gide: *Dostoevsky* (New York: New Directions; 1961), p. 50.

[2] Phyllis Greenacre: *The Quest for the Father* (New York: International Universities Press; 1963), p. 10.

to social philosophy is important not for the sake of the logical contradiction involved, but because the inconsistency points to a source of his productiveness. Freud strove again and again to overcome this tension. His late social works can be seen as an attempt to bridge inner discontinuities. His theorizing was self-healing to the degree to which it helped to provide external coherence as a substitute for inner disharmonies. Ultimately of course the sources of creativity remain an enigma; but the experience itself is well known for its conflictedness. As Nietzsche put it, "the price of fruitfulness is to be rich in internal opposition; one remains young only as long as the soul does not stretch itself and desire peace . . . one must . . . have chaos in oneself to be able to give birth to a dancing star."[3]

## 4 The Test of Science

No one can write about psychoanalytic theory without touching on aspects of Freud's intellectual biography; it is not antiquarianism that prompts an interest in the origins of Freud's ideas, in the history of the psychoanalytic movement, and in the relation of Freud's social speculations to his clinical theories; these topics are relevant to the extent that psychoanalysis was Freud's own creation.

But one must also be able to distinguish Freud's lasting achievements from his own personality. For example, Freud himself took certain positions which later psychoanalytic experience has superseded; the scope of treatment based on psychoanalytic principles has expanded greatly beyond cases

[3] F. W. Nietzsche: *The Portable Nietzsche*, ed. Walter Kaufmann (New York: The Viking Press; 1954), pp. 129, 488.

Freud himself would have considered suitable. Freud had difficulties, because of unresolved problems of his own, in being tolerant of cases which present-day psychoanalysts customarily treat. Despite psychoanalysis's debt to Freud, it has by now acquired a life of its own. Although its origins lie in Freud's self-analysis, the theories he postulated are capable of being validated apart from his own personality. If psychoanalysis is to be considered a science, it must be verified apart from Freud's own biography. Biographical research, informed by psychoanalytic doctrine, can do much to place Freud as a figure in intellectual history, but cannot by itself solve the problem of the status of psychoanalysis as a science.

Surely part of Freud's criticism of his own social works arose from his fears of damaging the standing of psychoanalysis as a science. His ideas about religion, for example, might, he feared, overload "the psychoanalytic applecart."[1] The views expressed in *The Future of an Illusion*, he wrote to Pfister, "form no part of analytic theory. They are my personal views. . . . If I draw on analysis for certain arguments—in reality only one argument—that need deter no one from using the non-partisan method of analysis for arguing the opposite view."[2] Unless he made clear that his social theories were derived from his personal preoccupations, and not from the science of psychoanalysis, he feared that the baby would get thrown out with the bath, that the questionableness of his social thought would help undermine clinical psychoanalysis.

Freud's theoretical bent could at times take him far beyond verifiable experience. When he wrote on fields outside clinical psychoanalysis, he no longer had the same scientific

[1] Freud: *Psychoanalysis and Faith*, p. 92.
[2] Ibid., p. 117.

controls on his thinking that were available in his more
strictly psychoanalytic work. "The trouble with interpreting
the behavior of groups or absent persons is that they do not
respond with reactions that can be utilized to narrow the
interpretive range."[3] That Freud's speculative inclinations
led to some classic mistakes as well as to his great discoveries is important because it helps set limits to the relevance
of his work for political thought. Everything that Freud
wrote does not have equal standing within the tradition of
psychoanalysis. It is not only that clinical psychoanalysis
has a logical independence from Freud's own social theories, but that Freud's speculative impulses led him to theories that can be easily ridiculed.

One could take, for example, Freud's belief, qualified and
agonized though it was, in thought-transference. Nowadays
analysts are prone to write off Freud's interest in telepathy,
either as an example of a genius's eccentricity or as a trivial
diversion. It is one of the merits of the Jones biography
that it faces this issue so squarely. The pioneers in the history of psychoanalysis were remarkably intrigued by tele-
pathic phenomena, at least partially out of identification
with Freud's intensely personal interest in the subject. It may
seem strange to us to hear of Freud going off with some of
his closest followers after a scientific congress to visit some
charlatan of a medium. But their openness to such nonsense
was part and parcel of their receptivity to new mental processes in general. If dreams could have meaning, as common
folk had all along assumed, might there not be something
in telepathy too?

We have here the necessary corollary of Freud's independent spirit. Jones relates this "credulousness" to the

---

[3] van den Haag: *Passion and Social Constraint*, pp. 184–5

"characteristically receptive nature of genius."[4] There is a shading here which we tend to miss, largely because of our immense debt to Jones and the Stracheys for what we know about Freud's mind. Their own rationalism and skepticism have made Freud less interesting than he really was. For to describe Freud's torment over the existence of thought-transference as a consequence of his gullibility is to put it in unduly negative terms. This side of Freud should not be described as if people were somehow able to put something over on him; his interest in telepathy was part of the strain of the believer that he had within him. This active, questing, anti-rational part of Freud's mind has been underplayed, while his sharp-wittedness and laconic humor have been pushed into the limelight.

The speculative drive that sent Freud beyond his contemporaries must have been difficult to tolerate at the time. Breuer, for example, could not keep up; "Freud's intellect is soaring at its highest. I gaze after him as a hen at a hawk."[5] Fliess could be so essential to Freud, as a speculative ally, precisely because of his willingness to see things freshly. "Fliess had the power to suspend the scientific superego for Freud."[6] Although Freud was indebted to Fliess for his stress on human bisexuality, Fliess's theory relating the nose to menstrual cycles, and his numerology, were just so much hot air.

But a theorist needs the ability to detach himself from conventional reality, to dissolve the relationships others can see; and he needs friends whose minds are similarly able to

---

[4] Ernest Jones: *Sigmund Freud: Four Centenary Addresses* (New York: Basic Books; 1956), p. 30.

[5] Jones: *Sigmund Freud*, Vol. I, p. 266.

[6] David Bakan: *Sigmund Freud and the Jewish Mystical Tradition* (New York: Van Nostrand; 1958), p. 63.

liquefy past categories. Fliess performed this function for Freud; and later Ferenczi did too. Groddeck was still another; his ideas about psychosomatic medicine were at the time without substantial verification. For Freud's more balanced friends it was an exasperating experience. "The state of mind that leads you to encourage Groddeck," Pfister wrote to Freud, "is exactly the same as that which made you the discoverer and pioneer of psychoanalysis."[7]

Freud's tendency to go beyond confirmed evidence resulted in more than the one unhappy experience of telepathy; his postulations of the primal horde and the origins of Moses both, in my opinion, fall into this category. There is also Freud's mistake in his study of Leonardo; he constructed a considerable portion of his thesis around a childhood memory of Leonardo's of a vulture inserting its tail into his mouth. Freud relied for his interpretation on a German translation of Leonardo's notebooks and on a Russian historical novel, which both used the word *Geier*—meaning "vulture"—for the Italian *nibio*—"kite."[8]

The bird which the artist remembered as having inserted its tail in his mouth was not a vulture, but a kite. . . . A kite is also a rapacious bird, but no eater of carrion and looks quite different from the vulture. [Pfister had "seen" the outlined form of a vulture in one of Leonardo's paintings.] More important, it is not the bird represented by the Egyptians in the hieroglyph for "mother," to which folklore attributes only a female sex; nor is it the bird which is cited by the Church fathers in connection with the Virgin birth.[9]

In short Freud had been a "plunger" all right in his study of Leonardo; he had founded his argument on one child-

[7] Freud: *Psychoanalysis and Faith*, p. 81.

[8] *Standard Edition*, Vol. 11, p. 61 (editor's note).

[9] Meyer Schapiro: "Leonardo and Freud," *Journal of the History of Ideas*, Vol. 17, No. 2 (April 1956), p. 151.

hood memory, which turns out to be very different from what Freud had supposed. His thesis was founded on sand.

Freud himself cautioned his followers about his theoretical bent. When he first put forward the concept of a death instinct, Freud prefaced his remarks by saying that "what follows is speculation, often farfetched speculation, which the reader will consider or dismiss according to his individual predilection." [1] Of telepathy Freud wrote to Jones: "When anyone adduces my fall into sin, just answer him calmly that conversion to telepathy is my private affair like my Jewishness, my passion for smoking and many other things, and that the theme of telepathy is in essence alien to psychoanalysis." [2] And Freud is reported, in private, to have dismissed the primal parricide notion as just something he thought up one Sunday afternoon. [3]

What saved Freud again and again was the strength of his hold on reality. His imaginative leaps were tested ultimately against the real world. In good part this was not fortuitous; it was a consequence of Freud's immersion in clinical work. Freud's ideas were always related to his patients; his therapeutic practice provided him with a firm foothold in practicality. "I was driven forward above all by practical necessity." [4] For example, James Strachey has clarified Freud's use of the concept of the unconscious:

It should be made clear at once . . . that Freud's interest in the assumption [of the unconscious] was never a philosophical one—though, no doubt, philosophical problems inevitably lay just around the corner. His interest was a *practical* one. He found that without making that assumption he was unable to explain

[1] *Standard Edition*, Vol. 18, p. 24.
[2] Jones: *Sigmund Freud*, Vol. III, pp. 395–6.
[3] Personal communication from Dr. Abram Kardiner.
[4] *Standard Edition*, Vol. 11, p. 22.

or even to describe a large variety of phenomena which he came across. By making it, on the other hand, he found the way open to an immensely fertile region of fresh knowledge.[5]

In his day-to-day therapeutic work, Freud paid scrupulous attention to details. It was typical of him to take a trifle and realize its significance. Every slip, every pause, etc., was interpreted for its possible meaning. What was remarkable about Freud's work as an analyst was that "his capacity for fruitful theorizing was on a level with his clinical genius."[6] "It was one of the special qualities of Freud's genius to combine in a unique manner intuitive understanding of the meaning of unconscious content with a capacity for conceptual deduction of a general abstract nature."[7]

Freud's pupil Ferenczi, who also had an abstract mind, once maintained that he had at his disposal "the minimal number of cases necessary for a generalization, namely two."[8] Freud thought that one case was in principle enough. "Naturally a single case does not give us all the information that we should like to have. Or, to put it more correctly, it might teach us everything, if we were only in a position to make everything out. . . ."[9] Even in his early work with Breuer Freud had taken the same attitude:

The immediate question . . . was whether it was possible to generalize from what he had found in a single case. The state

[5] Ibid., Vol. 14, p. 162 (editor's note).

[6] Heinz Hartmann: "The Development of the Ego Concept in Freud's Work," *International Journal of Psychoanalysis*, Vol. 37, Part 6 (1956), p. 428.

[7] Elizabeth R. Zetzel: "An Approach to the Relation Between Concept and Content in Psychoanalytic Theory," *Psychoanalytic Study of the Child*, Vol. 11, p. 102.

[8] Sandor Ferenczi: *Further Contributions to the Theory and Technique of Psychoanalysis* (London: Hogarth Press; 1926), p. 319.

[9] *Standard Edition*, Vol. 17, p. 10.

of things which he had discovered seemed to me to be of so fundamental a nature that I could not believe it could fail to be present in any case of hysteria if it had been proved to occur in a single one.[1]

In part this was an aspect of the heritage of romanticism, which stressed how a single man can experience within himself, by means of his intuition, the whole range of human emotions. Yet the confidence in a single case was also a rational assessment of the relation between theory and practice in science. "Newton did not require a hail of apples to develop a new frame of reference. . . ."[2]

Whatever Freud's links with romanticism or natural science, what ultimately preserved his intellectual contact with reality was not only his immersion in clinical details, but his insistence on using the scientific method as an investigatory standard. When he speculated, he was aware of it; he knew when a theory had been confirmed, and when it was still open to verification. *The Interpretation of Dreams* is Freud's finest example of scientific theorizing. His theory of dreams is the best illustration of his imaginative capacities working in tandem with scientific procedures. It has been well said that

it is characteristic of Freud's work that from an observation whose contents one may call improbable or unexpected, he drew a huge array of conclusions. . . . It was a *tour de force*, when Freud derived the approximate structure of the psychic apparatus from the investigation of a phenomenon as ephemeral as the dream.[3]

[1] Ibid., Vol. 20, p. 21.

[2] George Devereux: "Logical Status and Methodological Problems of Research in Clinical Psychiatry," *Psychiatry*, Vol. 14, No. 3 (August 1951), p. 330.

[3] Kurt Eissler: "Freud and the Psychoanalysis of History," *Journal of the American Psychoanalytic Association*, Vol. 11, No. 4 (October 1963), p. 678.

Freud opened *The Interpretation of Dreams* with a lengthy section on what others had said about dreaming. Most of these explanations conflicted with one another, and none had been very elaborately developed. After a painstaking exposition of his own theory of dreams, Freud was able to subsume all the other theories within his; his theory not only offered an explanation of dreaming, but did so in a way that combined all previous theories into a more elegant synthesis. He could conclude:

My treatment of the problem of dreams has found room for the majority of these conflicting views. I have only found it necessary to give a categorical denial of two of them—the view that dreaming is a meaningless process and the view that it is a somatic one. Apart from this, I have been able to find a justification for all these mutually contradictory opinions at one point or other of my complicated thesis and to show that they had lighted on some portion of the truth.[4]

Freud's theory of dreams is the best example of his innocence of mind, his willingness to try to explain what others had largely ignored as unworthy of serious investigation. At the same time it illustrates his commitment to science; there could be no more perfect example in the history of science of one theory superseding others by explaining the same phenomena in a more simple and elegant system. "Of all forms of mental activity the most difficult to induce . . . is the art of handling the same bundle of data as before, by placing them in a new system of relations with one another by giving them a different framework. . . ."[5]

Freud's dream theory has importance beyond these methodological points. It was in fact the crucial link in

---

[4] *Standard Edition*, Vol. 5, p. 588.

[5] Herbert Butterfield: *The Origins of Modern Science* (New York: Macmillan; 1952), p. 1.

his whole system, and the crux of the contention that psychoanalysis increases our understanding of human psychology. Freud thought that his dream theory was the "most valuable of all the discoveries it has been my good fortune to make. Insight such as this falls to one's lot but once in a lifetime."[6] What Freud proposed was a revision of the ancient notion that dreams had prophetic significance; dreams represent not the future, but what we wish to be the future. Freud distinguished between two layers within dream life, the manifest dream and the latent dream. It is the latter that contains our deepest wishes; the manifest dream content is the product of the various defenses of the mind which disguise the latent dream thoughts and dramatize them in visual terms, working on memory residues of the preceding day. Only by interpreting the manifest dream content through free associations can the disguises that the dream work has introduced be undone, and the original latent dream thought be laid bare.

In the light of our discussion of Freud's metapsychology in Chapter I, his theory of dreams will seem familiar. What happens when we sleep is that we relax our mechanisms of control; there is no need to be careful about expressing our impulses since we are asleep, hence even the most barbaric desires are no threat to anybody. They are less of a threat to ourselves to the extent that dreaming is a process cut off from reality. Dreams are in a sense hallucinations of our wishes. By fulfilling our impulses, they help to preserve our sleep. Dreaming can be looked at from the economic point of view; "the principle function of the mental mechanism is to relieve the individual from the tensions created in him by his needs."[7] Jokes serve the same purpose as

[6] *Standard Edition*, Vol. 4, p. xxxii.
[7] Ibid., Vol. 13, p. 186.

dreams: "Dreams serve predominantly for the avoidance of unpleasure, jokes for the attainment of pleasure; but all our mental activities converge in these two aims."[8]

While during sleep our ego controls, or defenses, are relaxed, they are still present and potentially active. They are responsible for the dream work, which keeps the desires within us sufficiently disguised to protect our sense of security. When an impulse in a dream becomes damaging to our self-respect, our ego can resort to anxiety as a danger signal, sometimes even overriding our wish to sleep by waking us up. Anxiety plays an essential role "as a signal to the censorship leading to the mobilization of the various defenses taking part in the distortions of the dream work."[9]

That this theory of dream life fits Freud's metapsychology will be readily apparent. One should emphasize therefore that Freud's dream theory was one of his earliest constructions, and metapsychological considerations, while there from the start, were not fully developed until many years later. There is a possibility here that in conceptualizing Freud's thought we will neglect issues of historical sequence, and his formulations will seem all the more arbitrary. We have already twisted Freud's thought by reorganizing it for the dual purpose of understanding what psychoanalysis has to contribute to the study of politics, and of establishing limits to the relevance of his work. In the rest of this study Freud's work will be organized topically around certain recurrent themes. Such distortions are to some extent inevitable if we are to pluck from Freud what is relevant to political and social thought. But it should

---

[8] Ibid., Vol. 8, p. 180.

[9] Elizabeth R. Zetzel: "The Concept of Anxiety in Relation to the Development of Psychoanalysis," *Journal of the American Psychoanalytic Association*, Vol. 3, No. 3 (July 1955), p. 374.

be possible to minimize them, provided we keep in mind the development of psychoanalytic doctrine as we discuss the late works of Freud.

The systematic quality of Freud's thought makes possible such a treatment of his ideas. Despite the tensions within it, there is a conceptual inner core which permits us to radiate outward. Freud's dream book is important here not for the particular mechanisms described in it, but for the extent to which his analysis of dreaming links up with the rest of psychoanalysis, the extent to which he viewed man as essentially a dream-making creature. For example, dreaming—which is an aspect of "normal" psychology—is the model for understanding all kinds of psychic "abnormalities." "The dreams which we produce at night have, on the one hand, the greatest external similarity and internal kinship with the creations of insanity, and are, on the other hand, compatible with complete health in waking life."[1]

The hallucinations of psychotics can be understood in much the same way as the latent dream content can be unraveled. A psychotic thinks, to put it broadly, the way nonpsychotics dream. Like dreams, neurotic symptoms and slips of the tongue are understood as compromise-formations between conflicting wishes, or between wishes and our sense of self-esteem. The symbolizing of dream life can be found in the symptomatic acts of everyday life, as well as in the antics of the insane. For the purpose of understanding Freud's social theory one need not be too detailed about other aspects of his work. What one should remember is that the theory underlying clinical psychoanalysis hangs together. According to Freud, "an unbroken chain bridges the gap between the neuroses in all their manifestations and normality."[2]

Freud's theories are scientific to the extent that they increase our understanding of psychic life. For "in the last analysis the justification of every scientific generalization is that it enables us to comprehend something that is otherwise obscure."[3] "The central criterion of whether or not a study is a true science is its capacity to infer the unknown from the known."[4] Certainly Freud shared none of the hostility toward science characteristic of much romanticism. In fact his willingness to conceptualize, his eagerness to build systems, clearly demonstrated his decisive departure from the anti-Enlightenment romantic tradition.

Instead of fulfilling the romantic ideal of diversity, Freud constructed a system which, while evolving over time, remained remarkably static. It really seems that in a deep sense Freud never changed his mind. A seminar was almost organized once at the Chicago Psychoanalytic Institute to study discarded concepts in Freud, but it was found that there were none. There is almost nothing new in Freud; one sees a shifting light playing over the same mind, revealing various facets. As Mann has written of Goethe, "the world even of so mighty a spirit, however spacious it is, is a closed world, existing within limits. It is a unit, where the motifs repeat themselves and the same presentation recurs at large intervals of time."[5]

Since psychoanalysis is a system, it cannot be tested at every level; it is enough if at certain crucial points it can be verified. The whole point of a theory is that it takes off from

[2] Ibid., Vol. 7, p. 171.

[3] Ernest Jones: *Papers on Psychoanalysis* (Boston: Beacon Press; 1961), p. 73.

[4] Berlin: "History and Theory," p. 17.

[5] Mann: *The Beloved Returns*, pp. 72–3.

the facts, that it leads to hypotheses which, if tested and confirmed, lead us to confidence in the initial theory.

The test of a new idea is . . . not only its success in correlating the then-known facts but much more its success or failure in stimulating further experimentation or observation which in turn is fruitful. This dynamic aspect of science viewed not as a practical undertaking but as development of conceptual schemes seems to me to be close to the heart of the best definition [of science].[6]

An obvious example from within the history of psychoanalysis is the postulation of the existence of infantile sexuality. Freud described the early erotic stages from his analysis of adults. "Subsequently these retrospective reconstructions were substantially validated by direct observation of the behavior of children."[7] What matters here is not so much the findings themselves, as their theoretical relevance.

One of the greatest of Freud's discoveries was the fundamental *importance* of the eroticism of childhood—the fact of its existence was not discovered by Freud, but as so often in the history of science well-known facts excited little interest because nobody knew how to assess their importance.[8]

That not all psychoanalytic theory can be confirmed is entailed simply by the nature of any creative theory; an abstraction is impressive to the extent that from a small amount of evidence it can point, for theoretical reasons, to a whole range of facts whose importance had previously been overlooked. Any large-scale system involves circularities at one level or another; the issue is whether or not the

---

[6] James B. Conant: *On Understanding Science* (New York: Mentor; 1953), p. 37.

[7] Arlow, in *Psychoanalysis, Scientific Method and Philosophy*, p. 207.

[8] Talcott Parsons: "The Incest Taboo in Relation to Social Structure," *The British Journal of Sociology*, Vol. 5, No. 2 (June 1954), p. 109.

system as a whole leads in a meaningful direction. Because Freud was a great system-builder it is possible to pilfer his ideas for our own concerns. The most appropriate place to begin is with Freud's own applications to social theory. Having understood their relation to the main body of psychoanalysis—the clinical core—we can now examine more closely Freud's own contributions to social philosophy.

*CHAPTER III*

# Religion: Realism and Utopianism

## Neurosis

Freud was preoccupied with religious questions throughout his life. Although there are occasional comments on the social psychology of religion in his earlier works, only in later years did this interest come to the forefront in his writings; in each of the last three decades of his life he wrote a book centering on a different facet of the psychology of religion. Since these treatises introduce most of the main themes of Freud's own applications of psychoanalysis, the question of religion serves as a useful introduction to the rest of his social reflections.

As for Freud's personal outlook on religion, there is plenty of evidence that he had a completely negative view toward all religious practices. An atheist and a freethinker, Freud presided over a "totally non-religious . . . household."[1] He liked to think of himself as a "wicked pagan."[2] Like many others, Freud was disturbed by the enormous quantity of senseless human suffering in the world, and could not correlate this suffering with sin. He could not reconcile the conception of a good God with our human experience. The essence of the religious outlook, he felt, was a "pious illusion of providence and a moral world order, which are in conflict with reason."[3] Instead of accepting ethics as derivatives of God's commands, Freud sought a naturalistic ethical system, "a kind of highway code for traffic among mankind. . . ."[4]

While godless, Freud was very much a Jew. He was brought up as a Jew, and throughout his life his associates were primarily Jewish. Freud was so conscious of psychoanalysis's support among Jews that one of his main reasons for choosing Jung as his successor to lead the movement was that Jung was Gentile; Freud was fearful that his movement would succumb to the label the Nazis eventually hurled at it, "the Jewish science." Although from our experience with Nazism it is possible to exaggerate the quality of nineteenth-century Viennese anti-Semitism, Freud's academic career was certainly not helped by his Jewishness. On several occasions he went so far as to attribute some of the resistance to his doctrines to a veiled form of anti-Semitism.

That Freud was, as he once put it, "in his essential nature a Jew"[5] is perhaps the aspect of his personality which his biographer Ernest Jones, a Gentile and a skeptic, was least competent to understand. Nevertheless, reading between the

---

[1] Anna Freud, in Freud: *Psychoanalysis and Faith*, p. 11.
[2] Freud, ibid., p. 17.
[3] Ibid., p. 129.
[4] Ibid., p. 123.
[5] *Standard Edition*, Vol. 13, p. xv.

lines one can see the cultural importance of the Jewish religion for Freud. His humor, for example, was characteristically Jewish. Before the Nazis would permit Freud to leave Vienna they asked him to sign a statement testifying to the quality of the treatment he had received at their hands; Freud complied, but asked if he could add one sentence to the document—"I can heartily recommend the Gestapo to anyone."[6] This is the humor of the downtrodden and can be found among Negroes as well; its essential character is to snatch an ironic victory from the blackest defeat.

Since Freud's Jewishness is one of the less explored aspects of his character, our knowledge of the origins of psychoanalysis is proportionately deficient. We do know, though, that Freud was proud of his Jewishness, and that he attributed a good deal of his own intellectual independence to his Jewish origins. "To profess belief in this new theory called for a certain degree of readiness to accept a situation of solitary opposition—a situation with which no one is more familiar than a Jew."[7] Much like Veblen, Freud felt that the marginal social position of Jews gave them a fulcrum of detachment, a freedom from local prejudices, as well as an inner directedness, which went far to account for their great intellectual productivity in an alien world.

These biographical fragments are an essential background to Freud's own studies on the psychology of religion. As a "completely godless Jew,"[8] culturally a member of an ancient religion though an unbeliever, Freud could reject God for himself and still retain a sensitivity to the emotional implications of religion. He was aware, for example,

---

[6] Jones: *Sigmund Freud*, Vol. III, p. 226.

[7] *Standard Edition*, Vol. 19, p. 222.

[8] Freud: *Psychoanalysis and Faith*, p. 63.

of the possible constructive functions of religion; he referred to it as "sublimation in its most comfortable form."[9]
Freud appreciated the help that religion could give the
growing child. As he wrote of a patient in one of his case
histories,

> in the present case religion achieved all the aims for the sake of
> which it is included in the education of the individual. It put a
> restraint on his sexual impulses by affording them a sublima-
> tion and a safe mooring; it lowered the importance of his family
> relationships, and thus protected him from the threat of isolation
> by giving him access to the great community of mankind. The
> untamed and fear-ridden child became social, well-behaved, and
> amenable to education . . . religion did its work for the hard-
> pressed child—by the combination which it afforded the believer
> of satisfaction, of sublimation, of diversion from sensual processes
> to purely spiritual ones, and of access to social relationships.[1]

While religion could, under certain conditions, help stifle
neurosis, the difficulty was that those very conditions which
made religion a possible constructive resolution of psychic
conflicts seemed to be dissolving as modern history pro-
gressed. Freud thought that there had been an "extraordinary increase in neuroses since the power of religions has
waned. . . ."[2]

What matters most for our purposes is the extent to
which Freud could build on his empathy for religion and
use psychoanalysis to extend our understanding of religious
phenomena. In his first sustained attempt to apply psychoanalysis to religion, "Obsessive Actions and Religious Practices" (1907), Freud pointed out that one can find the
notion of a ceremonial in two apparently different contexts,

[9] Ibid., p. 16.
[1] Standard Edition, Vol. 17, pp. 114–15.
[2] Ibid., Vol. 11, p. 146.

in the activities of pious believers and in the protective devices of obsessive acts. In the second case, an activity could serve the psychological function of warding off an impulse and fulfilling the punishment with which that impulse is unconsciously linked. Only by repeated performance of the obsessive act can the self-deception be maintained, the guilt satisfied. The resemblance to certain religious practices, such as those of the Catholic Church, lies in the pangs of conscience, the privacy, and the conscientiousness with which both religious rituals and obsessive acts are performed. (Living in Catholic Austria, Freud had less experience with Protestantism, which had internalized many of the rites of the Catholic Church.)

The sense of guilt of obsessional neurotics finds its counterpart in the protestations of pious people that they know that at heart they are miserable sinners; and the pious observances (such as prayers, invocations, etc.) with which such people preface every daily act, and in especial every unusual undertaking, seem to have the value of defensive or protective measures.[3]

In comparing a social institution like religion to an emotional disorder like a neurosis, Freud was giving a new twist to the tradition of drawing parallels between the individual and society. From Plato on, philosophers had drawn directly on their conceptions of individual man for their social theories. Freud's innovation was to focus on the emotional components of the psyche, and especially on pathological disorders.

Superficially an emotional disorder might seem unstructured, and hence very unlike a social institution such as religion. Yet, no matter how confused the irrational may appear, there is always a curious kind of logic to it; on a

[3] Ibid., Vol. 9, pp. 123–4.

deep level a neurosis is a very highly articulated organization of psychic forces. Neurotic disturbance is a "frantic
and inappropriate *reorganization*, and not primarily a disintegration and disorganization. . . ."[4] Symptoms are "the
products of an attempt to heal the underlying trouble,"[5]
though they disturb and discomfort the ego in its functioning. The reconciliation of inner forces that constitutes
a neurosis achieves its stability at the expense of the individual's ego. While in this sense a neurosis can be crippling to the individual, it is nonetheless a structured
compromise, and can be compared organizationally—or so
Freud assumed—with any large-scale social institution.
Hence "the neuroses are social structures; they endeavor to
achieve by private means what is effected in society by collective effort . . . a case of hysteria is a caricature of a work
of art . . . an obsessional neurosis is a caricature of a religion, and . . . a paranoic delusion is a caricature of a
philosophic system."[6]

Freud distinguished between obsessive acts and religious
ceremonials by describing obsessionality "as an individual
religiosity and religion as a universal obsessional neurosis."[7] He was not, to be sure, identifying the one with the
other; the religious person not only need not be personally
obsessional, but may, as we have seen, sublimate very well.
The significance of the comparison between religion and
obsessional neurosis lies in the similarity of the different
human needs these structures fulfill, and not in whatever
anti-clerical implications one might draw. In the case of

---

[4] George Devereux: "Psychiatry and Anthropology," *Bulletin of the Menninger Clinic*, Vol. 16, No. 5 (September 1952), p. 174.

[5] Jones: *Papers on Psychoanalysis*, p. 373.

[6] *Standard Edition*, Vol. 13, p. 73.

[7] Ibid., Vol. 9, pp. 126–7.

hysterical neuroses, Freud had thought that the suppressed drives which were being warded off by defensive actions were primarily sexual in nature; in the case of obsessive, and also religious acts, the suppressed trends were largely "self-seeking, socially harmful instincts. . . ."[8] In renouncing their aggression, men turned over the energy of their hostilities to religion. "Vengeance is mine, saith the Lord."

We have here in this early essay the nucleus of Freud's approach to religion. Religion is treated as an outcome of human needs. The resemblance of some religious practices to certain neurotic symptoms is the point of departure, leading to an examination of the ways in which religious ideals have been transformed into their opposites. For Freud could strengthen the analogy of religion to obsessional neurosis by pointing out how often the outer religious forms obliterate the inner religious intention, as with any other self-defeating neurotic structure. In fact, certain religions forwarded the very ends they were originally pledged to oppose; for example, Christianity launched the Inquisition as an instrument of the religion of love. It is a basic psychoanalytic rule that the result of an action, whatever the conscious motive, sheds light on the underlying intention; "in human affairs the effect of an action frequently betrays the motivation of that action."[9] If religion has led to intolerance and aggression, may it not be that these were the very forces underlying religion in the first place?

Freud himself did not go much further with these particular ideas about the inner meaning of certain religious acts. The essay does suggest, though, not only Freud's application of the psychoanalytic approach to a particular so-

[8] Ibid., p. 125.
[9] Eissler: "The Chicago Institute of Psychoanalysis," p. 152.

cial institution, but also the concept he later developed of the function of all cultural life.

In the development of the ancient religions one seems to discern that many things which mankind had renounced as "iniquities" had been surrendered to the Deity and were still permitted in his name, so that the handing over to him of bad and socially harmful instincts was the means by which man freed himself from their domination.[1]

The underlying principle is that "a progressive renunciation of . . . instincts . . . appears to be one of the foundations of the development of human civilization."[2] Freud had long before argued that the explosiveness of the sexual drives could be tamed only by cultural restrictions; here, for the first time, he sees that the social order is founded on renounced aggressive forces as well.

It was no accident that Freud could now see the place of noneurotic, and specifically aggressive, drives in social life. In scrutinizing religion he saw that it dealt with aggression by projecting it onto an external deity; at the same time, religion also helped relieve the psychological guilt entailed by aggressive wishes. The notion that guilt lies in the intention, whatever the act, is basic to the Christian view. In a sense Freud was translating a religious belief into his psychoanalytic system. He held that men's feelings about their aggressive drives were founded on Solomon's maxim that "as a man thinketh in his heart, so is he." "Psychoanalysis agrees with religion that guilt attaches almost as much to aggressive wishes as to aggressive acts."[3] Freud's point was not that men should be held morally responsible

[1] *Standard Edition*, Vol. 9, p. 127.

[2] Ibid.

[3] Karl Menninger: *Love Against Hate* (New York: Harcourt, Brace; 1942), pp. 216, 193.

for their evil thoughts, but only that, psychologically, men think and feel themselves to be reprehensible for their evil wishes.

From the beginning Freud had been clear about the need for society to control men's sexual drives; it was only later, however, that he took full account of the extent of human destructiveness in need of social control. In a sense this was a more difficult task for culture than the handling of erotic needs, since aggression, unlike libido, is normally incapable of being fully discharged.[4] If aggression has to be expressed indirectly, then it can build up to explosive heights, which makes our anger all the harder to reconcile with our self-esteem. Pent-up aggression can entail considerable guilt; this suppressed aggression can be "made over" to the super-ego, and expressed in self-punishment. If the Christian religion has assuaged human guilt at all, this is in part because of its insight into the psychology of human aggression, the way we unconsciously confuse aggressive wishes with murderous deeds.

The twofold character of Freud's account of human drives, the existence of both erotic and aggressive impulses, is paralleled by the complexity of his attitude toward authority. On the one hand cultural restrictions can be too demanding, can do violence to human needs; and yet on the other hand authority is helpful in enabling the individual to cope with the power of his passions. We will see later that as psychoanalysis elaborated its notions about aggressive drives, it came to a deeper appreciation of the uses of the social order.

In this early period before World War I, Freud was still primarily concerned with clinical problems, and the im-

---

[4] Hartmann, Kris, and Loewenstein: "Notes on the Theory of Aggression," *Psychoanalytic Study of the Child*, Vol. III/IV, p. 21.

portance of unfulfilled sexuality in the origin of neuroses still loomed large. He was then insisting on the fulfillment of erotic emotions, in order to stave off neurotic solutions for suppressed needs. Similarly, he took an iconoclastic view of the functions of religion. In his study of Leonardo, Freud saw a relation between Leonardo's scientific independence and his irreligiousness:

When anyone has, like Leonardo, escaped being intimidated by his father during his earliest childhood, and has in his researches cast away the fetters of authority, it would be in the sharpest contradiction to our expectation if we found that he had remained a believer and had been unable to escape from dogmatic religion. Psychoanalysis has made us familiar with the intimate connection between the father-complex and belief in God; it has shown us that a personal God is, psychologically, nothing other than an exalted father, and it brings us evidence every day of how young people lose their religious beliefs as soon as their father's authority breaks down. Thus we recognize that the roots of the need for religion are in the parental complex; the almighty and just God, and kindly Nature, appear to us as grand sublimations of father and mother, or rather as revivals and restorations of the young child's ideas of them. Biologically speaking, religiousness is to be traced to the small human child's long-drawn-out helplessness and need of help; and when at a later date he perceives how truly forlorn and weak he is when confronted with the great forces of life, he feels his condition as he did in childhood, and attempts to deny his own despondency by a regressive revival of the forces which protected his infancy. The protection against neurotic illness, which religion vouchsafes to those who believe in it, is easily explained: it removes their parental complex, on which the sense of guilt in individuals as well as in the whole human race depends, and disposes of it, while the unbeliever has to grapple with the problem on his own.[5]

[5] *Standard Edition*, Vol. 11, p. 123.

Instead of merely relating religious to neurotic ceremonials as in his earlier essay, religion in this later work is treated more broadly as an infantile defense against helplessness. In other words, a small child is objectively a helpless creature; this insecurity is regularly overcome by an inner sense of magical omnipotence. As the child grows into an adult, an index of his sense of inadequacy is his continued inability to face life without projecting that childish sense of all-encompassing control onto God. In Leonardo's instance, Freud saw his ability to do without the crutch of religion as a corollary of his general intellectual ability to stand on his own two feet.

## 2   Crime and Punishment

In *Totem and Taboo* (1912–13) Freud studied a religious system, not in order to point out the element of infantile wish-fulfillment, but to extend our understanding of the nature of civilization itself. Tactically, though, the book was an opening shot in the quarrel with Jung. Already distressed by Jung's rivalry, especially in his use of comparative religion and mythology, Freud hoped that "the most daring enterprise . . . [he had] ever ventured" would "serve to make a sharp division between us and all Aryan religiosity."[1] It is generally a good principle in intellectual history, and even more so with Freud, to keep in mind a writer's opponents; in *Totem and Taboo* the direction of Freud's thoughts on religion was channeled by his attempt to apply clinical psychoanalysis as he had already developed

[1] Jones: *Sigmund Freud*, Vol. II, p. 353.

it, rather than to reconstruct it in the light of various religious systems, as Jung was to do.

It is curious that *Totem and Taboo* has had so little impact on political theory. Its theoretical importance has been obscured both by the inadequacies of the evolutionary anthropology Freud relied upon, and by the issue of the "historical" reality of the primal crime. Basically he was hunting about for weapons to express some cherished ideas. Within political theory it is familiar to rescue social contract thinkers from the test of historical truth by interpreting their ideas as moral theories, or as logical fictions having explanatory value. In Freud's case his argument can be reconstructed as a psychological theory, entirely apart from the problem of the actual occurrence of a primal deed. One could, if one wanted to throw stones, have a field day with Freud's Lamarckianism; but since we are interested in Freud for what he has to say about human psychology, we will focus on how he extends our understanding of people.

Freud begins by linking totemic religion with the institution of taboos. According to certain "savage" customs, the totem, as ancestor, defines blood relations. All those descended from the same totem are involved in a complicated set of exogamy rules; these rules establish which relationships are defined as incestuous. Violations of the incest restrictions entail severe punishment; sometimes these rules are so internalized that no outside agency needs to enforce them. Oedipus, for example, blinded himself for violating his society's incest rules. Since totemic religion involves both worship of the common ancestor and the exogamous taboos, "totemism is thus both a religious and a social system."[2]

---

[2] *Standard Edition*, Vol. 13, pp. 103–4.

A taboo is by itself a social institution. Its purpose is directed against "liberty of enjoyment and against freedom of movement and communication."[3] Nonliterate tribes, with all their restrictive regulations, are highly sensitive to incest. There would seem to be a contradiction between their extensive efforts to avoid incest, as well as the enormous range of sexual life included within the category "incest," and their greatly heightened "horror" of incest. Such peoples "are probably liable to a greater temptation to it and for that reason stand in need of fuller protection."[4]

Extensive efforts to control oedipal strivings, according to Freud, provide an index of their strength. We have here a classic instance of ambivalence, and again Freud was drawn to the parallel of obsessional prohibitions. An obsessive neurotic, who is so afraid of killing someone that he performs actions designed to guard himself from committing murder as well as to expiate the guilt for the horrid wish, is similarly torn. On the one hand he feels the violent desire, on the other he cannot reconcile this with his sense of self-esteem. Just as a protective device like a personal taboo would be unnecessary unless the emotion guarded against were very powerful, so social taboos would be unnecessary unless there were a strong initial inclination to perform the forbidden act. As Frazer put it, "It is not easy to see why any deep human instinct should need to be reinforced by law. . . . The law only forbids men to do what their instincts incline them to do; what nature itself prohibits and punishes, it would be superfluous for the law to prohibit and punish."[5]

If we can accept the idea that a prohibition draws its

---

[3] Ibid., p. 21.
[4] Ibid., p. 9.
[5] Ibid., p. 123.

strength from the temptation, then we can see how the
danger of a violation lies in the possibility of imitation by
others. "If the violation were not avenged by other members they would become aware that they wanted to act in
the same way as the transgressor."[6] To be sure, we also
rationally identify with the victim; we are all aware of
the old-fashioned fear that motivates us to lock our doors
at night. Psychoanalysis points instead to fears which we
have good reason to censor from ourselves.

Although the psychology of punishment must seem a
digression from Freud's theses in *Totem and Taboo*, we
are not interested in Freud's studies in religion for their
own sake, but for what is relevant in them for political
theory. The existence of unconscious processes does alter
any rationalistic approach to punishment; punishment is
not solely for the criminal. "The object of punishment," as
Nietzsche so clairvoyantly saw, "is to improve him *who
punishes*. . . ."[7] Often the "improvement" may involve
warding off from within ourselves the forbidden impulse.
Hence "we are unconsciously indignant," Ferenczi noted,
"that the criminal dared to do something which we all unconsciously had the greatest inclination to do."[8] At the
same time, in punishing the offender there is an opportunity
of vicariously committing the very crime that is to be pun-
ished. "The punishment will not infrequently give those
who carry it out an opportunity of committing the same
outrage under colour of an act of expiation."[9] And to complete an irrational cycle, in order to punish ourselves for the

[6] Ibid., p. 33.

[7] F. W. Nietzsche: *Joyful Wisdom* (New York: Ungar; 1960), p. 199.

[8] Ferenczi: *Further Contributions to the Theory and Technique of Psychoanalysis*, p. 431.

[9] *Standard Edition*, Vol. 13, p. 72.

forbidden impulses as well as for our own misdirected pen-
alties, we need to punish criminality even more.

We have here the description of a classic vicious circle,
the well-known scapegoat mechanism. Ruth Eissler has recently restated the conundrum which a psychoanalytic understanding of criminal acts and punishment poses for us:

For society in general [nowadays] there remains only one justifiable outlet for aggression, which can be rationalized on the
basis of morality and which can provide the desired relief by
externalizing inner conflicts without creating conscious guilt
feelings. This is the persecution of the wicked, the criminals, that
group of individuals who commit violence, who break the laws.
. . . But if this is the case, if society needs criminals as scapegoats,
then what are the chances for a rational prevention of
[crime]. . . ?"[1]

Although Freud was not himself concerned with squar-
ing his psychoanalytic understanding with a liberal theory
of punishment, his theories obviously pose difficulties for the
traditional utilitarian theory of punishment. This tradition,
which stems from Bentham, has hypothesized a rational
group of legislators fixing sanctions of appropriate hardship
to deter rational men from breaking the law. In a recent
textbook, for example, it is maintained that "the strongest
utilitarian case for punishment is that it serves to deter potential offenders by inflicting suffering on actual ones. On
this view, punishment is not the main thing; the technique
works by threat."[2]

Yet on utilitarian grounds alone it is proper to inquire

[1] Ruth Eissler: "Scapegoats of Society," in *Searchlights on Delinquency*, ed.
Kurt Eissler (New York: International Universities Press; 1949), p. 295.
[2] S. I. Benn and R. S. Peters: *Social Principles and the Democratic State*
(London: Allen and Unwin; 1959), p. 181.

into the actual results of this technique. How effective is punishment as a deterrent? The authors of this same textbook make a bow toward what we know about the irrational springs of conduct by specifying that punishment as a deterrent can be effective "only in respect of *deliberate* acts."[3] For in any other state of mind the criminal "would be unlikely to take much account of the threat of punishment."[4]

Yet this formulation will not do for those concerned with incorporating Freud's findings within a modern theory of punishment. His point was not that some criminals are so overcome by their unconscious as to be unable to act "deliberately." Such a description would presumably cover only those whom a rationalistic psychology would itself be inclined to consider "insane." But to the extent that we are all neurotic, our egos are beset with conflicting feelings and ambivalences. As Freud put it,

All our social institutions are framed for people with a united and normal ego, which one can classify as good or bad, which either fulfills its function or is altogether eliminated by an overpowering influence. Hence the juridical alternative: responsible or irresponsible. None of these distinctions apply to neurotics.[5]

In discussing Freud's earliest essay on religion, we have already touched on a possible connection between aggression and irrational suffering. There Freud pointed out how one's own suffering—in this instance criminal punishment—can relieve one's guilt feelings. There is, according to Freud's metapsychology, a close relationship between the id and the superego; the energy of the superego is traced

[3] Ibid., p. 191.
[4] Ibid.
[5] *Standard Edition*, Vol. 20, p. 221.

to internalized aggression. Yet the link between these two psychic structures is not merely one of origins. The superego can also be bribed into permitting instinctual gratification. One's own punishment, that is to say the gratification of the superego's need for suffering, frequently acts as a relief. An external catastrophe can satisfy an individual's neurotic need to suffer; "when fate inflicts suffering there is less need for the self-punishing functions of the neurosis."[6]

Thus excessive punishment of oneself may permit forms of psychic relief. Providing the suffering is intense and our ego is weak, we are permitted a wide range of acts which our consciences would otherwise forbid. It is in this sense that the superego can be bribed by punishment; one's conscience can be disarmed by means of a "voluntary acceptance of some suffering."[7] "The superego can easily be hoodwinked; once its punishing tendencies are gratified, its eyes remain shut."[8] The psychoanalytic point is that self-suffering is sought because it relieves one of guilt; but the relief of this superego anxiety also permits the gratification of impulses which otherwise would be barred by conscience. "The aim of the superego—that is, self-punishment, suffering—is achieved through arousing a repressed instinctual drive."[9]

Freud specified, as early as 1915, a class of criminals motivated by a "sense of guilt." Instead of punishment acting as a deterrent on these men, their deeds were committed "principally because they were forbidden, and because their

[6] Jones: *Papers on Psychoanalysis*, p. 186.

[7] Franz Alexander and Hugo Staub: *The Criminal, the Judge, and the Public* (New York: Collier Books; 1962), p. 63.

[8] Franz Alexander: *The Scope of Psychoanalysis* (New York: Basic Books; 1961), p. 215.

[9] Loewenstein: "A Special Form of Self-Punishment," p. 59.

execution was accompanied by mental relief for the doer."[1]
Freud traced the origin of the guilt to infantile parricidal
and incestuous wishes. The criminal suffered "from an oppressive feeling of guilt, of which he did not know the
origin, and after he had committed a misdeed this oppression was mitigated. His sense of guilt was at least attached
to something. . . . It is as if it was a relief to be able to
fasten this unconscious sense of guilt on to something real
and immediate."[2] One such criminal is quoted in a recent
study as saying, "My only feeling when put in jail was
relief."[3]

Overwhelmed by guilt and unable to find himself, he committed
his crimes as a means of inducing social authority to ease his
conflict; punishment from without was substituted for punishment from within. . . . Being exposed and imprisoned helped to
cleanse him of guilt and to weaken somewhat the forces of
conscience.[4]

If psychoanalytic theory offers an explanation of the need
for punishment, Dostoevsky offers the best examples of this
type of suffering. In general Dostoevsky was the master
analyst of unconscious guilt feelings. In the character of
Ivan, in *The Brothers Karamazov*, we see a man create
his own accusatory double in order to handle his guilt over
death wishes toward his father. In Raskolnikov, in *Crime
and Punishment*, a man acts out his irrational guilt by attaching it to an external crime, in this instance a murder,
and then proceeds slowly to give himself away to the public authorities. The opposition of Ivan's doubts to Ras-

[1] *Standard Edition*, Vol. 14, p. 332.
[2] Ibid., p. 332; Vol. 19, p. 52.
[3] Daniel J. Levinson: "Criminality from a Sense of Guilt," *Journal of Personality*, Vol. 20, No. 4 (June 1952), p. 405.
[4] Ibid., pp. 422–3.

All criminality, needless to say, is not psychopathic. Some criminals may form a specific subculture, such as American gangsterism. Or criminal behavior may represent the most readily accessible means of defying social injustices. Other kinds of criminals, such as those who do not get caught, may be tempted by the pleasure of a close shave with the law, rather than by actual imprisonment. It may be as pleasurable to play with death as to experience the more classical forms of masochism. It is important to realize how inadequate the Benthamite model is for dealing with all these varieties. However, rational self-interest can also lead to crime where there is little or no chance of getting caught. Surely we have a lot of corporation hanky-panky in America today partly because of the low risk of being found out.

The utilitarian theory of punishment does not rely solely on deterrence. It also rests on the usefulness of preventing further crimes by locking some people up, as well as on the hope of being able to reform these criminals during confinement. On utilitarian grounds, however, it is possible to question how effective these techniques really are. There is an inherently degrading aspect to imprisonment; and if you humiliate a man, he is apt to respond by humiliating himself further. One need only think of the life of a prisoner—the idleness, the self-hatred, the homosexuality—to ponder the adequacy of the psychological basis of Benthamite thinking on punishment. Prison authorities could in principle become enlightened, but it would in practice require tremendous social expense even to try to accomplish realistic reformatory goals through punishment.

No amount of psychologizing, however, need lead us to abandon punishment as a rational instrument of social policy. But we must be ready to rethink the justifications for punishment, with whatever help psychological understanding can give. It may still be possible to adopt the utilitarian position for the sake of a social fiction that is more or less useful. But motivation for criminality cannot be traced only to a series of rational miscalculations over the risks and costs of criminal acts. When a problem as important to liberal thinking as the most severe deprivation of human freedom is at stake, one is entitled to expect greater psychological realism in our justification of punishment.

In fact, utilitarian reasoning has recently been under something of a cloud, and philosophers have felt a growing cordiality to the old retributionist theory of punishment. This turn to Kant, away from Bentham, has been largely on logical grounds rather than because of the inadequacies of utilitarian psychology. For example, "the theories of reform and deterrence . . . both would on occasion justify the punishment of an innocent man, the deterrent theory if he were believed to have been guilty by those likely to commit the crime in the future, and the reformatory theory if he were a bad man though not a criminal."[7] In other words, whatever use Bentham may be in justifying the institution of punishment, he fails when one considers individual breaches of law instead of the legal system as a whole.

The grounds for not punishing an innocent man must be derived from some notion that only legally defined crime demands punishment; "guilt is a *logically* necessary condition of punishment."[8] Likewise, the grounds for punishing a grave crime like murder more heavily than a trivial crime like stealing must be traced to some notion of proportion; the talionic rule, an eye for an eye, a tooth for a

[7] J. D. Mabbott: "Punishment," *Mind*, Vol. 48 (1939), p. 152.
[8] Anthony Quinton: "On Punishment," in *Philosophy, Politics, and Society*, ed. Peter Laslett (Oxford: Blackwell; 1956), p. 88.

tooth, is a useful standard in assessing the extent of retribution for any particular violation of law. It ensures legal
justice; the criminal has so much punishment coming to
him and no more, administered in specified ways and under
set circumstances. The retributionist theory of punishment
is thus in a sense an argument for channelling and restraining vengeance in civilized ways. "In limiting both crime
and punishment by a system of rules, this policy aims at
protecting individuals against arbitrary governmental action."[9]

Yet the Kantian tradition, like the Benthamite one, is
not exempt from a psychoanalytic critique. Unconsciously
we are all too ready to employ the talionic law; whatever
its uses in logically determining that the punishment fit
the crime, psychologically men are all too apt to respond
to crime by primitive retaliation. Presumably one of the
aims of civilized society is to prevent barbaric resort to the
talionic standard, to preclude matching the murder of President Kennedy with the murder of his assassin.

While Freud was not concerned with the theory of punishment in any systematic way, the manner in which his
system alters our previous thinking about crime is a good
example of how a close reading of his works reveals fresh
possibilities for political thought. The concept of the unconscious need not entail a wholesale rejection of punishment as an institution. Punishment can still be seen as a
"corollary of law breaking."[1] To the extent that societies
need rules for social control, then the coercion of punishment is entailed as an instrument of social policy. To the
extent that punishment is a rational procedure, we must
remember that "any increase in the number of conditions

[9] Shklar: *Legalism*, p. 152.
[1] Mabbott: "Punishment," p. 161.

required to establish criminal liability increases the opportunity for deceiving courts or juries by the pretence that some condition is not satisfied."[2]

But we must abandon those aspects of the theory of punishment which are grounded on an unreal picture of human nature. Otherwise, how can criminal law successfully live up to its function of maintaining certain standards of behavior? It behooves us to be clearer about the extent to which we foster lawbreaking, the degree to which criminals seek out their own suffering, the sense in which a criminal code "increases the fear of the external police but decreases the inhibiting influence of the internal controlling factor of human personality, that of conscience."[3] The utilitarian theory of punishment can be tested by the degree to which men approximate the ideal type of rational conduct; and the retributionist argument must face the extent to which the talionic law is merely a piece of unconscious barbarism. The psychoanalytic view of crime and punishment entails a reconsideration of the classic arguments behind the institution of punishment. Presuming, that is, that humane liberalism will not rest content with the mere pleasures of vengeance and retaliation.

## 3 Authority

Our elaboration of the psychoanalytic contribution to understanding punishment, while logically an offshoot from Freud's discussion in *Totem and Taboo*, was far from his immediate concern. Instead of focusing on the psychology

[2] H. L. A. Hart, in *Philosophy, Politics and Society*, ed. Peter Laslett and W. G. Runciman (Second Series) (Oxford: Blackwell; 1962), p. 174.

[3] Alexander and Staub: *The Criminal, the Judge, and the Public*, p. 243.

of punishment for the infraction of social rules, Freud was primarily interested in pointing out the extent of ambivalence underlying all such authoritative restrictions. In order to illustrate the latent desires in any society, Freud discussed the various taboos on the dead: that a dead man's name cannot be invoked, or his possessions used, or, in our society, his character spoken ill of—all these superstitions spring, Freud thought, from a fear of evil spirits. The dead man will take offense and retaliate. The unconscious mechanism behind such morality is projective; for a man's death magically fulfills all one's own aggressions toward him. "In the view of the unconscious thinking, a man who has died a natural death is a murdered man; evil wishes have killed him."[1] Since it is unacceptable to us to acknowledge our aggression once that aggression has unmistakably been fulfilled, we project it onto the dead: it is they who harbor the aggression, they who will take offense unless we preserve certain moral customs.

In a brief discussion of the authority relationship between rulers and ruled, Freud pointed out that similar ambivalent feelings could be found. We surrounded rulers, both primitive and modern, with a host of taboos; ostensibly these measures are designed for the benefit of both rulers and ruled. By carefully protecting the lives of rulers we make it possible for them to exercise their power for the benefit of society. But we also make their lives miserable with these very protective devices.

The ceremonial taboo of kings is *ostensibly* the highest honor and protection for them, while *actually* it is a punishment for their exaltation, a revenge taken on them by their subjects. The

[1] *Standard Edition*, Vol. 13, p. 62.

experience of Sancho Panza (as described by Cervantes) when he was Governor of his island convinced him that this view of court ceremonial was the only one that met the case.[2]

Freud explicitly suggests here that the ambivalence between the positive and negative poles of the subject's attitude to his ruler is grounded on a deep emotional relationship, that to his father; "much of a savage's attitude to his ruler is derived from a child's infantile attitude to his father."[3] Just as Freud thought that God was rooted in the adult's yearning for the security of his father's protection, so the divinity that doth hedge a king had a similar familial origin.

That secular authority has an irrational quality of majesty has been well known in political theory. We still think in the historical shadow of "the subject-ruler relationship of our monarchical past, in which authority was sanctified and resistance required more than a merely pragmatic justification."[4] Freud's contribution was to focus on the enduring human needs involved in authority relationships, and hence on the childish emotions and fantasies which we extend around political figures.

Recently political scientists have become interested in the way in which the child becomes socialized into political life. Their findings go far to confirm these hypotheses of Freud. For example, one research project indicates that "the child's political world begins to take shape well before he even enters elementary school. . .";[5] "children tend to view

[2] Ibid., p. 51.
[3] Ibid., p. 50.
[4] Shklar: *Legalism*, p. 71.
[5] David Easton and Robert D. Hess: "The Child's Political World," *Mid-West Journal of Political Science*, Vol. 6, No. 3 (August 1962), p. 230.

all significant authority, political or otherwise, as similar
to an ideal parental model. . . . By idealizing authority
. . . the child is able to allay the fears and anxieties of its
own dependent state."[6] Another study found that

the prevailing [American] adult skepticism and distrust of
politics and the politician simply did not seem to be present in
the grade school sample . . . the more negative attitudes toward
political leaders are chronologically late arrivals whereas the
firm impression that leaders are important people emerges early
and almost unconsciously—years before the child has more than
a smattering of political information. . . .[7]

These early and positive ties to the political system are
relevant for later political behavior. They would, for example, help to explain the basis of the sense of community
which can endure within a nation despite transitory dis-
agreements.

   Recent political history illustrates that political authority
can thrive on irrational needs for security. The U-2 incident
under Eisenhower, or the Bay of Pigs invasion under Kennedy, were hardly masterpieces of foreign policy. Yet both
crises seemed to provoke, according to the polls, increased
public support for the incumbent Presidents; intense insecurity can preclude a more rational public response.

The awareness of national peril seems inevitably to inspire an
anxious sense of dependence upon the Presidency, unbridled by
the strict appraisal of logic or fact. And this sense—of both
danger and dependence—may be greatly quickened, in fact, by
a manifest lapse in presidential leadership.[8]

   [6] Ibid., p. 243.
   [7] Fred I. Greenstein: "The Benevolent Leader," *The American Political
Science Review*, Vol. 54, No. 4 (December 1960), pp. 935, 942.
   [8] Emmet John Hughes: *The Ordeal of Power* (New York: Atheneum; 1963),
p. 332.

Political leaders are not the only foci of such processes; ideological systems as well can thrive on such insecurities, as can harsh distinctions between in-groups and out-groups or projective scapegoating.

The relation between the public world and inner psychological needs can become quite complex. The hypothesis of the existence of infantile roots behind authority relationships does not preclude a person's being "submissive toward one person or type of ideas and rebellious toward another."[9] And a political style or attitude can compensate for, rather than mirror, one's childhood emotional patterns. Grieving for a dead President may fulfill a great variety of private needs. These complications, however, need not alter the general notion that loving overestimation, combined with murderous hate, are often directed toward our political leaders.

One might grant that Freud discovered a uniform human nature beneath cultural varieties, and yet still think that whatever universals could be discerned would be so primary as to have a tenuous relation to social life. Freud himself focused on the special problem of the relation of totemism to exogamy rules. He related the two historically; on the basis of the evidence he selected, Freud thought that totemism was older than exogamy. "Totemism constitutes a regular phase in all cultures. . . ."[1] The crucial problem to be explained, he thought, was how an animal came to be the totem of the clan in the first place; how a clan could claim its ancestry from an animal, revere and honor it, and yet at certain festivals consume it in a feast, indulg-

9 L. S. Kubie: "Psychiatry in Relation to Authority and Freedom," in *Freedom and Authority in Our Time*, ed. Lyman Bryson, et al. (New York: Harper; 1953), p. 388.

1 *Standard Edition*, Vol. 13, p. 108.

ing in unfettered instinctual gratification. And these periodic violations of normal taboos somehow reinforced the unity of the clan.

The key, Freud argued, lay in the animal phobias of children. Freud had already traced, in his clinical work, the common childhood terror of animals to the conflicts of the oedipal stage. By displacing the terror and hatred of his father onto an animal, the little boy can externalize an inner conflict; the negative side of his oedipal feelings need no longer conflict with his affection for his father, the positive side of the Oedipus complex. The boy thereby relieves the inner tension of his ambivalent feelings toward his father. At some point the child often playfully identifies with the animal, displacing the positive aspect of his oedipal feelings onto the animal as well. Now he wants to behave like the animal, much as in real life he wants to grow up like father.

Freud therefore took quite literally the totem as the "ancestor" of the clan; the totem animal stands for the clan's oedipal feelings, the positive side expressed in the usual homage, ritual, etc., and in the identification with the totem animal by wearing his skins. The negative aspect of the clan's ambivalence was expressed by the ritual of the totem meal, at which in a riot of instinctual release the usual reverence for the totem animal was suspended. The identification was maintained by the incorporation of the totem meal; by eating the totem animal the clan expressed its hostile feelings combined with its positive ones, for the totem animal was not simply destroyed, but lovingly taken into the self.

Freud had already written of God the father, and of the relationship of the rulers to the ruled as founded on the father-child relationship; now he applied this parallel to a nonliterate society. The clan totem stood for the father, and therefore attached to itself the corresponding emotional ambivalence. But Freud pushed his argument one step further. He claimed that once, or repeatedly, the primal crime of parricide had actually been carried out.

He was aware of how far from his original position he was going. "Then [in *The Interpretation of Dreams*] I described the wish to kill one's father, and now I have been describing the actual killing; after all it is a big step from a wish to a deed."[2] Starting from a suggestion of Darwin's about early man living in small hordes, Freud postulated that one such group was ruled by an autocrat who monopolized the females. Eventually the sons banded together, slew the father, and then ate him. The totem feast represented a repetition of this primal deed.

The rest of Freud's story is very much like the old rationalistic social contract theory of the origins of society. The brothers soon found that social order required communal restrictions, that it was necessary to agree upon some body of rules to replace those of the father. By reimposing the father's rules, by accepting the notion that instinctual renunciation is socially necessary, at one and the same time they expiated their guilt and tried to "appease the father by deferred obedience to him."[3]

The totemic system was, as it were, a covenant with their father, in which he promised them everything that a childish imagination may expect from a father . . . while on their side they undertook to respect his life. . . . In thus guaranteeing one another's lives, the brothers were declaring that no one of them must be treated by another as their father was treated by them jointly. . . . To the religiously based prohibition against killing

[2] Jones: *Sigmund Freud*, Vol. II, p. 354.
[3] *Standard Edition*, Vol. 13, p. 145.

the totem was now added the socially based prohibition against fratricide.[4]

The origin of morality lies in ambivalence; once the aggression was satisfied, love remained, and that led to remorse and the renunciation of instinctual gratification.

Surely this tale of the origin of social life is that aspect of *Totem and Taboo* which entitled it to Freud's label of a "Just-So Story."[5] There is simply no evidence for the existence of such hordes. But there are also some strictly logical difficulties in Freud's argument; for no more than the traditional social contract thinkers does Freud succeed in reaching the origins of human society. Like them he is unable to extrapolate man into a state of nature. The point can be made by simply examining the logic of a covenant. There is, as many have pointed out, an inherent circularity in the social contract reasoning; contract theory assumes "the logical priority of the obligation to keep a promise."[6] To *promise* is after all a very complicated social act; it assumes a common language, or at least a set of symbols of communication held in common. The logic of being able to promise to obey common rules already assumes the existence of social life.

In extenuation of *Totem and Taboo*, one must admit that Freud was trying to deal with one of the most basic issues in political theory. Much like Hobbes before him, and yet from a different starting point, Freud wanted to explain the sources of social cohesion. Given man as Freud saw him, social order was problematic to an extreme; hence the need for the ritual of the totemic feast to reinforce social unity. Not only were the sexual drives divisive, but

[4] Ibid., pp. 144, 146.
[5] Ibid., Vol. 18, p. 122.
[6] Richard Peters: *Hobbes* (London: Penguin Books; 1956), p. 196.

aggressive impulses drove men apart. "Sexual needs are not capable of uniting men in the same way as are the demands of self-preservation."[7] What initially held society together, Freud thought, was a utilitarian covenant that instinctual renunciation was preferable to anarchy.

The inadequacies of the "covenant" as an explanatory concept of social cohesion soon became as evident to Freud as to us, and he was to return to the problem in *Group Psychology and the Analysis of the Ego*. But at least the utilitarian argument went part way in legitimizing coercion. Like Rousseau before him, who was also impressed by the "chains" on men, Freud was preoccupied with justifying society, with finding a standard that would support civilized life, and at the same time enable him to condemn particular institutions as inappropriate. Over and over again Freud claims that society is unnecessarily restrictive. Civilized life could aid self-fulfillment by helping men handle their aggressive drives, but always Freud questioned whether the price might not be too high, whether the constructive erotic drives might not thereby be excessively blocked.

Much of the difficulty with *Totem and Taboo* can be extracted by treating it as Freud handled the seduction fantasies of his patients in 1897. It is as if the revolutionary in Freud had to find in the past grounds for revolt against the father, once in the form of indignation at his sexual maltreatment of children, then at his monopoly of the females in the primal horde. Freud seems not quite able to accept his own theory of the power of psychic realities; since he had not completely convinced himself of the strength of fantasies, he had to have a "real" trauma, a "real" murder of the primal father. If we treat the primal crime as a fantasy, if we accept the oedipal conflict as a

[7] *Standard Edition*, Vol. 13, p. 74.

psychic truth, then we have less difficulty in accepting his argument. Freud himself was tempted by this alternative possibility: "The mere existence of a wishful *phantasy* of killing and devouring him, would have been enough to produce the moral reaction that created totemism and taboo. . . . In their childhood they had these evil impulses pure and simple, and turned them into acts so far as the impotence of childhood allowed."[8]

In a sense, in all his historical speculations, Freud was simply using a characteristic mental habit of the nineteenth century, shared by anthropologists of his time, of "translating 'essence' into 'origin,' so that the statement 'this is the essence of the situation' becomes 'this is how it began.' "[9] In terms of the history of political theory, such a procedure has an ancient heritage, extending throughout the history of the concept of the state of nature. In addition, as we have earlier cautioned, one should remember that Freud was writing this book as part of his quarrel with Jung. As is well known in intellectual history, one's opponents have a tendency to set the categories of debate. In this instance, Jung's own phylogenetic speculations must have helped to stimulate similar impulses within Freud's mind. Within Freud's system as a whole, it is logically possible to remove these elements, and translate Freud's phylogenetic stages into ontogenetic ones; one can thereby avoid the whole issue of the inheritance of acquired characteristics.

But there is enough of interest in *Totem and Taboo* to minimize the problem of the historical existence of the primal crime. Freud viewed society very much in dynamic

---

[8] Ibid., pp. 160–1.

[9] Stanley Edgar Hyman: *The Tangled Bank* (New York: Atheneum; 1962), p. 366.

terms; forces are at play, often in conflict. Just as Freud could see how useful criminality could be, how society might even foster disobedience, so he could see the pleasure of vengeance beneath our upright moralism. It is the dynamism in life, the compulsions, the hidden ways in which we are driven in one direction or another, that mark all of Freud's social thinking. Freud had a strong sense of the passionate elements in life, those undercurrents of feeling that we evade at our peril.

This very awareness of the energic content of forces, of their impelling strength, of the potentially limitless character of human passions, makes Freud's description of authority relationships so vivid. In focusing on the authority relationship, whether child and father, subject and ruler, or man and society, Freud links himself to a central concern of political theory. In fact, both Bodin and Filmer had insisted on the family as the point of departure for understanding political society. However rationalistic Freud might sound because of his use of covenant theory, in the last analysis he belongs in the tradition of those thinkers who reject a belief in the possibility of a state of nature. The essence of this trend is the belief that society is not willed into being by men's rationality, but that it is a given, natural phenomenon. To the extent that family life is the model for authority relationships, we are born political creatures.

What is unique about Freud's point of view is that he always talks about authority in inner terms, that he always strives to see the meaning authority has for the internal needs of men. Patrick Henry's "Give me liberty or give me death" is, according to Freud, superlatively untrue to human experience. Man wants both liberty and restraint, and the tensions between conflicting needs comprise human tragedy. Freud's description of social restrictions, of the coercions of life, is so intensely real because he sees the extent to which outer authority is linked to our inner needs. Society is coercive precisely because its rules are internalized, are taken into the self; and at the same time society is useful in helping to keep some sort of balance between various forces. Just as a child needs parental restrictions to handle his aggression, just as he needs to be stopped before the full horror of his murderous impulses becomes evident to him, so social restraints assist man in handling his aggression, both by providing vicarious forms of release, and by reinforcing his inner controls over drives which are alien to his inner security.

## 4   The Voice of Reason

It was essentially an Enlightenment idea that environmentalism was the hope of the future, that by institutional changes, man could be changed. Focusing on the solitary individual, by examining the soul of man, many have felt they could only despair of radical social changes. Institutional reformism has become associated with a neglect of individual psychology. However, Freud's thoughts on religion illustrate the notion that social radicalism can draw on depth psychology. Freud begins with a view of human nature very unlike a *tabula rasa*; although he postulates basic human drives, these can be satisfied in a variety of ways. An understanding of depth psychology need not, therefore, entail any social conservatism. The one form of social coercion Freud felt to be humanly unnecessary was religion. Our study of Freud's views on religion not only opens up psychoanalytic theories of punishment and au-

thority, as in *Totem and Taboo*; it also points to the underlying utopianism Freud maintained, despite the commonplace about the "grimness" of his view of man.

In *The Future of an Illusion* (1927) we see a narrow
slice of Freud's mind which is revealing of his whole cast
of thought. In this book Freud stresses that inner instinctual
core which strains beyond culture's reach. It is true that
Freud's theories emphasize the divisions within the human
mind; Freud differs from the classical liberal tradition to
the extent that he sees man not as a unit, but as an opposed self. Yet it is also true that Freud thought that deep
within man there was an unbreakable nucleus, a central
portion of the self ineluctably in opposition to society. Freud
once wrote that "for most people there is a limit beyond
which their constitution cannot comply with the demands
of civilization."[1] In that sense, "every individual is virtually
an enemy of civilization."[2]

If there is some kind of inner human nucleus, if man's
instinctual dispositions set limits to culture's demands, then
an empirical basis exists for the individualism of the
liberal tradition. It is possible to assert that society is asking for too much; the standard of individual self-fulfillment
is always at hand. It is in this sense that Lionel Trilling is
quite right in placing Freud within the tradition of "humane liberal thought."[3] It is principally Freud's Enlightenment heritage which moves him to denounce religious
belief in so bold, and yet rather superficial, a manner. The
"almost passionately impatient enthusiasm for science"[4] in
Freud, noted by his daughter Anna, is another mark of

[1] *Standard Edition*, Vol. 9, p. 191.

[2] Ibid., Vol. 21, p. 6.

[3] Lionel Trilling: *Freud and the Crisis of Our Culture* (Boston: Beacon Press;
1955), p. 41.

[4] Freud: *Psychoanalysis and Faith*, p. 11.

this heritage. *The Future of an Illusion* can best be understood as a passionate restatement of the Enlightenment ideals of reason and progress.

Freud's case against religion is brief and devastating, reminiscent of the style of Voltaire and Diderot. Religions "have been able to effect absolute renunciation of pleasure in this life by means of the promise of compensation in a future existence. . . ."[5] Human helplessness is at the root of religious belief; man needs religion because of his failure to outgrow the dependency of childhood. "The whole thing is so patently infantile, so foreign to reality, that to anyone with a friendly attitude to humanity it is painful to think that the great majority of mortals will never be able to rise above this view of life."[6] Religion is an illusion, not in the sense that it is necessarily erroneous, but in the sense that it is the product of wish-fulfillment. The "fairy-tales of religion"[7] are a product of emotional insecurities; God the father is needed to allay the deepest fears of man.

Nor is religion a genuine buttress to civilization. "In every age immorality has found no less support in religion than morality has."[8] Moreover, religion is potentially a Trojan horse; because it is a wish-fulfillment, because it is based on irrational fears, its unreality may eventually undermine the civilization it currently supports.

Civilization runs a greater risk if we maintain our present attitude to religion than if we give it up. . . . Is there not a danger here that the hostility of . . . [the] masses to civilization will throw itself against the weak spot that they have found in their task-mistress?[9]

5 *Standard Edition*, Vol. 12, p. 223.
6 Ibid., Vol. 21, p. 74.
7 Ibid., p. 29.
8 Ibid., p. 38.
9 Ibid., pp. 35, 39.

This is Freud at his most rationalistic; it is also, in a sense, Freud the therapist and scientist. As a therapist Freud was not noteworthy, by today's standards, for being accepting or tolerant. And that was his greatness, for he expected people to change, to overcome themselves. Illusions are dangerous, no matter how comfortable; the only reliable standpoint is the truth.

"In the long run nothing can withstand reason and experience, and the contradiction which religion offers to both is all too palpable."[1] This is not Freud the resigned stoic; he is here rejecting both the ideals of classical antiquity and those of Christianity, in favor of the faith of the *philosophes*. Freud sweeps aside possible objections to his radical position on religion: the weight of the past, the consolations of belief. He even ignores his earlier and far more profound analysis of religion, which related it to fears of death and guilt. "Ignorance is ignorance. . . ."[2] and that is all there is to it. Superstition is intolerable. "There is no appeal to a court above that of reason."[3]

Here again, as in his earlier reflections on religion in *Totem and Taboo*, Freud is continuing his running intellectual battle with Jung. Before, we related Freud's phylogenetic speculations to Jung's system-building; now Freud confronts Jung's religious views, without mentioning his name openly. Jung had proceeded from an acceptance of the psychic reality of religious beliefs; religion was useful to man, it was valuable because of its instrumental possibilities. This kind of religious pragmatism has been offensive to devout believers as well as to Freud the scientist. In intellectual history, Santayana's criticism of William James's

[1] Ibid., p. 54.
[2] Ibid., p. 32.
[3] Ibid., p. 28.

"will to believe" is the classic rebuttal of Jung's kind of religiosity:

To be boosted by an illusion is not to live better than to live in harmony with the truth; it is not nearly so safe, not nearly so sweet, and not nearly so fruitful. . . . Believe, certainly . . . but believe rationally, holding what seems certain for certain, what seems probable for probable, what seems desirable for desirable, and what seems false for false.[4]

Freud's quarrel with Jung never really subsided. Jung symbolized to Freud the mystical undercurrent within psychoanalytic work; Jung was far less disciplined a scientist than Freud, and far less interested in developing a therapeutic technique that could be communicated to others. Since, as Freud himself wrote, "to many physicians . . . psychotherapy seems to be a product of modern mysticism. . . ,"[5] it was perfectly understandable for him to be preoccupied with scientific standards. But it must seem inconsistent of Freud to rely on scientific truth to attack religion, while being himself quite superstitious about telepathy. Freud's efforts to dispel mysteries, whether of psychoanalysis or of religion, his insistence on the cold rational light of truth, were these not efforts to master his own tendencies toward the occult?

Whatever his motivation, Freud's tract on religion rings with the sharp clarity of a *philosophe*. It would be far better, Freud thought, to admit the human origin of cultural restrictions, than to sanctify with supernatural origin rules which are after all constructed for man's benefit. Why stunt men's intelligence with religious fantasies? Why not demand that they grow up, that they accept their limita-

---

[4] George Santayana: *Character and Opinion in the U. S.* (New York: Anchor Books; 1956), pp. 53–4.

[5] *Standard Edition*, Vol. 7, pp. 257–8.

tions, that they relinquish childish faith in an omnipotent being? It is admittedly true that men now rely on this crutch, "but have you asked yourself whether they *must* be like this, whether their innermost nature necessitates it? . . . Think of the depressing contrast between the radiant intelligence of a healthy child and the feeble intellectual powers of the average adult."[6] Freud goes on to a paean of optimism, a lyrical testimony to his faith in man's reason. "By withdrawing their expectations from the other world and concentrating all their liberated energies into their life on earth, they will probably succeed in achieving a state of things in which life will become tolerable for everyone and civilization no longer oppressive to anyone."[7] Condorcet could not have asked for more.

Marx, of course, stigmatized religion as the opium of the people. And before him, Feuerbach had come very close to Freud's psychoanalytic position. Not only did he hold that the "fundamental dogmas of Christianity are realized wishes of the heart,"[8] but he specifically related these wishes to dream life: "religion [is] the dream of waking-consciousness; dreaming is the key to the mysteries of religion."[9] An entire rationalist tradition has held that when men "project or objectify human characteristics as a non-existent God . . . [they] frequently deny themselves real satisfactions and indulge instead in imaginary ones."[1]

The universal state of childhood helplessness leads not only to the origins of a social myth like religion, but also to an increased understanding of the functions of mythology.

[6] Ibid., Vol. 21, p. 47.

[7] Ibid., p. 50.

[8] Quoted in H. B. Acton: *Illusion of the Epoch* (London: Cohen & West; 1955), p. 117.

[9] Quoted in ibid., p. 118.

[1] Ibid., pp. 117–18.

Social myths can be analyzed in terms of the childish needs they satisfy. The activities of gods and legendary heroes are extensions of some of our most basic hopes and fears. Granting their unifying function and the needs they fulfill, we can also stand aside and look at them more critically, to see the extent to which they are unnecessarily stultifying.

Freud's rationalism can be seen in his view of psychoanalytic treatment. He tended, for example, to view transference phenomena as mistakes, misperceptions which could be corrected if the patient was sufficiently educatable. "Nothing in life is so expensive as illness—and stupidity."[2] Freud was more rationalistic in his therapeutic approach than psychoanalysts tend to be today. He relied very much on verbalized insight as a therapeutic agent, and objected to supportive psychotherapy for not expecting enough of the patient's capacity to tolerate the truth. Freud proposed rational distance from one's emotions.

In Freud's social philosophy, reason was itself a unifying force. Men can grow up; by thinking through their conflicts, by facing reality, they can enrich their existence. A world without religion is a "treasure to be dug up capable of enriching civilization. . . ."[3] Freud gave a new twist to the rationalist tradition by locating the state of nature in childhood. The "treasure" to be unearthed is the child's capacity for seeing the fullness of reality without the protective devices he resorts to as he frees himself from familial help. "There is no period at which the capacity for receiving and reproducing impressions is greater than precisely during the years of childhood."[4] In his appreciation of the

2 *Standard Edition,* Vol. 12, p. 133.
3 Ibid., Vol. 21, p. 48.
4 Ibid., Vol. 7, p. 175.

sensitivity and empathy of the small child, Freud overcame the narrowness of his own rationalistic tendencies.

The young child can afford this intelligence, and at the same time needs it more. He can afford it in the sense that parental figures are available to help if the insecurities of independence become too intense; adults are available as allies when experience becomes too overwhelming. At the same time the child needs to see life more directly than at later periods; just because his defenses are not yet internalized, just because the parental figures have not yet been introjected, he cannot afford to be intellectually lazy. What is unique about childhood is that intelligence is in the direct service of emotional needs.

The intelligence that the world loses through adult neurosis is exactly what it loses through religious superstition. Freud's dream was to recapture the naïveté and zest of childhood. As Keniston has put it, "The adult abandons a world of directness, immediacy, diversity, wholeness, integral fantasy and spontaneity. He gains abstraction, distance, specialization, dissociated fantasy and conformity."[5] Freud's was a protest against inauthenticity, an appeal to man's original inner unity. By abandoning neurotic defenses against anxiety, by cleansing the social order of religion, the most creative impulses of childhood could be liberated.

In the enthusiasm of his radicalism, Freud betrayed a certain superficiality in terms of human needs that is akin to eighteenth-century utopianism. If men have always projected their feelings onto the gods, why is that so illegitimate? All of us project, just as Freud did with his early

[5] Kenneth Keniston: "Alienation and the Decline of Utopia," *American Scholar*, Vol 29 (Spring 1960), p. 172.

patients; it can be a means of mastering our anxieties, and of finding external support for our aspirations. Religion is human; Freud was so intolerant of the infantile and the regressive that he had difficulty understanding their functions. His concentration on the practices, rites, and observances of religion, to the neglect of such ecstasies as the "oceanic feeling," reflects his own inability to understand religious feelings.

There is about *The Future of an Illusion* a glossiness of surface, an impassioned dispassion, which for all its importance for tracing Freud's intellectual roots, is quite alien to the rest of his social thought. In *Totem and Taboo*, when Freud was a decade and a half younger and without the cancer he later acquired, we find less of this rejection of the human. In this earlier book he displayed a far deeper understanding of the origins of religion. "The chief starting point of this theorizing must have been the problem of death."[6] Whereas in *The Future of an Illusion* Freud described the boundless potentialities of society, in *Totem and Taboo* he emphasized society's guilty intensity.

Society was now based on the complicity in the common crime; religion was based on the sense of guilt and the remorse attaching to it; while morality was based partly on the exigencies of this society and partly on the penance demanded by the sense of guilt.[7]

The difference between the profound grasp of the nature of religious feeling in *Totem and Taboo* and the moral utopianism of *The Future of an Illusion* illustrates the essential duality of Freud's whole outlook, his union of conservatism and radicalism. Mannheim has contrasted the way

[6] *Standard Edition*, Vol. 13, p. 76.
[7] Ibid., p. 146.

in which "bourgeois liberalism was much too preoccupied with norms to concern itself with the actual situation as it really existed," with conservatism's emphasis on "the notion of the determinateness of our outlook and our behavior."[8] Both the realism of conservatism and the idealism of the Enlightenment can be identified in Freud's work.

Freud could side-step, temporarily, the relation of death to religion because for himself personally an afterlife was not necessary. He was of course throughout his life preoccupied to an exceptional degree with thoughts about death. His sagelike endurance of his cancer for the last sixteen years of his life only enhances for posterity his lifelong concern with how to face death. His solution for himself was a stoic one. "To tolerate life remains, after all, the first duty of all living beings. . . . If you want to endure life, prepare yourself for death."[9] The biographical element in Freud's thoughts on religion, his ability to dodge an issue because of personal strengths and weaknesses, reminds us again of the different status of clinical and applied psychoanalytic material within his work: "in itself psychoanalysis is neither religious nor irreligious, but an impartial tool. . . ."[1]

## 5  A Hero in History

The last book Freud completed before he died, *Moses and Monotheism* (1934–8), was as eccentric and stimulating as any product of his imagination.

8 Karl Mannheim: *Ideology and Utopia* (New York: Harvest Books; n.d.), pp. 221–2, 229.

9 *Standard Edition*, Vol. 14, pp. 299–300.

1 Freud: *Psychoanalysis and Faith*, p. 17.

*Moses and Monotheism* is a conspicuous exception to the usual run of Freud's works. One of the most . . . distinctive features of Freud's books is their fascinating architectonic structure. A whole book is unfolded before the reader as a single great syllogism; not a sentence superfluous, not a word may be omitted without damaging the whole. Such is not the case here. . . .[1]

Freud's followers have in general neglected this book, partly no doubt because the diaspora of psychoanalysts from Vienna was already underway when it was appearing, and hence Freud's pupils found it harder to consider as a group. It would be too simple to lay the blame for the book's uncertainties either on Freud's advanced old age or on the difficult external circumstances under which it was composed. While it is true that the argument is curiously repetitious, in other works Freud was throughout his extreme old age capable of the greatest conciseness and logical organization. The confused sequence in this work gives us formal grounds for suspecting that Freud was not at one with his thesis. The book is generally acknowledged to be a very gross distortion of the Biblical text.[2] Yet if it was historically a bad book, why did Freud write it? Even as rationalistic a philosopher as Bertrand Russell can see that "in the study of nominally abstract thinkers, it is their mistakes that give a key to their personality."[3]

It is well known that the figure of Moses had a special fascination for Freud. In 1914 he had anonymously pub-

---

[1] M. Wulff: "An Appreciation of Freud's *Moses and Monotheism*," in *Max Eitingon: In Memoriam*, ed. M. Wulff (Jerusalem: Israel Psychoanalytic Society; 1950), p. 141.

[2] Bakan: *Sigmund Freud and the Jewish Mystical Tradition*, p. 164. Cf. also Salo W. Baron: "Book Review of *Moses and Monotheism*," in *Psychoanalysis and History*, ed. Bruce Mazlish (Englewood Cliffs, N. J.: Prentice-Hall; 1963), pp. 50–5.

[3] Bertrand Russell: *Sceptical Essays* (London: Allen and Unwin; 1956), pp. 33–4.

lished an essay, written in the same month as his polemic against Adler and Jung, on a statue of Moses by Michelangelo. Freud obviously identified with Moses because of "the conflict which is bound to arise between such a reforming genius and the rest of mankind."[4] Freud saw the statue as a representation of the Moses who had triumphed over his anger at the Jews' worship of the golden calf. In this light he called the artist's creation "a concrete expression of the highest mental achievement that is possible in a man, that of struggling successfully against an inward passion for the sake of a cause to which he has devoted himself."[5]

Whatever this interpretation may say about the statue, it reveals a good deal about Freud's own state of mind at the time when he wrote this essay. He was still suffering bitterly from the loss of some of his followers, especially Jung. If Freud was not fully expressing his anger and disappointment, we can be sure that the "cause" for which he restrained himself was the psychoanalytic movement itself.

At the same time this essay hints that Freud was at least partly aware of the way in which his personality threatened to interfere with and undermine his own movement. The characterization of Michelangelo and Pope Julius II, which Freud draws in order to establish Michelangelo's motivation for selecting the figure of Moses for Julius' tomb, might well explain why Freud himself chose this statue to interpret at that period in his life:

Julius II was akin to Michelangelo in . . . that he attempted to realize great and mighty ends, and especially designs on a grand scale. . . . He desired to bring about single-handed what was not to happen for several centuries, and then only through the con-

[4] *Standard Edition*, Vol. 13, p. 221.
[5] Ibid., p. 233.

junction of many alien forces; and he worked alone, with im-
patience, in the short span of sovereignty allowed him, and used
violent means. He could appreciate Michelangelo as a man of his
own kind, but he often made him smart under his sudden anger
and his utter lack of consideration for others. The artist felt the
same violent force of will in himself, and, as the more introspec-
tive thinker, may have had a premonition of the failure to which
they were both doomed. And so he carved his Moses on the
Pope's tomb, not without a reproach against the dead pontiff,
as a warning to himself, thus, in self-criticism, rising superior to
his own nature.[6]

Freud saw himself as struggling with a heroic task in history, the triumph of psychoanalysis, and at some level he
must have realized by now that his aggressive means might
endanger his own ultimate aim.

Two decades later Freud returned to Moses with his book
on the rise of monotheism. As a matter of course Freud
utilized the technique of psychoanalysis, which is "ac-
customed to divine secret and concealed things from de-
spised or unnoticed features, from the rubbish-heap . . . of
our observations."[7] Freud began his thesis with a crucial
initial detail—Moses' name was an Egyptian one. By rein-
terpreting various biblical legends, Freud found support for
the idea that the actual historical facts were reversals of
what we have come to believe. Instead of God choosing the
Jewish people to worship Him and obey His command-
ments, Moses—an Egyptian aristocrat—chose the Jewish
people in order to perpetuate an earlier Egyptian monotheism. As Freud developed this historical reconstruction,
at various points in his argument he acknowledged the
tenuousness of the "web" he was spinning. As he put it, he

[6] Ibid., pp. 233–4.
[7] Ibid., p. 222.

felt "like a dancer balancing on the tip of one toe."[8] Despite the obvious objection to his enterprise—the almost nonexistent basis in historical fact—Freud drove his thesis on in a daredevil way. It must have been like the pleasure of skating on thin ice.

*Moses and Monotheism* reinstated the bogeyman of the seduction theory and *Totem and Taboo*. The Egyptian Moses, according to Freud's reconstruction, proved to be too hard a taskmaster. He was a great leader, and his teaching was culturally superior to all other available religions; none had so completely faced the fact of death. This religion did without a whole range of magic and ritual. "The deity disdained sacrifice and ceremonial and asked only for faith and a life in truth and justice. . . ."[9]

But Moses' religion was too demanding, and his personality too irascible. The Jews rose up, slew him. They acquired a second leader, also called Moses, and a cruder religion; it was only the first Moses' retinue, the Levites, who maintained the original monotheistic religion. The Moses of legend is a fusion, as in a dream, of two figures, the earlier Egyptian and a later Moses. The earlier religion, kept alive by the first Moses' followers and prophets, slowly overcame the later crude doctrines. Moved by collective guilt over the parricide, the Jews returned to the earlier religious system of the Egyptian. As in the "deferred obedience" of the sons of the primal horde, the death of the leader ensured the success of his teachings.

Freud's original title for *Moses and Monotheism* was *The Man Moses, A Historical Novel*; in conversation he used to call the book "my Moses-novel."[1] It may well seem

---

[8] Ibid., Vol. 23, p. 58.
[9] Ibid., p. 51.
[1] Wulff: "An Appreciation of Freud's *Moses and Montheism*," p. 142.

fantastic that a man who considered himself a scientist
could venture so rashly into historical reconstructions, in
*Totem and Taboo* as well as here. As Freud aged and
gradually made his leave-taking with human beings, he
turned his novelistic talents away from case histories and
directed them onto world history. But outside clinical psychoanalysis, without the test of science, Freud's thought
could depart radically from reality.

To the extent, though, that Freud's social speculations
lack objectivity, they can be all the more revealing about
his subjective complexes. For this was a book close to his
heart.[2] As we have noted already, Freud identified with
Moses. He interpreted the reception of the first Moses' religion in terms of the opposition to psychoanalysis that he
himself had experienced: "the new truth awoke emotional
resistances. . . ."[3] Freud too felt that it was his mission to
lead people out of slavery and oppression. According to
legend Moses had been slow of speech: as operation suc-
ceeded operation on Freud's cancerous jaw, he too had difficulties in speaking. By the end of his life Freud was a
legendary figure in his own lifetime, as Moses was a legend
in history.

Yet much as Freud admired Moses, his psychoanalytic
work was in a sense directed at undermining him. Freud's
message was in large measure one of liberation of instinctual life, of rebellion against the Mosaic law.[4] This negative
pole of Freud's feelings toward Moses as the leader of the
Jews was expressed by his whole interpretation of Moses as
an Egyptian, which robbed the Jewish people of their crea-

---

[2] Robert Waelder: "Historical Fiction," *Journal of the American Psychoanalytic
Association*, Vol. 11, No. 3 (July 1963), p. 635.

[3] *Standard Edition*, Vol. 23, p. 67.

[4] Bakan: *Siegmund Freud and the Jewish Mystical Tradition*, p. 164.

tive leader. The thesis that Moses was an Egyptian was in fact seen by many as anti-Semitic bias on Freud's part. The figure of Moses could satisfy both the positive and negative poles of Freud's Oedipus complex; on the one hand Moses could be admired as a great ethical teacher, while on the other hand he could be—through textual ingenuity—deprived of his position as a Jewish hero; "the distortion of a text," Freud wrote, "resembles a murder. . . ."[5]

I believe that a full-scale effort to understand this book would greatly enhance our understanding of Freud's psychoanalysis. The comments here will be limited by the over-all objective of understanding Freud's social thought; since *Moses and Monotheism* is one of his important contributions to social theory, even a partial unraveling of its mysteries should be instructive. The book is illuminating largely because of the circumstances under which it was written, the last years of Freud's life. As his health deteriorated, his inner conflicts and his struggles to master them became more exposed. In his life, of course, Freud attained great final serenity; he was really heroic in enduring physical suffering. Yet areas of his personality were being restricted by physical pain and consciousness of approaching death. Alongside the extraordinary display of courage and self-discipline in his life, one finds a partial loss of mastery in his work. As he noted a few years before he died, "threads which in the course of my development had become intertangled have now begun to separate. . . ."[6] Tragically, the greatness of his work had lain in the amalgamation of his talents.

The novelistic character of Freud's Moses book is especially illuminating on the problem of his relation to Juda-

[5] *Standard Edition*, Vol. 23, p. 43.
[6] Ibid., Vol. 20, p. 71.

ism. What was Freud doing in making Moses a Gentile? There is of course a long history of myths of leaders who are outsiders; yet there were more personal forces at work in the development of Freud's Moses thesis. After his seventieth birthday in 1926, Freud wrote in a letter that "the Jews altogether . . . have celebrated me like a national hero, although my service to the Jewish cause is confined to the single point that I have never denied my Jewishness."[7] Freud was rather understating the extent of his acknowledged Jewishness by omitting to mention, for example, his active membership in Jewish organizations. Yet it is in some sense true that it took the arrival of the Nazis to turn Freud into a Jew.

My language is German. My culture, my attainments are German. I considered myself German intellectually, until I noticed the growth of anti-Semitic prejudice in Germany and German Austria. Since that time, I consider myself no longer a German. I prefer to call myself a Jew.[8]

The problem was the same for a whole generation of Central European Jews; having lost their religious faith, they lost their protective shield against anti-Semitism. They could not ignore it as easily as their ancestors might have; it was so much pointless suffering, and they had not the consolation of the faith of their fathers.

No wonder then if Freud resented being deprived of his cultural identity, and being forced, once it had become a disadvantage, to shout his Jewishness. Would it not be a fitting revenge, if his identity as a Jew was not quite comfortable to him, to take away the Jewish identity of the

[7] Freud: *Letters*, p. 369.
[8] George S. Viereck: *Glimpses of the Great* (London: Duckworth; 1930), p. 34.

greatest of the Jews? By making Moses an Egyptian, was not Freud saying that he could retain Moses as a model only if Moses was not Jewish? For the truth of the matter was that Freud's Jewishness, which had been used against his career and his science, was not unstained by shame and guilt in his own eyes. Making Moses an Egyptian was one way of accomplishing a fantasied conversion.

The same mechanism appears in a short article on anti-Semitism which appeared in 1938. As evidence of Freud's failing literary powers, he was unable to use the form of a dialogue or a dialectic for his narrative, as he had once done so freely. Instead he resorted to the rather clumsy device of commenting on a long quotation from a Gentile on anti-Semitism. Yet Freud cannot find the source of this passage. Both Ernest Jones and Anna Freud concluded that it was in fact a self-quotation on Freud's part.[9] The implication, however, is that Freud was here, as in the Moses book, identifying with a Gentile.

The sources for Freud's ambivalence about his Jewishness are no doubt multiple; it would be only in Freud's tradition if we glanced mainly at his relation to his father. Freud describes his father as a kindly man; but as a child Freud was deeply disappointed by his father's unheroic passivity in the face of an anti-Semitic insult.[1] There was of course nothing of this passivity in Freud himself when he grew up; his son Martin records an incident in which Freud bravely charged into a hostile crowd which had been shouting anti-Semitic abuse, an uncanny reversal of Freud's own father's behavior.[2] But there was a willed quality to

---

[9] Letter from Anna Freud to Ernest Jones, August 25, 1956 (Jones Archives).

[1] *Standard Edition*, Vol. 4, p. 197.

[2] Martin Freud: *Glory Reflected* (London: Angus & Robertson; 1957), pp. 70–1.

Freud's identity as a Jew, a strained denial of the shame his society expected from him.

Jewish self-hatred is not confined to Freud alone; yet Freud's alienation from his father as a Jew may help explain why he was able to discover the Oedipus complex, as well as why a generation of American Jewish intellectuals, at a similar cultural distance from their fathers, have been so attracted by his psychological system. There was in Freud a yearning toward self-overcoming; his lifelong desire to get to Rome can be interpreted symbolically, as the wish to transcend the religion of obedience to the father by the religion of love.[3] Of course Freud's own thoughts on religion reveal a heavy patriarchal bias; and he offers no analysis of the conception of the Madonna. Freud was intolerant of human feelings only when he was himself threatened in some way.

Freud felt guilt toward his father, and not only over the religious question; this would be a psychological truism, were it not relevant to Freud's work, and specifically to his Moses book. Like other creative men, Freud must have been bewildered about his intellectual origins; compared to the talents of his own family, Freud seemed to have sprung from nowhere. The child may plead pathetically to be told where he came from; but to a genius this torment is reinforced by the gulf between his own capacities and any identifiable familial background. It should come as no surprise that Freud should indulge in fantasies of self-creation, since he had soared so far beyond his natural family.

A man who has to obliterate his parents does so at a cost, and can never be quite at ease about it. Freud came back again and again to the fantasy of being raised fatherless. In his book on Leonardo, he even recounts the Egyptian

[3] I owe this suggestion to Dr. Charles Rycroft.

legend of vultures being impregnated by the wind; Leonardo was a vulture-child in being raised apart from his
natural father. And so was Oedipus, and the Moses of
legend as well. When necessary Freud's fantasies ensure
that the true father always turns out to be a man of high
rank; as with Oedipus it was a king, so with Moses Freud
made it an aristocrat. He even speculated that Shakespeare
was not the man of humble origins at all, but instead the
Earl of Oxford. These were the ego models that Freud
needed to sustain him in his work. "A genius finds his family from among heroes. . . ."[4], and is thereby reassured of his
own immortality. These fantasies represent a special version
of the oedipal complex, the son seeking "to supplant his real
father by an ideal father created in his phantasy . . . the
wish to have begotten oneself . . . to be one's own father."[5]

If Freud unconsciously thought of himself as his own
father, then one can see the source of much of his trouble
with his pupils; for if one is both one's own ego and also
one's own father, then to be challenged by opposition means
that the very gods from within one's soul are being affronted. One can tolerate criticism of oneself that becomes
intolerable when directed toward one's father image. Furthermore, if one has replaced one's father by oneself, if one
has spread one's own ego over the idols from one's infantile
past, then one is left with a good deal to atone for. Freud
had to create a whole new family, the psychoanalytic movement, to make up for the family he denied.

Freud could not finally become his own father until he
could have his own sons. Natural born sons would not do;

[4] Eva Rosenfeld: "Dream and Vision," *International Journal of Psychoanalysis*, Vol. 37, Part I (1956), p. 100.
[5] Karl Abraham: "Amenhotep IV," in *Clinical Papers and Essays on Psycho-analysis* (London: Hogarth Press; 1955), p. 288.

they had to have the qualities of immortality associated with genius. So Freud made symbolic sons of his most promising pupils. But of course Freud's quarrels with his pupils constituted the tragedy of his public life. He might have been thinking of himself when he wrote of "the benefactor who is abandoned in anger after a time by each of his *protégés*, however much they may otherwise differ from one another, and who thus seems doomed to taste all the bitterness of ingratitude. . . ."[6]

The succession theme, the torment about the lack of an heir, and the anxiety about the future of his creation, psychoanalysis, permeate Freud's treatment of the Moses theme. Freud's essay on the Moses of Michelangelo (1913) was written at a turning point in his career, the stage at which he had to become centrally concerned with caring for the future of psychoanalysis. Freud later referred to the year 1912 as "the very climax of my psychoanalytic work. . . ."[7] Once the break with Jung was final, Freud had to labor hard to make a success of the psychoanalytic movement. Our successes are founded on our failures; only through the creation of a psychoanalytic movement could Freud fulfill his aspirations and heal his inner wounds.

How can one be so sure of the image of Jung behind the man Moses? When they were on good terms, Freud referred to Jung as his "son and heir." As Jones put it, "Jung was to be the Joshua destined to explore the promised land of psychiatry which Freud, like Moses, was only permitted to view from afar."[8] In a letter to Ferenczi shortly after the split with Jung, Freud returned to the problem of finding a successor, if not in one man then in the whole movement

[6] *Standard Edition*, Vol. 18, p. 22.
[7] Ibid., Vol. 20, p. 72.
[8] Jones: *Sigmund Freud*, Vol. 2, p. 33.

of psychoanalysis. "Let us carry on our work with calm self-confidence. That assurance that the children will be provided for, which for a Jewish father is a matter of life and death, I expected to get from Jung; I am glad now that you and our friends will give me this."[9]

One incident between Jung and Freud should further illustrate the background to Freud's book on Moses. The occasion was a confrontation between them in 1913 at Munich, near the end of their relationship. Jung gave the account of what happened to a *Time* reporter many years later:

... the name of Amenhotep IV had arisen in the conversation as the founder of a religion. Freud remarked that he was the one who had scratched out his father's name on the monuments. "Yes, he did," replied Jung, "but you cannot dismiss him with that. He was the first monotheist among the Egyptians. He was a great genius, very human, very individual. That is his main merit. That he scratched out his father's name is not the main thing at all." At that point, added Jung, Freud fainted.[1]

In this meeting the problem of death wishes toward the father appears clearly as one fraught with great anxiety for Freud. On the basis of our earlier investigations we would assume this to result on the one hand from his own fantasies of having annihilated his real father, and on the other hand from his anxieties about what Jung, his spiritual son, might correspondingly wish to do to Freud himself. His fainting not only makes plain the severe anxiety Freud associated with the question of even just spiritual patricide; but it can also be regarded as a type of death—a fantasied pre-enactment of his succumbing to Jung's presumed mur-

[9] Freud: *Letters*, p. 308.

[1] Letter from Lester Bernstein to Ernest Jones, November 26, 1954 (Jones Archives). Cf. also Jung: *Memories, Dreams, Reflections*, p. 153.

derous wishes. Furthermore, Amenhotep IV's founding of
a monotheistic religion, and Moses' transmission of this to
the Jews, was sufficiently like Freud's position as discoverer
of psychoanalysis vis-à-vis his leading disciple Jung, to form
an associative link between twentieth-century psychiatry
and ancient Egyptology. For Freud Egypt stood for the ex-
otic and distant past which his psychoanalysis was designed
to decipher.

Freud had initially picked Jung as his successor for two
reasons, aside from Jung's brilliance. First of all he had a
position in the world of hospital psychiatry, in which Freud
lacked training, and could promise new territory for the application and development of Freud's theories. In other
words he offered Freud standing in a wider scientific community. Secondly, Jung was a Gentile, and could lead psychoanalysis in a world which Freud considered at bottom
anti-Semitic. The loss of Jung was bitter since Freud had
such opportunistic motives in picking him in the first place.
There were hints of anti-Semitism in Jung even before the
split with Freud; by the thirties Jung was actually collaborating with the Nazis. (He justified his actions as designed to protect psychotherapy in Germany, which may
actually have been the case; but it was still collaboration.)

By making Moses an Egyptian, Freud in a sense recap-
tured a Gentile, Jung, as leader of his movement, and he
could die with the hope that his movement would be preserved. This interpretation of Freud's Moses theme so much
in terms of his ambivalence over his religion and his difficulties with his father and his pupils does not preclude
other compatible lines of approach. Freud could not have
been unaware that Schiller wrote an essay on "The Mission of Moses," and one could use that link to German
culture to explore a very different side of Freud's mind. It

is enough for us to see in Freud's treatment of Moses the personal character of his involvement. As Freud wrote about his Moses manuscript in 1935 to Lou Andreas-Salomé: "I remain silent. It is enough that I myself can believe in the solution of the problem. It has pursued me through my whole life."[2]

While the intensity of Freud's personal emotional involvement with the Moses image helps to account for the rambling character of *Moses and Monotheism* and his inability fully to come to terms with his thesis, it would be unfortunate to overlook the quality of many of the ideas themselves. Freud's social thought is of course not only of interest to the student of Freud's psychology, but is always relevant to political theory as well. In a sense this book has suffered a fate similar to that of *Totem and Taboo*; Freud's insistence on a particular historical reconstruction has blinded observers to the merits of other aspects of the argument.

Whatever the gross failures of Freud's tale of Moses, and whatever the origins of Freud's argument in his emotional life, his particular thesis illustrates an aspect of clinical psychoanalysis which has importance for the applications of Freud to the study of history. In everyday psychoanalytic practice, Freud engaged in the reconstruction of past events. On the basis of dreams, fantasies, associations, slips, as well as conscious memories, Freud formed hypotheses about the very early life of each of his patients. His theory of the stages of infantile sexual life, now widely accepted, was not based on the direct observation of children, but was reconstructed from the analyses of adult patients.

In some instances there were spectacular confirmations of bold reconstructions. For example, in Marie Bonaparte's

[2] Jones: *Sigmund Freud*, Vol. 3, p. 194.

analysis, on the basis of her analytic material and in particular her attitude to money, Freud concluded that very early in her childhood she had witnessed intercourse between two family servants, accompanied by an exchange of money. When she returned home, she confronted her old servant with the story, and confirmed that he used to have sexual relations with her nurse in the child's presence when she was less than a year old.[3] This is a classic example of the verification of a particular psychoanalytic hypothesis, retrodiction rather than prediction. However far Freud's special skill in such retrodictions went beyond that of other analysts, reconstructing the past is an everyday psychoanalytic practice.

The methodology of *Moses and Monotheism* was simply an extension onto the world-historical plane of a common psychoanalytic procedure. This principle behind the study of Moses may well be its main contribution to political thought, entirely apart from the issue of its mistaken application to Jewish history. Kurt Eissler has pointed out that it is possible

to read a people's history as if it were the history of an individual, with the goal in view of uncovering what his particular history conceals—that is, what it contains as its "repressed" content . . . the psychoanalysis of a people, by unearthing the unconscious factors at work in their history, may bring mastery to them, and lead to the sort of action that guarantees preservation. . . .[4]

---

[3] Marie Bonaparte: "Notes on the Analytic Discovery of a Primal Scene," *Psychoanalytic Study of the Child*, Vol. 1, pp. 119–25. For other examples, cf. "Kardiner Reminisces," *Bulletin of the Association of Psychoanalytic Medicine*, Vol. 2, No. 4 (May 1963), pp. 61–4; and Choisy: *Sigmund Freud*, pp. 6–7.

[4] Kurt Eissler: "Freud and the Psychoanalysis of History," *Journal of the American Psychoanalytic Association*, Vol. 11, No. 4 (October 1963), pp. 689, 682.

The possibilities of this application of psychoanalysis to history can be seen in any major attempt to understand a nation's history; by understanding the past, by bringing to consciousness various forces whose importance has been neglected, history can be overcome, the past can be mastered, repetition avoided.

In this sense Louis Hartz's *Liberal Tradition in America*,[5] for example, is in the tradition of the methodology of *Moses and Monotheism*. As Marvin Meyers has pointed out, "It is basically . . . a study of the unconscious mind of America, conditioned by a peculiar historical and social experience. . . . The substance of American political thought . . . lies in the unarticulated premises of the society and culture rather than in the logic of books."[6] Hartz links the pervasive triumph of democracy in America to a psychic reality, liberalism; "fundamentally we are dealing with a psychic matter, the transforming impact of an idea. . . ."[7] By understanding the nature of America's liberal consensus, Hartz hopes to make it possible to articulate a political philosophy relevant for our time. Through understanding the roots of the American inhibition in political theorizing, he believes we may be able to overcome the limitations of the past and engage in constructive theorizing.

Not only is Hartz's basic aim analogous to Freud's, but much of Hartz's thesis can be reconstrued as an essentially psychoanalytic interpretation. His basic point is that politi-

[5] Louis Hartz: *The Liberal Tradition in America* (New York: Harcourt, Brace; 1955).

[6] Marvin Meyers: "Louis Hartz, *The Liberal Tradition in America*," *Comparative Studies in Society and History*, Vol. 5, No. 3 (April 1963), p. 264.

[7] Louis Hartz: "The Rise of the Democratic Idea," in *Paths of American Thought*, ed. Arthur M. Schlesinger, Jr., and Morton White (Boston: Houghton Mifflin; 1963), p. 44.

cal thought arises out of conflict. The comparative absence
of social conflict in this country when viewed against the
European experience is responsible for the relative thinness
of American political thought. The great social upheaval
that faced the ante-bellum South was alone responsible for
a flowering of political theorizing. The assumption, and it
seems to me that it is at bottom a psychoanalytic one, is that
men think, politically as elsewhere, only when they are
forced to do so. America has been permitted a degree of
intellectual lassitude impossible under more stressful conditions.

Furthermore, Hartz's account of the history of what he
calls the cosmopolitan approach to American history is a
further confirmation of the uses of the psychoanalytic interpretation of history. The basic American trauma was
the separation from European life: "The decisive moment
in American history is the time of the great migration of
the seventeenth century. . . ."[8] This is the key, according
to Hartz, to the American past: "A bourgeois trip that was
taken in the seventeenth century which everyone has forgotten."[9] The memory traces of the connection to Europe,
just as in a classic case of hysteria, were never entirely
blotted out; the relation of American history to that of
Europe was fitfully and partially remembered. "The early
nationalists were far more cosmopolitan than the Progres-
sives, for when these patriots celebrated the freedom and
equality of the American experience they had in mind a Europe where those virtues did not exist."[1] After a long latency
period, in our own time events have forced on us an aware-

---

[8] Hartz: "The Rise of the Democratic Idea," p. 43.

[9] Ibid., p. 50.

[1] Hartz: "Comment," *Comparative Studies in Society and History*, Vol. 5, No.
3 (April 1953), p. 279.

ness of the cosmopolitan point of view. Now the original trauma (America's relation to Europe) has been remembered, and the repressed could complete its return.

The strengths of *Moses and Monotheism* are not exhausted by the possibilities for large-scale historical interpretations. We find here a re-emphasis of the themes of *Totem and Taboo*, along with a deepening conception of religious experience, instead of merely the radicalism of *The Future of an Illusion*. God as a father figure is emphasized, not for the sake of debunking religious belief, but to increase our understanding of the concept of God. Monotheism represented a cultural advance, for example, since "now that God was a single person, man's relation to him could recover the intimacy and intensity of the child's relation to the father."[2] In relating God to the childhood past, Freud was prepared to see more fully religion's power, instead of simply brushing it aside as a neurosis. Moreover, he could now realize the importance of religious institutions as defenders of protest: "it is precisely the institution of the Catholic Church which puts up a powerful defence against the spread of this [Nazi] danger to civilization. . . ."[3] He retained, however, his essentially iconoclastic viewpoint; now that he had more understanding for religion and was not content with dismissing it as ignorance or superstition, he was emboldened to jettison his careful distinction in *The Future of an Illusion* between religion as illusion rather than delusion:

We have long understood that a portion of forgotten truth lies hidden in delusional ideas. . . . We must grant an ingredient such as this of what may be called *historical* truth to the dogmas of religion . . . which, it is true, bear the character of psychotic

[2] Quoted in Jones: *Sigmund Freud*, Vol. III, p. 352.
[3] *Standard Edition*, Vol. 23, p. 55.

symptoms but which, as group phenomena, escape the curse of isolation.[4]

Freud advanced in his feeling for religion by elaborating its relation to the problem of death, rather than continuing to view it simply as a response to helplessness. Why was a son, Christ, required to be sacrificed? To atone for the murder, in fact or fantasy, of the father: "through the idea of the redeemer, he [St. Paul] exorcized humanity's sense of guilt. . . ."[5] The origin of religious ethics lay in "the sense of guilt felt on account of a suppressed hostility to God."[6] Surely this interpretation is more sensitive, if only in its emphasis on guilt feelings, than the cry of *The Future of an Illusion* that ignorance is ignorance.

Freud also had a number of ideas here of more strictly political significance. In a sense, *Moses and Monotheism* is a study in political leadership. What intrigues Freud about Moses is his status as a great man. He is impressed by "how impossible it is to dispute the personal influence upon world-history of individual great men, what sacrilege one commits against the splendid diversity of human life if one recognizes only those motives which arise from material needs. . . ."[7] What Freud considered remarkable about Moses was his ability to impose his teachings on the Jewish people. Just as in psychoanalytic therapy the analyst becomes an authority figure, on whom the patient can project his superego functions, so for the people at large their political leaders are allotted the role of superego.

This is scarcely as farfetched as it might sound. The behavior of ruling elites has been correlated with the life of

4 Ibid., p. 85.
5 Ibid., p. 88.
6 Ibid., p. 134.
7 Ibid., p. 52.

the populace at large before. For example, de Grazia relates the international marriages of upper-class Americans to the increased industrial strife in late-nineteenth-century America.[8] And Franz Alexander has connected the decline of the upper classes to the coming of World War I. "The external authorities, the living representatives of our internal standards, were discredited, and the unconscious forces swept through the barriers of the conventional code."[9] Leaders have the responsibility to reinforce superego controls, if only by the example of their character.

No matter what one may think of the reality behind Freud's picture of Moses, or of his effect on his people, Freud's belief in the possibilities of leadership and his emphasis on the function of leaders as a collective superego are of enduring interest. Freud's growing understanding of social forces is in general impressive. For example, in accounting for the rise of monotheism in Egypt, he correlates it with the political conditions of the time; "monotheism grew up as a by-product of imperialism: God was a reflection of the Pharaoh who was the absolute ruler of a great world-empire."[1]

In the course of developing his theory of the rise of Jewish monotheism, Freud gives his most sustained treatment of the place of tradition in maintaining the continuity of culture. It was the strength of the philosophy of the early Moses that sustained the Jews throughout their trials. This Jewish religion formed the character of the Jewish people, "through its rejection of magic and mysticism, its invitation to advances in intellectuality and its encouragement of

---

[8] Sebastian de Grazia: *The Political Community* (Chicago: The University of Chicago Press; 1963), pp. 115 ff.

[9] Alexander: *The Western Mind in Transition*, p. 188.

[1] *Standard Edition*, Vol. 23, p. 65.

sublimations. . . ."[2] Freud traced the pride and self-confidence of Jews to their highly civilized religious tradition.

The psychic mechanisms of conscience by which Freud thought that tradition was maintained form a fundamental part of psychoanalytic thinking. That political systems endure over time, that one generation succeeds another with certain habits of political behavior unimpaired, though often taken for granted require explanation. Even if Freud were entirely wrong about the role of Moses, the underlying mechanism for the maintenance of *any* tradition is of interest to political thought.

According to Freud's final formulations, the superego in the individual is the consequence of his overcoming the oedipal stage. When, at around four to six years of age, the child's passionate loves and hates reach their apex, he must renounce his aims if he is to retain the love of his parents (or their substitutes) and avoid their punishment. While relinquishing the personal objects of his passions in the real world, the child makes up for this loss by incorporating his parents within himself. Thus we have the foundations of an individual's superego, both of his aspirations and of the restrictions on his impulses. The love and hate he would have directed outwardly toward his parents he now directs at himself; the hostility and love are internalized, providing the energy to support this new psychic structure.

A child's super-ego is in fact constructed on the model not of its parents but of its parents' super-ego; the contents which fill it are the same and it becomes the vehicle of tradition and of all the time-resisting judgments of value which have propagated themselves in this manner from generation to generation. . . . Mankind never lives entirely in the present. The past, the tradi-

[2] Ibid., pp. 85–6.

tion of the race and of the people, lives on in the ideologies of the super-ego. . . .[3]

At times, much like Jung, Freud postulated a collective unconscious, an "archaic heritage" of genetically transmitted memory traces. While such pre-Darwinian thinking lay behind Freud's theory of symbolism, by and large his clinical work was much less preoccupied with such genetic notions than was Jung's. For the purposes of political theory, what counts is the extent to which Freud illuminates the sources of the power of tradition. According to Freud, society acts through the family; in each individual family custom gets internalized into each new member of society. Nor do these processes happen on a random basis. It is possible to speak of national character, even of modal personality structures: as Inkeles has said,

National character refers to relatively enduring personality characteristics and patterns that are modal among the adult members of a society . . . in any national population there is likely to be substantial variation in modal personality patterns, even though for any given nation this variation may cover only a narrow part of the world-wide range.[4]

It is possible to pin-point the relevance of social character for political life by using the concept of the superego to analyze the dominant values of any cultural unit. Parsons has been especially interested in this aspect of Freud's system. "Moral standards constitute, as the focus of the evaluative aspect of the common culture, the core of the stabilizing mechanisms of the system of social interaction

[3] Ibid., Vol. 22, p. 67.
[4] Alex Inkeles: "National Character and Modern Political Systems," in *Psychological Anthropology*, ed. Francis Hsu (Homewood, Ill.: Dorsey Press; 1961), pp. 173, 185.

... not only moral standards, but all the components of the common culture are internalized as part of the personality structure."[5] That there are characteristic inconsistencies, ambivalences, and inner conflicts within cultural superegos only makes them more readily analyzable in Freud's terms. The concept of the superego, then, is a bridge from within Freud's work to the social sciences, not only in the sense that it is a structure of the mind acquired "through a process of social interaction,"[6] but also in that the role of the superego demonstrates that Freud's psychology is not restricted to the understanding of so-called abnormal behavior. "One of the most common tendencies is to introduce personality factors in the hypothetical explanation of deviance but to assume that personality has little to do with the acceptance of prevailing norms."[7]

In any given nation, for example, there are shared political values and expectations, common heroes and villains. No matter how enlightened a citizen may be, he can never fully emancipate himself from certain national prejudices and symbols. An American may oppose one of his nation's wars, and find to his horror that he has secretly been pleased by American victories on the battlefield. Or, a citizen critical of many of his nation's values and policies may find himself unexpectedly defending his country while traveling abroad. Nationalism can be a very seductive force; it sets its limits on our intellectual and moral options in the most insidious possible way, from within. Devereux has written of "that portion of the total unconscious segment of

[5] Talcott Parsons: "The Superego and the Theory of Social Systems," *Psychiatry*, Vol. 15, No. 1 (February 1952), p. 18.

[6] Ibid., p. 23.

[7] Daniel J. Levinson: "The Relevance of Personality for Political Participation," *Public Opinion Quarterly*, Vol. 22, No. 1 (Spring 1958), p. 5.

the individual's psyche which most members of his given cultural community have in common."[8]

If one is not too put off by the story about Moses, this study of Freud's is not only revealing about himself and the origins of his ideas, but also contributes to our political thinking; it contains the underlying method for a psycho-analysis of history, a deepened feeling for religious experience, as well as the elaboration of the psychic mechanisms of custom and communal standards. If we find a disharmony between the historical fantasies and the social insights, perhaps this only reflects the more personal conflicts which moved Freud to argue his thesis. Freud himself felt "uncertain in the face of my own work; I lack the consciousness of unity and of belonging together which should exist between an author and his work."[9] Moses was the historical figure Freud chose both to admire and undermine; his unresolved oedipal feelings would not let him rest. In Freud's final social work we do not find the proverbial serenity of old age; there is a tone of hidden personal urgency. Freud wrote it, as he said, "with the audacity of one who has little or nothing to lose. . . ."[1] It has the recklessness of extreme old age.

Freud's studies on the psychology of religion led him far outside those phenomena which are strictly considered "religious." In order to trace the emotions supporting religion throughout the ages, Freud explored human helplessness and the need for omnipotence, aggressive wishes and the consequent guilt. He illuminated the unconscious mech-

[8] George Devereux: "Normal and Abnormal," *Some Uses of Anthropology*, ed. Joseph Casagrande and Thomas Gladwin (Washington, D. C.: The Anthropoligical Society of Washington; 1956), pp. 26–7.

[9] *Standard Edition*, Vol. 23, p. 58.

[1] Ibid., p. 54.

anisms at work in punishment, authority relationships, and social cohesion; and he extended our understanding of the historical process, of the way culture is psychologically transmitted. To the extent that despite his realism Freud still insisted that religion was a piece of psychic infantilism to be overcome, and that God was an unnecessary neurotic crutch, we can see glimmerings of an ideal of individual self-fulfillment, the importance of which will become evident only as we examine the remainder of his system.

CHAPTER IV

# Politics: Social Controls

## War and Aggression

Freud wrote two short but directly political essays, both on war, one in 1915 and the second in 1932. The conclusions of these essays are not original contributions to political theory. But in the course of Freud's thinking here he demonstrates, even if only in an elliptical way, some of the central themes of his social applications of psychoanalysis: the hypocrisy of contemporary society, the uses of societal coercion, the impoverishment of modern life, and the primary character of aggressive drives. Furthermore, we can see here the beginnings of trends of thought in psychoanalysis that have been fully developed only in the years since Freud's death.

The first of the two essays on war was written under the impact of the outbreak of World War I. Freud was at first quite chauvinistic, patriotically siding with the Central

Powers, and against those who were the accomplices of the
Czar. He experienced an upsurge of Social Darwinian
sentiments: "Life is impoverished, it loses in interest, when
the highest stake in the game of living, life itself, may not
be risked . . . war is bound to sweep away . . . [the] conventional treatment of death. . . . Life has . . . become interesting again; it has recovered its full content."[1] Theo-
dore Roosevelt or Justice Holmes might have said exactly
the same thing. The significant point is not that Freud
stands out here as very much the nineteenth-century gentleman, confident that war has raised the stakes of life, but
rather that he was haunted, like Max Weber, by the impoverishment of modern life. Later, in *The Future of an Illusion,*
Freud expressed his concern that modern society was emotionally freezing men, that the spontaneity in life was being
ground away. The point here is very much the same, although
the drives he is talking about now are exclusively the aggressive ones.

Freud was perceptive in his reaction to World War I in
that he felt it was a turning point in modern history;
"no event has ever destroyed so much that is precious in
the common possessions of humanity, confused so many of
the clearest intelligences, or so thoroughly debased what is
highest."[2] Freud was of course not alone in his shock at
the war; Henry James, for example, was convinced that
the world he knew would never be the same again. Freud's
response was distinctive in that the war provided intellectual fodder for the evolution of psychoanalysis.

World War I did not produce Freud's focus on aggression any more than his cancer was later directly responsible
for his theory of a death instinct. Aggression was there in

[1] *Standard Edition*, Vol. 14, pp. 290–1.
[2] Ibid., p. 275.

the 1890's as a component of the oedipal conflict, in the little boy's death wishes toward his father. But it is true that some of Freud's pupils, like Adler and Stekel, were readier to elaborate theoretically the place of aggression in mental life. Freud later admitted that his reluctance to embark along these lines was due to his own inner resistances. At the time of his quarrels with Adler and Stekel, Freud was treating aggression as the sadistic component of the sexual instinct. Before his first essay on war, we have encountered aggression in Freud's social applications of psychoanalysis in the early essay relating religion to guilt feelings over death wishes. The tale of the primal crime also illustrates his preoccupation with human barbarousness.

Instead of the disillusionment a civilized man might feel at the horrors of war, or at the credulous mass belief in atrocity stories, Freud thought his general view of man had been confirmed. "The deepest essence of human nature consists of instinctual impulses which are of an elementary nature, which are similar in all men and which aim at the satisfaction of certain primal needs . . . the primitive mind is, in the fullest meaning of the word, imperishable."[3] Freud had always held that "our unconscious will murder even for trifles. . . ,"[4] just as he had thought that men tend to believe what they want to believe. If the aggressive and wish-fulfilling aspects of people were now harshly revealed, this meant only that psychoanalysis had been right all along. "In reality our fellow-citizens have not sunk so low as we feared, because they had never risen so high as we believed."[5]

Wartime hostilities illustrated Freud's view of the nature

[3] Ibid., pp. 281, 286.
[4] Ibid., p. 297.
[5] Ibid., p. 285.

of social restraints. "Civilization has been attained through the renunciation of instinctual satisfaction, and it demands the same renunciation from each newcomer in turn."[6] As he had argued in *Totem and Taboo*, the very existence of social restrictions points to our underlying tendency to violate them. "What no human soul desires stands in no need of prohibition; it is excluded automatically."[7] While renouncing his own murderous impulses, man could vicariously fulfill them in the state's aggressions; just as he could renounce the talionic code for himself, provided legalized punishment operated on the same principle. "The state has forbidden to the individual the practice of wrong-doing, not because it desires to abolish it, but because it desires to monopolize it. . . ."[8]

War caused a malignant regression, both within the contending countries and within each individual. It lifted restraints all across the board. Aggression was sanctioned now, murder was legitimized, and those impulses within men which had been held under control were reactivated. This of course illustrated Freud's developmental perspective, for according to psychoanalysis no stage of the life cycle is ever completely overcome. Outside events can always reawaken those most elemental drives of men. And this is true even under the impersonal conditions of modern warfare. Whatever the technological changes in warfare, combat stimulates aggressive fantasies of a regressive nature.

The most interesting aspect of this essay is not Freud's conclusion that wars are inevitable, which he himself would shortly revise; but rather that here, as in his brief comments

[6] Ibid., p. 282.
[7] Ibid., p. 296.
[8] Ibid., p. 279.

on the function of leadership in reinforcing superego controls, we get a glimpse into the psychoanalytic view of the directive aspects of social controls. Throughout Freud's work we find him insisting on the high price man pays for civilization and pleading for a more tolerant attitude to spontaneity. Usually Freud takes this stance when he is talking about the erotic drives. But here, where he is specifically considering aggression, the constructive uses of civilized restraints are in the forefront: "The maintenance of civilization even on so dubious a basis [contemporary hypocrisy] offers the prospect of paving the way in each new generation for a more far-reaching transformation of instinct which shall be the vehicle of a better civilization."[9] Self-fulfillment and spontaneity may be relevant standards when discussing erotic needs, but they are less adequate when it comes to aggression. After all, as Kenneth Keniston has pointed out, "one can 'spontaneously' commit murder and 'authentically' press a guided missile button."[1]

No matter how favorable the family environment, a certain proportion of aggressiveness is inevitable in the growing child. Anna Freud has maintained that

the infant develops hostile as well as loving feelings toward the mother over and above the hostility which is aroused whenever the mother frustrates the child's wishes . . . aggression . . . [is] an inborn instinctive urge which develops spontaneously, in response to the environment but . . . not produced by environmental influences.[2]

Aggression is both primary and environmental, in that the external world elicits that which is innate. Learning to

[9] Ibid., p. 285.

[1] Keniston: "Alienation and the Decline of Utopia," pp. 184–5.

[2] A. Freud: "Notes on Aggression," *Bulletin of the Menninger Clinic*, Vol. 13 (1949), pp. 147–8.

handle destructive urges was for Freud an essential part of
child development. "By the admixture of *erotic* components
the egoistic instincts are transformed into *social* ones. We
learn to value being loved as an advantage for which we
are willing to sacrifice other advantages."[3] The child renounces his murderous wishes, the "advantage" of replac-
ing his father, in order to retain his father's love. Repression is not due just to fear, but also to love.

Emotional immaturity can be conceived as the failure to
achieve the integration of wishes; "the normal fusion between the erotic and destructive urges cannot take place
and aggression manifests itself as pure, independent destructiveness."[4] The intensity of the conflict over these
wishes points to the importance of the oedipal stage. The
oedipal conflict is agonizing precisely because while on
the one hand the child does have murderous desires, on the
other hand he also desperately needs parental love. For the
love of his parents he then internalizes and represses the aggression. While restrictions frustrate one aspect of the child's
desires, on another level they support his aspirations to become like his parents.

Freud saw the advantage to the individual of restrictions
and self-sacrifices, but the notion has become theoretically
more important to psychoanalysis since his death. The
whole issue of the role of authority links psychoanalysis
and traditional political theory: "The problem of political
philosophy, and its dilemma, is the reconciliation of freedom and coercion."[5] Many commentators have seen that

---

[3] *Standard Edition*, Vol. 14, p. 282.

[4] A. Freud: "Notes on Aggression," p. 151.

[5] Franz Neumann: *The Democratic and the Authoritarian State* (New York:
The Free Press of Glencoe; 1957), p. 116.

Freud hypothesized a basic conflict between the individual and society, between inner instinctual needs and outer repressive measures. Yet they have usually seen the conflict from one angle only, that of the damage done to individual development by the restrictive aspects of culture—be it by delusional religion which prevents men from "growing up" or by excessive sexual taboos which stunt men's optimum emotional development. What has been neglected is Freud's view that limit-setting can serve constructive functions as well; the psychoanalytic view of the positive functions of social controls is well illustrated by his essays on war.

The point can be made most sharply by considering more closely the process of child development. There was indeed a time in the history of psychoanalytic doctrine when the inclination was to view all suppressions as negative, all controls on the child as hindrances to his fulfillment. Anna Freud herself once considered the "question unanswered as to what would happen if the adults around a child refrained from interfering with him in any way."[6] The inclination was to "risk the chance of their being somewhat uncontrolled in the end instead of forcing on them from the outset such a crippling of their individuality."[7] Frustration, as by now we are all aware, can foster aggression: "Increased frustrations of essential libidinal wishes . . . abnormally increase the child's aggressive reaction to the normal and inevitable deprivation to which every infant is subjected from birth."[8] Nowadays, however,

The idea that the school child is best left alone, that he knows best what he needs and that the grown-up's intervention will

[6] A. Freud: *Psychoanalysis for Teachers and Parents*, p. 78.

[7] Ibid., p. 101.

[8] A. Freud: "Notes on Aggression," p. 151.

only do damage, is out-dated. . . . The external world represented by the educator [can provide] too little help in the difficult task of mastering their urges and in the anxiety aroused by them.[9]

We should seek to avoid those school situations, now all too prevalent, in which children are encouraged to give unlimited expression to their primitive drives without providing the educational direction whereby such expression is helped to become sublimation.[1]

By saying "No," one can help a child overcome the anxiety of his drives.

Whatever anarchistic tendencies there might have been within psychoanalytic theory were only short-lived. Although in *The Future of an Illusion* Freud himself writes of childhood as an idealized state of nature, ultimately it was one of his achievements to put an end to the notion of childhood as a Garden of Eden. He pointed out that "childhood is not the blissful idyll into which we distort it in retrospect. . . ."[2] A child's desires are of an intensity out of proportion to his biological and physical capacities, and he is assailed by murderous inclinations which terrorize him. One index of the connection within psychoanalytic thought between the child's aggressive impulses and the positive functions of restraints is that Freud sees the uses of culture precisely in his essay on war, when he is focusing on the psychology of aggression.

The practicing psychoanalyst and the wise parent have probably always known this, even if it was not until recently elaborated. The advance in understanding the importance of external controls for the child's development

[9] Ilse Hellman: "Psychoanalysis and the Teacher," in *Psychoanalysis and Contemporary Thought*, pp. 62, 61.

[1] Christine Olden: "Notes on Child Rearing in America," *Psychoanalytic Study of the Child*, Vol. 7, p. 391.

[2] *Standard Edition*, Vol. 11, p. 126.

The child needs help in restraining even his erotic drives, to the extent to which these are in the service of selfish motives. The boy, for example, wants to eliminate both father and siblings, and have his mother sexually all to himself. But, as Melanie Klein has pointed out,

It is obvious that if these impracticable wishes were fulfilled they would cause him the deepest feelings of guilt. . . . He himself actually wants to be restrained by the adults around him in his aggression and selfishness, because if these are given free reign he is caused suffering by the pain of remorse and unworthiness; and in fact he relies on obtaining this help from grown-ups, like any other help he needs.[7]

Klein's concept of the "depressive position" refers to that developmental stage when the child has the greatest difficulty in tolerating his own ambivalence "without feeling too anxious lest his hate prove stronger than his love."[8] The more normal the individual, the more he has mastered this conflict between love and hate, the more capable he is "of experiencing deprivation without being overwhelmed by hatred. His own hatred also . . . [is] less frightening as his belief increases that his love can restore what his hatred has destroyed."[9]

This trend in psychoanalytic thinking justifiably purports, I think, to be within the general framework of Freud's thought. It is at odds, however, with an earlier psychoanalytic generation's outlook on aggression. Aichhorn's school for delinquents was founded on a different understanding of aggression: as he wrote of one incident

[7] Ibid., pp. 74–5.
[8] Elizabeth R. Zetzel, in *Affective Disorders*, ed. Phyllis Greenacre (New York: International Universities Press; 1953), pp. 109–10.
[9] Hannah Segal: *Introduction to the Work of Melanie Klein* (London: Heinemann; 1964), p. 80.

was made possible on two fronts: the greater insight into the psychology of the aggressive drives (largely a contribution of Melanie Klein), and the growth of ego psychology. Susan Isaacs, writing of a school she ran, makes the point from the perspective of a deeper grasp of the psychology of aggression.

At first I was too passive in my treatment of situations of bullying and cruelty [by older children to the younger] in the hope that if the bullying elders were not interfered with the impulse would die a natural death. But I found that this did not happen. And that . . . was . . . because the impulse feeds upon itself rather than exhausts itself in fulfillment. When I ceased to remain passive and showed my disapproval, it was not only the younger children who were now saved from teasing, but also the elder, stronger children now became more contented. They now felt safeguarded against their own impulses.[3]

This viewpoint on aggression is like Edgar Allan Poe's concept of fear—terror can be self-fulfilling. An impulse can grow on itself, and become insatiable. "Once destructiveness appears, a kind of multiplier effect comes into play."[4] Intense emotions are self-propelling. "An emotion . . . has the tendency to accumulate new energy by activation of all memories which are closely related to it and whose contents support it."[5] The unacceptability of one's own desires entails self-alienation. "It is always the uncontrollable character of one's desire and aggression, and one's helplessness in face of these impulses, that is most dreaded."[6]

[3] Hellman: "Psychoanalysis and the Teacher," p. 63.

[4] John Schaar: *Escape from Authority* (New York: Basic Books; 1961), p. 263.

[5] Kurt Eissler: "Notes upon the Emotionality of a Schizophrenic Patient and Its Relation to Problems of Technique," *Psychoanalytic Study of the Child*, Vol. 8, p. 204.

[6] Melanie Klein and Joan Riviere: *Love, Hate and Reparation* (London: Hogarth Press; 1953), p. 39.

there, "aggression can rise only to a certain pitch. . . . Since we did not oppose the destructive behavior of the group, their aggression was bound to reach a climax."[1] Nowadays there would be a greater wariness among psychoanalysts of erring on the side of excessive indulgence. Without external controls, the child may be even harder on himself.

Klein's concern with the child's need for self-respect, his desire for outside help to stop his aggressive and sexual selfishness, links up with recent advances in ego psychology. The immediacy of childhood, the directness of contact with reality, are made possible by the fact that the child's defenses are not yet internalized. He can afford to be so responsive to life precisely because when he needs the safety of control, he can turn to his parents for outside help. In other words, "deprivation [discipline] supports the ego in its attempt to gain control of id impulses."[2] This is one of the theoretical sources of the psychoanalyst's neutrality. Instinctual frustration serves as an incentive to ego development; anxiety can stimulate as well as inhibit. Unfulfilled fantasies and longings are necessary for the growth of t' ego.

"Deprivation is necessary . . . in order to achiev e distinction between the self and the outside world."[3] ( er-wise, how would a child develop a sense of reality?

. . . in his development toward reality, the child has to learn to postpone gratification . . . while the child does not have to

[1] Quoted in *Psychoanalytic Pioneers*, ed. Alexander, Eisenstein, and Grotjahn, p. 353.

[2] Ernst Kris: "On Psychoanalysis and Education," *American Journal of Orthopsychiatry*, Vol. 18 (October 1948), p. 628.

[3] Beata Rank: "Adaptation of the Psychoanalytic Technique for the Treatment of Young Children with Atypical Development," *The American Journal of Orthopsychiatry*, Vol. 19, No. 1 (January 1949), p. 130.

learn everything the hard way, for many important functions this situation proves unavoidable. And there is certainly nothing to invalidate any of Freud's statements on the impact of situations of deprivation on the evolution of the reality principle. . . . The reality principle includes postponement of gratification and a temporary toleration of unpleasure . . . once the superego has been established, the child will often feel pride in foregoing a pleasure.[4]

Even in the case of the erotic drives, frustration is necessary in order to encourage sublimation; excessive instinctual gratification can lead to fixation at early developmental stages.

We want him [the child] to have control over his sexual drives, for if they are constantly breaking through, there is a danger that his development will be retarded or interrupted, that he will rest content with gratification instead of sublimating, with masturbation instead of learning; that he will confine his desire for knowledge to sexual matters instead of extending it to the whole wide world.[5]

In cases where a child's aggressive fantasies are fulfilled, either by the illness or the death of a parent, the child's guilt feelings are increased. Nothing could terrify a child more than to see its murderous wishes magically gratified. A contemporary novelist describes the emotional response of a preparatory school student who "accidentally" cripples his roommate; the murderously aggressive component in athletics becomes so patent that he is inhibited from play-

[4] Heinz Hartmann: "Comments on the Psychonanalytic Theory of the Ego," *Psychoanalytic Study of the Child*, Vol. 5, p. 78. Also, Hartmann: "Notes on the Reality Principle," ibid., Vol. 11, pp. 35, 36, 39.

[5] A. Freud: "Psychoanalysis and the Training of the Young Child," *Psychoanalytic Quarterly*, Vol. 4 (1935), p. 20.

ing any sports. "I wanted no more of sports. . . . I didn't trust myself in them, and I didn't trust anyone else. It was as though football players were really bent on crushing the life out of each other, as though boxers were in combat to the death, as though even a tennis ball might turn into a bullet."[6] Since each child experiences anxiety in coping with such impulses, it is not surprising that "almost any child who dares give an honest answer will indicate that he is waiting for better days when he grows up."[7] Observing children during air raids, Anna Freud found that "when it [the child] has only just learned to curb its own aggressive impulses, it will have real outbursts of anxiety when the bombs come down and do damage around it."[8] Ruth Eissler makes a similar point in her study of delinquency; in one case a murderer, an adolescent, left the following note at the scene of his crime—"Catch me before I kill more; I cannot control myself."[9] "Cases are known of people trying to be arrested in order to prevent themselves from committing a murder."[1]

What this means for child development, in practical terms, is a balanced psychic diet of indulgence and deprivation; any good psychiatric procedure includes common sense. "The complications of the psychiatric approach lie in the evaluation of the clinical data and in the elaboration of the theoretical system by means of which one arrives at

[6] John Knowles: *A Separate Peace* (New York: Dell; 1961), p. 102.

[7] Samuel D. Lipton: "On the Psychology of Childhood Tonsillectomy," *Psychoanalytic Study of the Child*, Vol. 17, p. 386.

[8] A. Freud and Dorothy Burlingham: *War and Children* (New York: International Universities Press; 1944), p. 28.

[9] Ruth Eissler: "Scapegoats of Society," p. 363.

[1] Melanie Klein: *Envy and Gratitude* (London: Tavistock Publications; 1957), p. 75.

one's conclusions."[2] Here the conclusion is that a different proportion of permissiveness and discipline are required at varying periods of the child's life. Lack of discipline, as well as an absence of instinctual gratification, can interfere with the growth of ego functions.

A similar principle can be drawn from psychiatric therapy. Just as children need a balance between discipline and permissiveness, so in clinical practice there is an acknowledged place for both the loosening of defenses and the strengthening of control mechanisms. For patients under orthodox psychoanalytic treatment, the analyst's task is largely to enable them to be more directly expressive. By being able to see his own anger, by exposing his aggressive wishes to the light of day, the patient can learn to master and channel these feelings. Through re-living the past in the analytic situation, he can regain his sense of childhood immediacy. Therapy helps by lifting defenses against reality, the distortions imposed on life that anxiety has engendered.

The ego, according to Freud's last formulation, responds to danger, whether internal or external, by the signal of anxiety. Instead of treating anxiety, as in his earlier work, as simply transformed or "dammed-up" libido, Freud saw it finally as a sign of approaching danger, a warning to the ego either to fight or flee. (Anxiety hence becomes a cause of repression rather than a result.) The obvious method of psychologically fleeing from an internal danger is to erect a defense against it: to repress it, or to project it, and so on. The psychoanalytic situation provides the security that enables the patient's ego to face its anxieties, and to abandon the various neurotic defenses it has used in the past.

---

[2] Grete Bibring: "Psychiatry and Medical Practice in a General Hospital," *New England Journal of Medicine*, Vol. 254 (1956), p. 370.

For other patients, though, the task of therapy is a suppressive one.[3] These patients need support for their defenses. In cases where only a transitory psychological problem is at issue, these patients may be relatively healthy; but in other cases—say, psychotics—the whole clinical problem may be that the customary methods of handling anxiety have collapsed, and the ego has had to resort to much more extreme defensive maneuvers against the overwhelming anxiety. Neurotic inhibition is not the worst that one can suffer from; "in schizophrenia the therapeutic aim must be directed at re-repression rather than at lifting of repression."[4] For the therapist the "gross major decision is whether the defenses of the ego are to be strengthened or broken through as a preliminary toward a reintegration of the ego."[5] The frequent misunderstanding of Freud's view of the conflict between social restrictions and the individual is in part due to the history of psychoanalysis. Waelder has explained the early anarchistic bias within psychoanalytic theory in terms of the early preoccupation with pathology, as opposed to the contemporary preoccupation with normal developmental processes. "It is true that in Freud's writings the restrictive aspect of culture is more amply discussed than the 'directive' aspect; but that is due to the fact that Freud's writings deal mostly with *psychopathology*, i.e., with maladjustments rather than with successful adjustments."[6] Yet inappropriate direction is certainly involved

---

[3] R. P. Knight, in *Psychoanalytic Psychiatry and Psychology*, ed. R. P. Knight and C. R. Friedman (New York: International Universities Press; 1954), p. 60.

[4] F. C. Redlich: "The Concept of Schizophrenia and Its Importance for Therapy," in *Psychotherapy with Schizophrenics*, ed. Eugene B. Brody and Frederick C. Redlich (New York: International Universities Press; 1952), p. 30.

[5] Merton M. Gill: "Ego Psychology and Psychotherapy," *The Psychoanalytic Quarterly*, Vol. 20, No. 1 (1951), p. 63.

[6] Waelder: "Psychoanalysis, Scientific Method, and Philosophy," p. 618.

in the etiology of severe psychic disorders. It is more honest, in my view, simply to admit that since Freud's death we have a greater theoretical understanding of psychic life. And this is due largely to the development of ego psychology, as well as to our more extensive understanding of the role of aggressive drives.

Nevertheless, while these issues have been refined and clarified only recently, for some of Freud's pupils the intellectual implications were there from the beginning. Even as early as 1907 we find Federn, who fittingly enough pioneered in the therapy of psychotics, recognizing that

our kind of education (through its forceful moral precepts) fulfills a good purpose in so far as it shields the child from sexuality and its torments for a long time. In addition, the powerful tendencies toward cruelty which are inherent in mankind are bridled by our Judeo-Christian upbringing. In spite of this, it is true that our moral education has to be changed.[7]

Only by seeing the psychoanalytic view of both the uses and dangers of the suppression and expression of human feelings, can we understand Freud's contribution to the conflict between the individual and society.

Freud is quite explicit about the uses of cultural controls in his second essay on war (1932). Again Freud can see the directive, positive aspects of cultural restraint when he is focusing on aggression. Here he refers to "a process of evolution of culture. . . . We owe to that process the best of what we have become, as well as a good part of what we suffer from . . . whatever fosters the growth of civilization works at the same time against war."[8] The point is not the

[7] *Minutes of the Vienna Psychoanalytic Society*, Vol. I, p. 117.

[8] *Standard Edition*, Vol. 22, pp. 214–15. Elsewhere Freud proposed that "Where id was, there ego shall be. It is a work of culture. . . ." Ibid., p. 80.

one Freud later argues in *Civilization and Its Discontents*, and elsewhere. It is not just that restrictions are inevitable, because of the conflicting passions of men, nor that we should face life with stoical resignation. It is clear here that restraints and restrictions serve inner psychic needs of a positive, constructive character.

This is an issue of considerable theoretical importance. Freud's contribution to our understanding of the relation of the individual to society is far more complex than has usually been assumed. It is often seen that Freud is ambivalent toward cultural restrictions, because the coercion which often stunts men's personalities is nevertheless the instrument which has made civilization possible in the first place. But it has not been noticed that implicitly within Freud's work, and quite explicitly in psychoanalytic theory since his death, limitations are shown to have a positive, directive aspect. Freud is always more articulate about the usefulness of restrictions when he is talking of the aggressive drives.

Earlier, in discussing *Totem and Taboo*, we saw that Freud thought civilized life presupposed renunciation of both sexual and hostile drives. Society compensated individuals for this deprivation by various forms of communal aggressiveness—in *Totem and Taboo* the vicarious satisfactions in punishment, and in his essays on war the institution of warfare. In addition, it is now possible to see the way in which communal restraints reinforce defenses within individuals and how the individual's self-controlling agencies are in need of outside support. Culture is not conceived only as a necessary evil providing a variety of compensations, but also as a useful buttress in providing its members with a needed sense of direction.

A similar argument within the history of political philosophy is advanced by Burkean conservatism. Horrified at the destructiveness of aggression, Burke called attention to the value of social restraints in delivering us from the slavery of our passions. "Government is a contrivance of human wisdom to provide for human wants. . . . Among these wants is to be reckoned the want, out of civil society, of a sufficient restraint upon their passions. . . . In this sense the restraints on men, as well as their liberties, are to be reckoned among their rights."[9] Institutions help to limit the range of our hostile passions, partly through accustoming us to them in a piecemeal way. The resemblance between Burke's thought and Melanie Klein's is striking; their affinity helps to explain the responsiveness of the English to one particular strand of psychoanalytic thought. Klein's psychology has thrived in England partially for cultural reasons.

This aspect of Freud's thought may lead in a conservative path, but the revisionist tendency to drop the innate character of aggression has led to plainly anarchistic conclusions. As John Schaar perceptively points out about Fromm's more recent work,

It is all but impossible for Fromm to come to terms with the restraining institutions of a society. . . . Gone is the earlier understanding that society aids as well as impedes the growth of human powers. Fromm . . . sees society only as a force which cripples, corrupts, confines. . . . Fromm's program . . . advocates the elimination of all convention and inhibition—all discipline, no matter how imposed.[1]

[9] Edmund Burke: *Reflections on the French Revolution* (London: J. M. Dent; 1953), pp. 57–8.
[1] Schaar: *Escape from Authority*, pp. 302, 311, 312–13.

There is a continuous strand of such thought as Fromm's from the Enlightenment through Tolstoy to our own day; Sir Isaiah Berlin has described the basis of this trend as the belief that "to direct is to spoil. Men are good and need only freedom to realize their goodness."[2] In Skinner's utopia, the premise is identical: "when a baby graduates from our Lower Nursery . . . it knows nothing of frustration, anxiety, or fear."[3] This faith in the individual's capacity for conflict-free development has been at the heart of the anarchist position.

These references to conservative and anarchistic notions, however, are intended mainly to highlight some of the possible ramifications within Freud's thought. Freud's second essay on war clarified his general point about the uses of cultural restraints, and specified the way in which human drives are culturally channelled. In it Freud abandoned his earlier view that human aggressiveness as a primary need inevitably entails war. In his first essay on war he had maintained that "war cannot be abolished; so long as the conditions of existence among nations are so different and their mutual repulsion so violent, there are bound to be wars."[4] In the second he recognizes that alternative cultural solutions are available for the same inner human needs; that it is possible to structure human aggressiveness in such a way as to avoid war. He now holds that "wars will only be prevented with certainty if mankind unites in setting up a central authority to which the right of giving judgment upon all conflicts of interest shall be handed over."[5]

2 Sir Isaiah Berlin: "Tolstoy and Enlightenment," *Encounter*, Vol. 16, No. 2 (February 1961), p. 38.

3 B. F. Skinner: *Walden Two* (New York: The Macmillan Co.; 1962), p. 98.

4 *Standard Edition,* Vol. 14, p. 299.

5 Ibid., Vol. 22, p. 207.

A search for the "moral equivalent" of war was also William James's solution to "pugnacity." Kluckhohn has related the actual implementation of a substitute for warlike brutality in a nonliterate society. "In Papua anthropologists utilized the principle of cultural substitution by introducing a pig instead of a human body in a fertility rite, a football to replace a spear in discharging hostilities between factions in a tribe."[6] In terms of modern political theory, Fourier is an example of a theorist who founded a reformist program on an instinctivist psychology. Human needs can be fulfilled through a variety of social channels.

While at first glance Freud's essays on war do not seem to amount to much from the point of view of political theory, a close examination of their implications reveals, beneath the straightforward surface, hints of exciting theoretical possibilities. Neither the early statement that war is inevitable, given human aggressiveness, nor the later proposition that a super-state is the only solution to evade war, constitute much that is very fresh for political thought. But these essays do point to the psychoanalytic view of the directive aspects of culture. They offer an opportunity to clarify the role of frustration in human development. Furthermore, they demonstrate with the issue of war how inner needs can be socially satisfied in a variety of ways. However we conceive the innate character of man, there is still room for social engineering. Acceptance of innate aggressiveness does not preclude indirect means of gratification. "Moral equivalents" are still possible for war. Freud's essays on war not only illustrate the way culture can help the individual achieve maturity, but also how it can be responsible for directing inner aggressions into constructive solutions.

[6] Clyde Kluckhohn: *Mirror for Man* (New York: Premier Books; 1957), p. 133.

## 2   The Past

Freud's essays on war also typify a major orientation within psychoanalysis which has relevance for political thought. The violence underlying civilized society has been seen by others. As a psychoanalyst Freud focuses on the unconscious manifestations of destructiveness. Freud links latent violence with his developmental view of man: "every earlier stage of development persists alongside the later stage which has arisen from it. . . ."[1] What distinguishes Freud's view from, say, Hobbes's, is that Freud's position is not a mechanical one; Freud looks at the hatred that exists beneath the social order in terms of its potential fusion with the more social drives as the individual matures.

Maturity, for psychoanalysts, is a matter of integrating various human needs. Even in the small child, "the aggressive strivings, if fused in the normal way with the libidinal ones, are socializing influences, rather than the opposite. They provide the initial strength and tenacity with which the infant reaches out for the object world and holds onto it."[2] Destructive hostility indicates a defusion of drives, a regression to an earlier developmental stage. The concept of regression originated in the field of neurology; for psychoanalysis it simply meant a "re-establishment of an earlier stage where conflict is less."[3] Rather than face the difficulties of maturity, the individual returns to earlier, less integrated ways of handling conflicts. The potentiality for

[1] *Standard Edition*, Vol. 14, p. 285.

[2] A. Freud: *Normality and Pathology in Childhood* (New York: International Universities Press; 1965), p. 180.

[3] G. L. Bibring, et al.: "A Study of the Psychological Process in Pregnancy," *Psychoanalytic Study of the Child*, Vol. 16, p. 19.

individual regression perpetuates the influence of the past, and helps explain the ever-present danger of violence. Instinctual defusion opens the door to loosening all inner controls on aggressiveness, and a return to less socialized stages of the past.

In Freud's clinical work the historical past always played a special role. Freud began his therapeutic work treating what were then known as "hysterical" patients; he explained hysteria in terms of failure to recall the past. Under hypnosis, early memories could be relived; the individual's increased knowledge of his past could produce symptomatic improvements. Freud concluded that "hysterical symptoms are derivatives of memories which are operating unconsciously";[4] for "hysterics suffer mainly from reminiscences."[5]

Although the technique for reviving memories grew more sophisticated over the years, the emphasis within psychoanalysis on each patient's individual history remained. Freud believed that "neurotics are anchored somewhere in their past. . . ."[6] Hysterics in particular "cannot get free of the past and for its sake they neglect what is real and immediate."[7] As Franz Alexander put it,

the mental apparatus resists fresh situations, alterations in reality which require fresh struggles and testing of reality. . . . Reality is only accepted so far as it can be mastered by automatisms: anything that is new or unexpected is rejected by means of flight.[8]

[4] *Standard Edition*, Vol. 3, p. 212.
[5] Ibid., Vol. 2, p. 7.
[6] Ibid., Vol. 16, p. 365.
[7] Ibid., Vol. 11, p. 17.
[8] Alexander: *The Scope of Psychoanalysis*, p. 211.

The task of therapy was to loosen these ties to the past and, by reviving early emotional experiences, free the individual from this bondage. The more distant the experience, the more it conflicted with an adult's sense of security and the more pathogenic it became. Freud, who collected ancient statuary, likened such memories to archeological artifacts: he liked to use the "equation of repression and burial, and of Pompeii and childhood."[9]

Nor was the importance of early emotional experiences restricted to the pathology of the neuroses. Freud even once held that the "little creature is often completed by the fourth or fifth year of life, and after that merely brings gradually to light what is already within him."[1] It is possible to avoid all Freud's phylogenetic constructs, and stick to ontogenetic development; "burdened with his past, the child is indeed anything but a blank sheet."[2] During his early years the child experiences his most intense emotions, for he is least equipped with defensive structures to protect himself from psychic injury. Psychoanalysts once liked to compare the young child to an embryo; damage at an early stage becomes magnified after further development. The psychological stages corresponding to the erotogenic zones (oral, anal, phallic), which have been popularized by Dr. Spock, are unimportant for our purposes. What does matter is the concept of a developmental sequence, the life cycle as a staircase toward maturity. Illness was defined as the failure to overcome a stage.

The importance of one's childhood past extended through all aspects of life. As Freud once wrote, "in mental life

<hr/>

[9] *Standard Edition*, Vol. 9, p. 85.

[1] Ibid., Vol. 16, p. 356.

[2] A. Freud: *Psychoanalysis for Teachers and Parents*, p. 74.

nothing which has once been formed can perish— . . . everything is somehow preserved and . . . in suitable circumstances (when, for instance, regression goes back far enough) it can once more be brought to life."[3] Freud thought that each of us carries within himself a resonance board, or a resounding box, so that when we see or experience something, all our past memories give their overtones to our experiences. When the patient's past distorts his relationship to his analyst, a transference neurosis has been established. "The essential core of clinical psychoanalysis relates to the revival of early conflicts through the medium of the transference neurosis."[4] Freud thought that "transference is merely uncovered and isolated by analysis. It is a universal phenomenon of the human mind, it decides the success of all medical influence, and in fact dominates the whole of each person's relations to his human environment."[5]

For psychoanalysis the importance of the past can be deduced from the initial view of the unconscious; to the extent that life is influenced by unconscious mechanisms, the past lives in the present; "it is a prominent feature of unconscious processes that they are indestructible. In the unconscious nothing can be brought to an end, nothing is past or forgotten."[6] Freud interpreted dreams as "derived from the past in every sense."[7] "Every dream was linked in its manifest content with recent experiences and in its

---

[3] *Standard Edition*, Vol. 21, p. 69.

[4] Elizabeth R. Zetzel: "The Theory of Therapy in Relation to a Developmental Model of the Psychic Apparatus," *International Journal of Psychoanalysis*, Vol. 46, Part I (January 1965), p. 39.

[5] *Standard Edition*, Vol. 20, p. 42.

[6] Ibid., Vol. 5, p. 577.

[7] Ibid., p. 621.

latent content with the most ancient experiences."[8] In Freud's final formulation of instinct theory, he postulated that "all instincts tend toward the restoration of an earlier state of things."[9]

Freud's stress on early experiences—his theory that fixations at early stages are at the bottom of mental illness, his insistence that every mental act be looked at in terms of the individual's history—form so important an aspect of the psychoanalytic system as to have been christened the "genetic point of view." Although Freud himself did not articulate this aspect of psychoanalysis, it has recently been put on a conceptual plane with the dynamic, economic, topographic, and structural points of view, and hence is now included by some as part of psychoanalytic metapsychology. "While the psychoanalytic theory is undoubtedly a genetic psychology, Freud apparently took this so much for granted that he saw no necessity to formulate a genetic point of view of metapsychology."[1]

In *Moses and Monotheism*, we saw how the past of an entire culture lived on in the present by the incorporation of cultural traditions within the superego of each member of society. On the clinical level we can now see that the past of the individual's own infancy and childhood persists similarly throughout his subsequent development. Within each man maturity is a tenuous achievement. A defusion of instincts, and a return to earlier developmental stages, are always possible. For Freud the passions of men lie just below the surface of life.

[8] Ibid., Vol. 4, p. 218.

[9] Ibid., Vol. 18, p. 37.

[1] David Rapaport and Merton Gill: "The Points of View and Assumptions of Metapsychology," *The International Journal of Psychoanalysis*, Vol. 40, Parts 3-4 (1959), p. 154.

## 3  Social Cohesion

Whenever Freud's ideas link up most directly with traditional concerns of political thought, we need to be most wary of misconceiving his intentions. The temptation to transform Freud into our own image becomes most acute exactly when his thought, on the face of it, connects with customary preoccupations of political philosophy. Here above all it is necessary to retain our original intellectual stance; if we are constantly on guard against yanking Freud too far from the context of psychoanalytic doctrine, it may prove possible to assess more adequately what he has to offer for political thought.

In the course of Freud's work, he tried by several approaches to solve the problem of how societies cohere. In *Totem and Taboo*, he resorted to a kind of social contract. Although men were driven by guilt over their aggressiveness to accept society, they did so in a rationalistic way for purposes of self-preservation. With the beginnings of ego psychology in *Group Psychology and the Analysis of the Ego* (1921), Freud offered an original explanation of the basis of social unity and of its dissolution. But his resolution of the problem can only be understood within the development of psychoanalysis. Hence particular attention must be paid to the state of psychoanalytic theory in 1921; otherwise the temptation is to construe Freud's thesis in terms alien to his own, to see it merely as a tract within the history of political theory rather than as an offshoot from within the theory of clinical psychoanalysis.

The starting point of his argument has misled interpreters. Freud found Gustave Le Bon's *The Crowd* a useful point of departure. Why do men behave in groups in ways so much more irrational than they would permit themselves as individuals? Le Bon's intuitive grasp of unconscious motivation, the vividness of his narrative style, and the fame of his book, all combined to make it a useful text to explicate. This was in fact a frequent expository technique of Freud's. He would begin his argument with either a couple of texts, as in *Totem and Taboo* and *Group Psychology and the Analysis of the Ego*, or with a whole compendium of authorities, as in *The Interpretation of Dreams* and *Jokes and Their Relation to the Unconscious*. He would then go on to integrate the same empirical phenomena into an original conceptual scheme. Therefore it is impossible to jump from Freud's use of Le Bon, in *Group Psychology and the Analysis of the Ego*, to any conclusions about Freud's "debt" to Le Bon.[1] Freud begins with a social thinker, Le Bon, and handles a standard issue, social cohesion; yet as one examines Freud's argument, the extent to which the work is an integral part of psychoanalysis becomes clear.

Freud's point of departure in *Group Psychology and the Analysis of the Ego* was the same as in the essays on war—regression. "In the mental operations of the group the function for testing the reality of things falls into the background in comparison with the strength of wishful impulses. . . ."[2] Freud defines "group psychology" broadly as concerned with "the individual man as a member of a race, of a nation, of a caste, of a profession, of an institution, or as a component part of a crowd of people. . . ."[3]

---

[1] Philip Rieff: "The Origin of Freud's Political Psychology," *Journal of the History of Ideas*, Vol. 17, No. 2 (April 1956), p. 246.

[2] *Standard Edition*, Vol. 18, p. 80.

[3] Ibid., p. 70.

One can describe all the irrationalities within these groups, which observers from Le Bon to Lippmann have noted, as regressive phenomena:

> . . . a group can only be excited by an excessive stimulus. Anyone who wishes to produce an effect upon it needs no logical adjustment in his arguments; he must paint in the most forcible colours, he must exaggerate, and he must repeat the same thing again and again. . . . [A group] is as intolerant as it is obedient to authority. It respects force and can only be slightly influenced by kindness, which it regards merely as a form of weakness. What it demands of its heroes is strength, or even violence. It wants to be ruled and oppressed and to fear its masters . . . groups have never thirsted after truth. They demand illusions, and cannot do without them.[4]

Within social groups men can renounce their maturity and return to earlier states of dependence and childish thinking.

What happens can be described as a split within the individual's ego ideal. ("Ego ideal" in the context of 1921 meant what we now mean by superego. The later term, it has been said, substitutes "a word of a more solemn ring, of darker or more tragic implications for a word of a more casual sound. . . .")[5] In groups a "splitting of the superego takes place, and as a member of the group the individual accepts moral standards that as a private person he would reject. . . ."[6] The individual regresses to the extent that "in obedience to the new authority he . . . put[s] his former "conscience" out of action, and so surrender[s] to the attraction of the increased pleasure that is certainly obtained from

---

[4] Ibid., pp. 78–80.

[5] Waelder: *Basic Theory of Psychoanalysis*, p. 188.

[6] Heinz Hartmann: "On Rational and Irrational Action," in *Psychoanalysis and the Social Sciences*, Vol. I, ed. Geza Roheim (New York: International Universities Press; 1947), p. 374.

the removal of inhibitions."[7] By the communal externaliza-
iton of superegos, group norms can support delinquent
conduct which private consciences could not tolerate. In
fact, of course, the existence of two moralities, public and
private, has been proclaimed before by writers like Thucy-
dides and Machiavelli; it is what Cavour meant when he
exclaimed what scoundrels we would be if we did for ourselves what we do for our country.

Yet if the new tie to the group is a stable one, a higher—
less instinctual—form of conscience is made possible. While
from the point of view of the individual it constitutes a
regression, from the point of view of the group as a whole
it may well mean that more exacting conduct is expected
of its members. The problem is largely an organizational
one; "how to procure for the group precisely those features
which were characteristic of the individual and which are
extinguished in him by the formation of the group."[8]

Freud takes as examples of the ethically successful organization of groups the Catholic Church and the Army. In
both cases there is a leader, Christ and the Commander-in-
Chief respectively, to whom obedience is due, and who in
turn treats his followers with equal affection. For Freud
the existence of a leader was the crucial point in understanding the psychology of the group. He recognized "the
possibility of a leading idea being substituted for a
leader. . . ,"[9] which he was later to illustrate with the
theory of how the communal standards of the Mosaic religion had held the Jews together. There had at any rate to
be a common focus to ensure a father surrogate. There

[7] *Standard Edition*, Vol. 18, p. 85.
[8] Ibid., p. 86.
[9] Ibid., p. 95.

would then be a sufficient motive for overcoming anarchistic drives. The members of the group would be doubly bound, not only to obey the leader but to respect each other as the leader's equal subjects.

Freud had formulated a new explanation for the sub-missiveness of the masses. Indeed men behaved irrationally in groups; it was the credulity of love. Phenomena associated with political obedience have long puzzled social thinkers. It is well known that "men's devotion to societies and institutions is usually out of proportion to their belief in their utility."[1] Instead of ascribing obedience to the magical powers of "suggestion," Freud traced it to libido: "we will try our fortune . . . with the supposition that love relationships (or, to use a more neutral expression, emotional ties) . . . constitute the essence of the group mind."[2] Social cohesion comes from libidinal ties inhibited in their aim. Only affection for others is sufficient to overcome self-love; for the sake of the leader the members of the group renounce their aversion to obedience.

Freud expressed this whole relationship in clinical concepts made possible by the growth of psychoanalytic ego psychology. Beginning with the metapsychological papers of the period around World War I, and then in the 1920's with *Group Psychology and the Analysis of the Ego* and later in *The Ego and the Id* and *The Problem of Anxiety*, Freud recast psychoanalytic theory in terms of the ego. In essence he was adding the structural point of view to his metapsychology. He was now interested in those unconscious mechanisms within the ego which are responsible for normal psychological development. Whereas he had earlier considered defenses against instinctual drives mainly

[1] Plamenatz: *The English Utilitarians*, p. 154.
[2] *Standard Edition*, Vol. 18, p. 91.

as neurotic distortions, he now saw them more in their function as adaptive sublimations.

One should not overlook within earlier psychoanalytic thinking the hints of this later perspective. "Freud's concept of psychoanalysis has from the very first, ever since the *Studies on Hysteria*, embraced the ego. . . , the forces of defence as well as those they oppose, whether they appeared as the censorship or under some other name. . . ."[3] Only in those days "defense" referred mainly to repression; as Freud put it, psychoanalysis first came to know the ego "only as a repressive, censoring agency, capable of erecting protective structures and reactive formations."[4] Whatever drives the ego had were largely negative ones: as in *Studies on Hysteria* the ego was responsible for maintaining self-deception, for keeping various human needs out of awareness. "In most of the great case histories . . . little is said about the ego."[5] "Only in the twenties was ego psychology explicitly defined as a legitimate chapter of analysis."[6]

Psychoanalysis' concern with ego psychology is sometimes attributed to its need to explain psychoses, which are accompanied by extreme regressions to earlier ego states. For example, magical thinking and general narcissism are more pronounced in the schizophrenias than in the neuroses; and in the melancholias, there is a splitting within the ego itself. Psychoanalytic understanding of war neuroses also helped provoke this change. In addition, the shift toward ego psychology among psychoanalysts was in part a response to their increased concern with therapeutic treat-

---

[3] Ernst Kris: "Book Review of *The Ego and Mechanisms of Defence*," *International Journal of Psychoanalysis*, Vol. 19 (1938), p. 141.

[4] *Standard Edition*, Vol. 18, p. 51.

[5] Hartmann: "The Development of the Ego Concept in Freud's Work," p. 432.

[6] Heinz Hartmann: "The Mutual Influences in the Development of the Ego and the Id," *Psychoanalytic Study of the Child*, Vol. 7, p. 9.

ment, as opposed to their original interest in more abstract understanding. The most healthy part of the patient's ego is that which is most readily available to the therapist as an ally.

For Freud himself the conceptual understanding of the ego came mainly after the loss of Adler and Jung. He was in a sense integrating the insights of his lost supporters within his own terminology. It was as if Freud were handling the loss of his followers by incorporating their insights into his evolving system in order magically to retain their support. For it was Adler who had stressed the individual's attempts to maintain self-esteem through a variety of "fictive-goals," overcompensations for feelings of inadequacy. Adler also stressed the importance of the "secondary gains" of neurotic illness, the uses to the individual's ego of remaining ill. "Adler's concept of man's struggle for self-assertion and power, and his understanding of the ways in which individuals utilize their own problems in the act of overcoming them, foreshadowed the Freudian 'ego psychology.' . . ."[7] A later ego psychologist explicitly acknowledged that his postulated "'instinct to master' is essentially the same as Alfred Adler's will to power."[8]

It is very hard to be original in psychoanalysis; each succeeding generation of psychoanalysts finds it difficult to invent new formulations. In the case of Jung's theories, Freud's pupils also later integrated some of a renegade's insights. For example, Ernst Kris's concept of "regression in the service of the ego"[9] is similar to Jung's insistence on

[7] Leon Edel: "Criticism and Psychoanalysis," *Chicago Review*, Vol. 5, No. 2 (Autumn 1961), p. 104.

[8] Ives Hendrick: "The Discussion of the 'Instinct to Master,'" *The Psychoanalytic Quarterly*, Vol. 12, No. 4 (1943), p. 563.

[9] Ernst Kris: "Art and Regression," *Transactions of the New York Academy of Sciences*, Series II, Vol. 6 (1943–4), pp. 236–50.

the "creativity" of the unconscious. Jung related the arche-
typal night journey, the descent into the unconscious, to
the ultimate growth of the personality. It is no accident
that Jung's theories have had such an appeal for literary
people nor that Kris came to psychoanalysis from art history. For in these areas the role of inspiration, of "creative
madness," is apparent. Under certain conditions, the release of primary unconscious impulses may lead to artistic
creativity. If, that is, the regression can be contained "in
the service of the ego," which is what Jung had meant by
the "descent into the unconscious." Under conditions of
ego strength one can contain the regression and use it for
artistic purposes; "the integrative functions of the ego may
include self-regulated regression."[1] If the ego should lack
that integrating capacity, it would simply be swamped by
unconscious impulses.

Acknowledging the contributions of Adler and Jung to
contemporary ego psychology, we must still add that in
Freud's most abstract view of the ego it functions as a
protective barrier against stimulation, whether from drives
within the psyche or from external reality. The ego's main
task is to keep on an even keel of psychological excitation; for this purpose anxiety is "a danger-signal given
by the ego as a warning against the danger of the approach
of a state of psychic helplessness in the face of overwhelming stimulation."[2] The ego is now treated as a coherent organization of psychic forces in its own right, perhaps
possessing a developmental cycle apart from that of the
drives. For our purposes here we need not compare alter-

[1] Karl Menninger: *Theory of Psychoanalytic Technique* (New York: Science
Editions; 1961), p. 49.
[2] Edward Glover: *The Technique of Psychoanalysis* (New York: International
Universities Press; 1955), p. 77.

native ego psychologies; it is enough to remember that *Group Psychology and the Analysis of the Ego* has to be understood as an aspect of the development of the structural point of view.

For Freud the character of the ego was a "precipitate of abandoned object-cathexes and . . . contains the history of those object-choices."[3] The growth of the individual's ego in relation to familial figures constitutes a crucial developmental link between the child and society. The growing child models itself on its parents and other adults whom he loves. By identifying with these figures, the child's ego can draw strength; the mental energy which formerly constituted the affection for these outer objects now goes toward the images of those objects left behind within the child's ego.

This mechanism of identification, which Freud describes in *Group Psychology and the Analysis of the Ego*, is a crucial concept in child development. "A little boy will exhibit a special interest in his father; he would like to grow like him and be like him, and take his place everywhere. We may say simply that he takes his father as his ideal."[4] We have already seen the relevance of this concept for understanding the "passing" of the oedipal stage. In addition, identification helps explain the basis for melancholic depressions. Having been disappointed in a love relationship, the subject, instead of simply relinquishing the object in the real world, regressively introjects it within his own ego. He magically identifies through incorporation with the object, rather than rationally accepting its loss. The self-reproaches that the melancholic directs to his own ego are explained by the hate he feels for an object which he can-

[3] *Standard Edition*, Vol. 19, p. 29.
[4] Ibid., Vol. 18, p. 105.

not give up. He is disappointed, he rages against the object; yet because the original relationship was made on a narcissistic basis, the object can be introjected into the self. Aggression which normally would be directed outside is redirected within. Dostoevsky understood this phenomenon with the uncanny intuition of the natural psychologist:

This sort of thing . . . often happens among the Japanese. A man who's been insulted goes to his adversary and says to him, "you've insulted me, and to pay you back I've come to rip my belly open before your eyes," and, having said that, he really does rip it open before his adversary's eyes and, I daresay, feels highly gratified, as though he had really revenged himself.[5]

Since Freud wrote his *Group Psychology and the Analysis of the Ego*, far more subtle psychoanalytic explorations of identifications have been possible. It has generally been admitted that in Freud's work the term identification covers a very wide variety of phenomena. But what Freud elucidated here, the notion of a divided ego, was of decisive importance for the future of psychoanalysis. He had previously written about the phenomenon of conscience and had used the concept of the "ego-ideal" to explain it. Now Freud's whole theoretical orientation began to shift; clinical phenomena would receive henceforth a more refined conceptualization. "Freud's early emphasis on pathogenic id tendencies and on the modes of the id demands as the most important factors in symptom formation gradually gave way to his increased interest in the ego and its repressed forces, as well as in identification, as factors leading to symptom formation."[6] Here in *Group Psychology and the Analysis of the Ego* Freud used the notion of a split

[5] F. Dostoevsky: *The Idiot* (London: Penguin Books; 1955), p. 208.
[6] Felix Deutsch, ed.: *On the Mysterious Leap from the Mind to the Body* (New York: International Universities Press; 1959), p. 37.

ego—the intellectual possibilities inherent in the division between the ego and the conscience—along with the mechanism of identification, to explain the character of group cohesion.

Freud's formula had great simplicity: "A number of individuals . . . have put one and the same object in the place of their ego ideal and have consequently identified themselves with one another in their ego."[7] Put less succinctly, Freud hypothesizes that each member of the group is able to introject into his ego ideal the same outer object, the leader. The tie that binds them to their fellow members is precisely the fact that they all have a common ego ideal. It is a libidinal tie, inhibited in aim, in the sense that the original choice of a leader was grounded in the child's love for his father, the child's need for authority. Yet it is a regressive bond, to the extent that an identification is a more primitive form of relationship to one's environment than an object relationship.

Freud could test his hypothesis by examples of panic states, where a group disintegrates after the loss of a leader.

It is of the very essence of panic that it bears no relation to the danger that threatens, and often breaks out on the most trivial occasions. . . . The loss of the leader in some sense or other, the birth of misgivings about him, brings on the outbreak of panic . . . the mutual ties between the members of the group disappear, as a rule, at the same time as the tie with their leader.[8]

People behave differently under the stress of panic; they lose their normal control over their primitive selves, become unable to tolerate delay or frustration, and confuse inner and outer realities as they regress. The collapse of

[7] *Standard Edition*, Vol. 18, p. 116.
[8] Ibid., pp. 96–7.

the group releases the hostility which had been bound up in the libidinal ties; instinctual defusion occurs. The Great Fear of the countryside of pre-revolutionary France becomes comprehensible. The insecurities which are satisfied by group life are revealed when the group ties exist no longer.

Fundamentally Freud was here simply extending the insights of *Totem and Taboo*. The group is seen as a revival of the primal horde.

The leader of the group is still the dreaded primal father; the group still wishes to be governed by unrestricted force; it has an extreme passion for authority; in Le Bon's phrase, it has a thirst for obedience. The primal father is the group ideal, which governs the ego in the place of the ego ideal.[9]

The family is still the prototype of authority relationships. As Freud later wrote, "What began in relation to the father is completed in relation to the group."[1]

Freud's description of the mechanism by which dependence on the father surrogate also unites one member of a group with another is an advance made possible by ego psychology—by the elucidation of the mechanism of identification in object relationships, as well as by the postulation of a "differentiating grade in the ego" (the ego ideal). In *Totem and Taboo* Freud proposed that guilt over their murderous deeds and wishes bound the members of a society together; in other words, conscience was seen as a reaction to aggressive drives. Now in *Group Psychology and the Analysis of the Ego* conscience is seen as a more positive aspect of the ego itself. Just as the child renounces his aggression not only because of fear of punishment but also

9 Ibid., p. 127.
1 Ibid., Vol. 21, p. 133.

because he wants his father's love, so the adult obeys not only as a reaction to guilt over aggression, but also because he can identify with his fellow citizens by means of a similar love for a common object.

It is by now clear that it is far too simple to consider Freud's thesis in *Group Psychology and the Analysis of the Ego* as an outgrowth of his "conservative snobberies."[2] David Riesman is equally far afield in thinking that here Freud "wants to justify contemporary authority by throwing over it the mantle of the primal father."[3] As becomes apparent when interpreted within its context, Freud's whole interest in the group "may be much more important in terms of his tendency to develop ego psychology than in terms of his interest in any scientific treatment of the group per se."[4] As Kris once pointed out, the book "was not written as a treatise in social psychology . . . [but] to clarify further the structural model of the personality which he was developing at the time."[5]

As we have said, no very solid conclusions about Freud's social views can be drawn from his citation of Le Bon. There is, to be sure, a strain within Freud's thought which suggests suspicion of the masses and disdain toward unintellectual Gentiles. Yet it is only a strain, and is in a sense an aspect of the whole Enlightenment rationalism behind psychoanalytic treatment itself. In *Group Psychology and the Analysis of the Ego* Freud retained the same classically liberal model of society he had used in *Totem and Taboo*.

[2] Rieff: "Psychology and Politics," *World Politics*, Vol. 7, No. 2 (January 1955), p. 300.

[3] Riesman: *Individualism Reconsidered*, p. 209.

[4] Fritz Schmidl: "Freud's Sociological Thinking," *Bulletin of the Menninger Clinic*, Vol. 16, No. 1 (January 1952), p. 9.

[5] Ernst Kris: "Some Problems of War Propaganda," *Psychoanalytic Quarterly*, Vol. 12 (1943), p. 394.

The state and the individual, with no groups in between, was the traditional liberal view. In order to sweep away the chaos of feudal restrictions, liberals had to rely on a sharp instrument—often a centralized monarchy—to undermine feudal institutions; hence Voltaire's theory of enlightened despotism.[6]

Liberalism repeatedly resorted to a top and bottom analysis of political society. While Freud does acknowledge that "each individual is a component part of numerous groups, [that] he is bound by ties of identification in many directions,"[7] he does not explore the implications for social unity of this multiplicity of ties. The model he is fascinated with is that of the leader and the led; and this can be traced, if one cares to use political categories, to his characteristic liberalism. It can of course be said of Freud's theory that it does little to explain day-to-day politics. Freud's intellectual commitment to the father-son relationship, as well as his retention of the liberal image of society, hinder him from seeing the functions of the vast range of social institutions that cushion the relationship of the individual to his leader. In other words, he did not see the variety of possibilities in group life.

But it is perhaps unfair to demand too much of any great theorist. Freud has offered us an original theory of the mechanism of social cohesion; in addition to common guilt and the need for self-preservation, there are aim-inhibited libidinal ties between members of society founded on their common identification with a leader. While Freud may challenge Hume's theory that habit is responsible for social unity, since "habit" is merely a descriptive and not an ex-

---

[6] I am indebted for this conception of liberalism to Professor Louis Hartz, Harvard University.

[7] *Standard Edition*, Vol. 18, p. 129.

planatory concept, psychoanalysis can supplement Weber's
theory of the importance of a shared belief in legitimacy.
It is enough to see how Freud adds to our understanding of
political psychology.


## 4   Ego Psychology

Just what the growth of the structural point of view might
mean for psychoanalysis has become clear only since Freud's
death. The full-scale development of ego psychology has in
fact been the central direction of psychoanalytic thinking
since the late 1930's. If one had to express in a phrase what
there was about Freud's earlier work which it has taken
a generation of psychoanalytic thinking to overcome, one
would single out his negativism. Stefan Zweig captured
this part of Freud's character: writing in 1933, he saw in
Freud

the expression of an indomitable, almost mordant will. In the
earlier portraits the glance was simply contemplative, but now
it is piercing and gloomy; the brow is deeply furrowed, as if
with bitterness and suspicion. The lips are narrowed, tensed, as
though he were uttering an emphatic "No," or coldly saying
"That is false." For the first time we are aware that a mighty
impetus, the severity of a formidable nature, are manifest in the
face, and we murmur to ourselves: "No, this is not a good, grey
old man, mellowed by the years, but an inexorable scrutineer, a
rigorous examiner, who will neither try to deceive nor allow
himself to be deceived."[1]

[1] Stefan Zweig: *Mental Healers* (London: Cassell; 1933), p. 272. As Jones
put it, "It was characteristically in negative resistance that his will displayed
unusual strength . . . 'No' could be a powerful word to him. In his old age
he would repeat the words *'nein, nein, nein,'* to the accompaniment of a vigorous shaking of the head. . . ." Jones: *Sigmund Freud*, Vol. 2, p. 428.

Freud demanded more of people, and sometimes he got it; he expected patients to be able to grow up. He was a nay-sayer, and not among the lovers of mankind. It is so characteristic of Freud, for example, to use a series of negatives in order to assert the positive. In a letter, for example, he writes that "there are times when one is not inclined to write, but I should not like not to be in contact with you."[2] He seems, moreover, to have been aware of his inner harshness; as he wrote of an etching completed for his seventieth birthday in 1926, it "strikes me as excellent. Others find its expression too severe, almost angry. Inwardly this is probably what I am."[3]

One does not have to look very far within early psychoanalytic theory to find the manifestations of these personal qualities of Freud in his work. The terminology has a marked negative cast to it; "pathography" rather than psychological biography, "organ psychosis" instead of psychosomatic medicine, and so on. Freud's whole system was designed to explain motivation when a person is in conflict, when the ego has relatively failed at its integrative task. As a therapist, Freud was preoccupied with pulling problems apart and tearing fixations asunder, on the assumption that the patient's ego would be able to put the pieces back together again. For Freud analysis was automatically synthesis; constructive processes were taken for granted. A centipede was once asked how he knew which foot to put forward next; he never, so the story goes, walked again.

Freud understood every conceivable means of self-deception; but he ignored many processes of self-healing. The main trend within recent years has been to correct this im-

[2] Quoted in *Psychoanalytic Pioneers*, p. 413.
[3] Freud: *Letters*, p. 370.

balance in psychoanalytic theory, and to focus on the ego as an agency integrating inner needs and outer realities. The ego has a unifying function, ensuring coherent behavior and conduct. The job of the ego is not just the negative one of avoiding anxiety, but also the positive one of maintaining effective performance. The ego's defenses are not necessarily all pathogenic; they may be adaptive as well as maladaptive. Adaptation is bedeviled of course by anxieties and guilts; but the ego's strength is not measured by the earlier psychoanalytic standard of what in a personality is denied or cut off, but rather by all the extremes that an individual's ego is able to unify.

It would of course be misleading to claim too widespread an agreement among psychoanalytic theorists about the course of recent thinking; but whatever the points at issue, a unity of mood prevails. Currently there is a greater preoccupation with what Freud would have called the life instincts, those curative tendencies or strivings for self-fulfillment. There was a radicalism, even a shocking quality, to many of the early psychoanalytic formulations; contemporary ego psychology has a tamer, more "healthy-minded" quality. It is not past fixations that matter so much, but present meanings and future possibilities.

One can illustrate this new trend in psychoanalytic thinking by a shift in the conceptualization of the psychology of dreams. Freud's focus was on the dream as the bearer of one's infantile past; it was, Freud thought, the normal prototype of the psychosis. The dream was conceived as a disturbance of the state of sleep, evidence of failure in that the ego is unable to fulfill its wish to sleep.[4]

---

[4] Kurt Eissler: *Medical Orthodoxy and the Future of Psychoanalysis* (New York: International Universities Press; 1965), p. 17.

The post-Freudian interpretation of dreams accepts, of course, the premise that dreaming is a meaningful mental activity. But whatever the structural similarities between a dream and a symptom, their functions are quite different. Dreaming is now seen as a healthy and necessary activity; there is even experimental evidence to prove the disturbing consequences of being deprived of one's dreams. While a dream may release instinctual wishes, as Freud first postulated, it also helps the ego to master problems. From the point of view of ego psychology, it makes sense that we should wake up with a feeling of wholeness from a good night's sleep; dreaming serves integrating needs, and to be cut off from one's dream life would endanger one's sense of continuity and integrity. Erik Erikson has done as much as anyone to shift psychoanalysis away from the view that dreaming is an index of ego weakness: "the dream must help us awake with a sense of wholeness, centrality, and competence—in other words, in an ego state of active tension. . . . As long as the sleeper can thus relax, dream well, and wake ready for action, do we really have a right to say that his ego in the state of sleep was "weak"?[5]

Freud himself was responsible for the beginnings of this shift within psychoanalysis toward ego psychology. Yet it came in the last years of his life, when more and more he took an abstract view of personality, as an object to be investigated rather than as a human being to be cured. In the hands of some of his followers, ego psychology has produced an abstract metaphysics, a language from which human emotions have almost disappeared. Freud's theoretical talents could lead to mechanical formalization and freez-

[5] Erik Erikson: *Insight and Responsibility* (New York: W. W. Norton; 1964), pp. 198–200.

ing of clinical realities. His late work was more human than
before, in the sense of accepting the place of external reality
and of an organizing ego within his system; and yet it was
less human and more sterile in that it had less contact with
living clinical details. The early case histories of Freud's,
no matter how unbalanced theoretically they now look, had
an unequalled richness and fullness to them; so many
levels in the patients are displayed simultaneously that they
seem to resemble short stories or novels. Freud's late work
needed to be more intellectually rounded, partly because it
lacked the roundedness of life itself. No one could say of
his last clinical works that they read like novels.

The one ego psychologist who is still able to write like
a novelist is Erikson. His place within psychoanalysis is
unique; his work has sanctioned new concepts and permitted people to think heterodox thoughts. When once a
man dares to think new ideas, we forget how much easier
it makes it for the rest of us. Erikson has emphasized the
sense of identity as an integrating agent, and the ways in
which a defective identity can be responsible for pathology
which once would have been traced to instinctual drives.

Rage, for example, can result from an individual's blocked
sense of mastery. Aggression can stem from an inability to
tolerate passivity and helplessness. Sometimes we would
rather be bad than weak. In Erikson's terms, aggressiveness
can be a defense against a sense of identity diffusion. The
concept of the ego's integrating needs is at odds with Freud's
image of the individual personality as a passive archeological mound, organized "in layers; as he [the individual]
grows he makes the past part of all future, and every environment, as he once experienced it, part of the present
environment."[6] Identity formation, which is founded on

[6] Erikson: *Young Man Luther*, pp. 117–18.

ideal prototypes, develops by its opposition to what Erikson calls negative identity, which is based on models of evil:

Negative identity . . . is composed of the images of that personal and collective past which is to be lived down and of that potential future which is to be forestalled. . . . Identity formation involves a continuous conflict with powerful negative identity elements: what we know or fear or are told we are but try not to be or not to see; and what we consequently see in exaggeration in others. In times of aggravated crises all this can arouse in man a murderous hate of all kinds of "otherness," in strangers and in himself.[7]

Because of ego psychology's explicit attention to the interaction of internal and external realities, it has opened up possibilities for interdisciplinary cooperation with the social sciences. To emphasize the way in which ego psychology has shifted psychoanalytic thinking, we can compare Kris's study of Nazi propaganda during World War II with Freud's own essays on war. As we saw earlier, Freud viewed wartime brutality primarily from the point of view of the instincts; wartime released the civilized inhibitions, and erotic and aggressive drives defused as society regressed. Instead of approaching the problem of brutality from the viewpoint of drive regression, Kris took his starting point within ego psychology. Sanctioned criminality, Kris argued, was a powerful cement for binding together German society in the war effort.

Brutality . . . is not mainly a direct expression of regression or of deterioration of standards. Brutality is part of planned psychological manipulation and is supposed to serve a number of purposes. One of the purposes is the intimidation of actual and potential opponents. Another is to give the impression of strength

[7] Erik Erikson: "Psychoanalysis and On-Going History," *The American Journal of Psychiatry*, Vol. 122, No. 3 (September 1965), p. 246.

and determination so frequently linked to ruthlessness. A third, we believe, is the attempt to create a feeling of complicity among the German people.[8]

Common participation in crime can be a powerful element in group identification; association in crime, by stimulating guilt feelings, promotes unity. The Nazis saw the social usefulness of their atrocities; Goebbels announced openly that "the annihilation of the Jewish race in Europe is now being fulfilled."[9] There is therefore a sense in which the Nazis made the Germans blood brothers. Through identificatory ties with the leaders, as well as by the actual commission of crimes, social solidarity could be reinforced. In this respect *Group Psychology and the Analysis of the Ego* had made intellectually unnecessary the primal deed of *Totem and Taboo*.

According to Kris, the Nazi propagandists wanted to get all they could from the atrocities; they not only reinforced guilt feelings among the Germans, but transformed them into fears of retaliation. "Dr. Goebbels . . . [embarked] upon an elaborate description of what Jewish revenge would be like in case of a German defeat."[1] German solidarity could be strengthened by projecting all the hostility underlying the German exterminations and the war effort onto the mythical Jewish enemy. German national self-esteem could be maintained by imputing all their hatred to a scapegoat; and German unity could be solidified by the common focus on an enemy. The ingenuity of the Nazis consisted in their daring attempt to stimulate fears of talionic revenge. "By announcing openly the plan for the an-

[8] Ernst Kris: "The Covenant of the Gangsters," *Journal of Criminal Psychopathology*, Vol. 4, No. 3 (January 1943), pp. 448–9.

[9] Quoted in ibid., p. 454.

[1] Ibid.

nihilation of the Jews he [Goebbels] wanted to transform the guilt feelings of the Germans into fear of retribution."[2]

Kris's thesis is in a sense an extension of Freud's argument in *Group Psychology and the Analysis of the Ego*. It demonstrates the way in which a common identification with a leader—Hitler—permits psychologically regressive acts. The leader became the superego; the individuals no longer had civilized consciences. Yet all their guilt over aggression remained. And it is this that potentially gives the leader so much leverage. He can "activate anxiety through guilt for his own advantage, not for the sake of the led."[3] Franz Neumann has elegantly formulated this device:

There are anxiety and an unconscious feeling of guilt. It is the task of the leader, by creating neurotic anxiety, to tie the led so closely to the leader that they would perish without identification with him. Then the leader orders the commission of crimes: but these are, in accord with the morality that prevails in the group . . . no crimes, but fundamentally moral acts. But the . . . superego . . . protests against the morality of the crimes, for the old moral convictions cannot simply be extirpated. The feeling of guilt is thus repressed and makes anxiety a nearly panicky one, which can be overcome only through unconditional surrender to the leader and compels the commission of new crimes.[4]

The importance of this thesis about totalitarian societies is not limited to the particular political systems involved. To the extent that every society and the groups within it are held together by mechanisms such as these—guilt feelings, scapegoats, identifications with leaders—every political community is open to the manipulation of the anxieties of the people. As Neumann puts it, "every political system

[2] Ibid., p. 457.
[3] Neumann: *The Democratic and the Authoritarian State*, p. 292.
[4] Ibid., p. 293.

is based on anxiety."[5] This is in a sense the fundamental psychological truth found in Freud's tale of the primal deed of *Totem and Taboo*. There he had seen to what extent all social restrictions are founded on guilt feelings; internalized aggression was seen as a socially cementing force. "Society was now based on complicity in the common crime; religion was based on the sense of guilt and the remorse attaching to it; while morality was based partly on the exigencies of this society and partly on the penance demanded by the sense of guilt."[6]

The development of ego psychology serves as a bridge to the social sciences precisely because of its attention to processes of adaptation; in terms of the example of social cohesion, the splits within the superego are not looked on solely from the standpoint of individually regressive acts, but rather from that of the consequences for the individual's relationship to the social unit as a whole. Acts may on one level constitute gratification of id impulses—here both loving dependence and destructive aggression—while they also, from the viewpoint of the ego and superego, serve purposes of social adjustment.

Adorno has extended our understanding of the ego mechanisms involved in totalitarian mass movements. His explicit starting point is *Group Psychology and the Analysis of the Ego*: "Freud, though he was hardly interested in the political phase of the problem, clearly foresaw the rise and nature of fascist mass movements in purely psychological categories."[7] Adorno stresses how primitive the identificatory ties between leader and led can become. Submitting to

[5] Ibid., p. 291.

[6] *Standard Edition*, Vol. 13, p. 146.

[7] T. W. Adorno: "Freudian Theory and the Pattern of Fascist Propaganda," *Psychoanalysis and the Social Sciences*, Vol. 3, ed. Geza Roheim (New York: International Universities Press; 1951), p. 281.

a totalitarian leader can solve more psychic conflicts than just what the security of a collective father figure can satisfy:

The primitively narcissistic aspect of identification as an act of *devouring*, of making the beloved object part of oneself, may provide us with a clue to the fact that the modern leader image sometimes seems to be the enlargement of the subject's own personality, a collective projection of himself, rather than the image of the father . . . by making the leader his ideal he loves himself, as it were, but gets rid of the strains of frustration and discontent which mar his picture of his own empirical self.[8]

The figure of the totalitarian leader can thus satisfy both aspects of a primitive wish, "to submit to authority and to be the authority. . . ."[9]

Ego psychology can help us understand the general role of political leadership. In a totalitarian state, say Hitler Germany, the identifications between leaders and led can be understood in terms of id and superego functions. "Totalitarian propaganda tries to sway the audience into participation; its preferred setting is the visible leader talking to the masses; it is modeled after the relations between the hypnotist and his medium."[1] As we have already seen, totalitarianism encourages not only pathological dependence on the leader, an acceptance of Hitler's standards, but also considerable instinctual release in sanctioned aggression.

In democratic states, on the other hand, the identifications between leaders and led ideally focus instead on ego functions. The task of the leadership stratum is to anticipate danger situations and to prove its competency by making factual information public. In this sense Churchill's

[8] Ibid., p. 288.

[9] Ibid., p. 290.

[1] Kris and Leites: "Trends in Twentieth Century Propaganda," *Psychoanalysis and the Social Sciences*, Vol. I, p. 404.

greatness in 1940 consisted in his ability to transform unknown danger "into a danger known in kind and extent.
He fulfilled those functions of leadership that can be compared to those fulfilled in the life of the individual by the
organization of the ego."[2]

Such a distinction between totalitarianism and democracy
is of limited value in helping to understand the actual political processes of specific states, which often contain elements
of both. But the more even distribution of ego and superego
components in the identificatory ties to democratic leaders
may have consequences in the degree to which rational responses to military setbacks are at all possible. One reason,
then, for the relative resilience of democratic states is the
extent to which their members have not resorted to the more
primitive mechanisms within the id and the superego.
Rather, they have allocated to leaders those functions of the
ego which as a group they are incapable of retaining for
themselves. In fact, it may well be that "the non-affective
identification with an institution (state) is less regressive
than identification with a leader."[3]

## 5    Freud's Political Psychology

It is proper to speak of Freud's "political psychology" only
in a very limited sense. It is merely our own political interests that have led us to ferret out Freud's political comments. Despite his youthful ambition to become a political
leader, as an adult he had very little emotional stake in
politics; he voted rarely, usually whenever there was a Lib-

---

[2] Ibid., p. 406–7.
[3] Neumann: *The Democratic and the Authoritarian State*, p. 282.

eral candidacy in his district. Freud's local interest in Viennese politics centered largely on the progress of the anti-Semitic movement. Politics never formed a very important part of his general intellectual concern. Max Eastman once asked him, "What are you politically?" "Politically I am just nothing," Freud replied.[1]

The one time that Freud was aroused on a strictly political issue was after the Versailles peace conference. Like other liberals, Freud felt that Wilson had betrayed his promises. In the late 1920's and early 1930's Freud collaborated with Ambassador W. C. Bullitt in writing a psychoanalytic study of the President. It remained unpublished until 1967. Since Freud was born in the same year as Wilson, and was beset by a similar combination of intolerance and idealism, one could have guessed that this study would reveal as much about Freud himself as his books on Leonardo and Moses. This study of Wilson can be considered the hidden ancestor of the tradition of psychoanalytic debunking, perhaps the only occasion on which Freud used psychoanalysis as a tool of social warfare.

Aside from World War I itself, the major political event of Freud's maturity was the Russian Revolution. Here Freud was always skeptical. He acknowledged "the grandeur of the plan [the U.S.S.R.] and its importance for the future of human civilization. . . ."[2] But as early as 1919 he felt that the inevitable suffering would outweigh the cultural benefits of the new regime. In part it was a matter of temperament, in part an outcome of psychoanalysis. According to Wortis, Freud remarked that "Communism and psychoanalysis go ill together."[3] He was right, in that the

---

[1] Max Eastman: "Differing with Sigmund Freud," p. 128.

[2] *Standard Edition*, Vol. 21, pp. 8–9.

[3] Wortis: *Fragments of an Analysis with Freud*, p. 161.

Communists had closed down the psychoanalytic movement in Russia just as it began to flourish (1929). To
Freud communism was another religion, offering suffering believers an illusory compensation in a future world.
Barbarism flourished again under the banner of progress. If
the confrontation of Marx and Freud is one of the conundrums of our time, Freud personally was willing to brush
the whole Marxist system aside. The task of doctrinal reconciliation was bequeathed to others.

At times Freud could utter historical sentiments that
strike us as downright reactionary. One good litmus test of
a man's political leanings is his attitude toward the French
Revolution. In his *The Interpretation of Dreams*, Freud
paused to remark:

. . . who . . . could fail to be gripped by narratives of the Reign
of Terror, when the men and women of the aristocracy, the
flower of the nation, showed that they could die with a cheerful
mind and could retain the liveliness of their wit and the elegance of their manners till the very moment of the fatal sum-
mons?[4]

Still, whatever Freud's romantic sympathy for the old
regime, whatever his doubts about the success of the Revolution in his own time, he retained a personal sympathy for
the underprivileged:

Anyone who has lived through the misery of poverty in his
youth, and has endured the indifference and arrogance of those
who have possessions, should be exempt from any suspicion of
having no understanding of or goodwill toward the endeavors
made to combat the economic inequality of men and all that it
leads to.[5]

[4] *Standard Edition*, Vol. 5, pp. 496–7.
[5] Jones: *Sigmund Freud*, Vol. III, p. 334.

Freud was in favor of greater economic egalitarianism, without expecting that it would produce significant alterations for the better in basic human nature.

None of these views is especially remarkable. What is unusual about Freud's political psychology, in the limited sense of his occasional asides or implicit assumptions, is the extent to which it is elitist; and this cannot be entirely explained by the preoccupations of psychoanalysis proper. Freud could think that it is "impossible to grasp the nature of a group if the leader is disregarded"[6] precisely because he was so great an aristocrat of the spirit and of intelligence. He felt that only the enlightened few could do without religion: "The analyst can of course make a bad technical mistake if he creates the impression of belittling this emotional demand [for religion], or calls on everyone to overcome a piece of infantilism which only a few are capable of overcoming."[7] And he could write in a letter that "I have found little that is 'good' about human beings on the whole. In my experience most of them are trash. . . ."[8] On the other hand, he retained the Enlightenment faith in reason and there was a deeply rationalist character to his thought. He did write *The Future of an Illusion*; and he never failed to ask of men "whether they *must* be like this, whether their innermost nature necessitates it?"[9]

Freud's elitism, his feeling that at present, at any rate, the few must set the example, lay behind a good deal of his social thinking. We have seen how large a place he allotted to creative political leadership in his hypothesis about Moses and the Jews; Moses had to be an Egyptian *noble-*

---

[6] *Standard Edition*, Vol. 18, p. 119.
[7] Freud: *Psychoanalysis and Faith*, p. 118.
[8] Ibid., p. 61.
[9] *Standard Edition*, Vol. 21, p. 47.

*man* if Freud's fantasies were to be retained. And in his essays on war, Freud on leadership sounds very much like Bagehot; he thinks it advisable to "educate an upper strata of men with independent minds."[1] As he once wrote,

It is only through the influence of individuals who can set an example and whom masses recognize as their leaders that they can be induced to perform the work. . . . One . . . gets the impression that civilization is something which was imposed on a resisting majority by a minority which understood how to obtain possession of the means to power and coercion.[2]

Still, he considered that "the ideal condition of things would . . . be a community of men who had subordinated their instinctual life to the dictatorship of reason."[3] He never abandoned this ultimate Enlightenment idealism.

This discrepancy between Freud's pessimism and his idealism was mirrored on a more abstract level in the tension between his political views and his religious ones. In the mythology of a nation, a political system has its secular gods. Freud was understandingly tolerant toward this sort of self-deception, while insisting that men outgrow their religious dependencies. Freud himself, in *The Future of an Illusion*, had asked "must not the assumptions that determine our political regulations be called illusions as well?"[4] There, he linked both religious and political superstitions: "So long as a person's early years are influenced not only by a sexual inhibition of thought but also by a religious inhibition and by a loyal [in regard to the Monarchy] inhibition derived from this, we cannot really tell what in

[1] Ibid., Vol. 22, p. 212.
[2] Ibid., Vol. 21, pp. 8, 6.
[3] Ibid., Vol. 22, p. 213.
[4] Ibid., Vol. 21, p. 34.

fact he is like."[5] In practice he never tried to reconcile these two aspects of his social thought; religion always seemed to Freud a more intolerable irrationality than political authority. In part this was no doubt a consequence of Catholic Austria, where the bureaucracy had a greater appeal for rationalists than the mysteries of the Church. Yet in theoretical terms, too, Freud was less hopeful of man's ability to do without illusions in political life. He was impressed by the "extent of man's inner instability and his consequent craving for authority."[6]

As a clinician, Freud was of course a meliorist as well as a scientist. In his role of a therapist he upheld the reality principle. "Men cannot remain children forever; they must in the end go out into 'hostile life.' "[7] As Freud described the analytic aim of psychic maturity,

The liberation of an individual, as he grows up, from the authority of his parents is one of the most necessary though one of the most painful results brought about by the course of his development. It is quite essential that that liberation should occur and it may be presumed that it has been to some extent achieved by everyone who has reached a normal state. Indeed, the whole progress of society rests upon the opposition between successive generations.[8]

Freud's whole therapy is aimed at liberation and independence.

It is therefore more than an exercise to relate Freud to the liberal tradition. As Erikson has pointed out, in Freud's day "nervous" patients were an exploited minority. In his

---

[5] Ibid., p. 48.
[6] Quoted in Jones: *Sigmund Freud*, Vol. III, p. 337.
[7] *Standard Edition*, Vol. 21, p. 49.
[8] Ibid., Vol. 9, p. 237.

respect for the dignity of his patients which made his discoveries possible, in his conviction that despite appearances
all men are psychologically brothers, and in his individualism—in all these ways it seems to me that Freud is indeed
a great heir of the Enlightenment. Sir Isaiah Berlin once
distinguished between liberals and conservatives by comparing them to claustrophobics and agoraphobics; liberals
always crave more space, while conservatives fear open
places.[9] By this standard, Freud is surely among those who
are ever demanding more freedom.

At the same time, however, we can see in the development of psychoanalysis how the open-ended quality of liberalism led to a revision of some of its most cherished
premises. For Freud represents an aspect of liberalism's self-
examination. It was after all an Enlightenment ideal to relate political values to human impulses, with the aim, as
Nietzsche exhorted, to achieve "the best that is in one."[1]

The trouble with the liberal tradition, of course, was its
narrowness of understanding, its difficulties which we have
encountered before in treating issues of human emotions.
The problem does not hinge on the alleged controversy in
intellectual history between pessimists and optimists regarding human nature. It is frequently maintained, for example,
that *The Federalist* papers exhibit a realism about human
motives, as well as a lack of utopianism about history, that
might well benefit contemporary political thinking. Yet in
comparison to Freud, *The Federalist* emerges as shallow on
human nature as much of the rest of liberalism. For while

---

[9] Sir Isaiah Berlin: *John Stuart Mill* (London: The Council of Christians and
Jews; 1959), p. 27.
[1] F. W. Nietzsche: *The Philosophy of Nietzsche* (New York: Modern Library;
1927), p. 561.

Madison and the others had a shrewd eye for human motivation, they lacked a sense of what Reinhold Niebuhr has called "the inordinancy of human lusts and ambitions."[2] Ambition can be made to counteract ambition, Madison tells us; human drives can be rearranged and engineered until a complicated clocklike mechanism of checks and balances emerges to ensure constitutionalism. This smacks more of a utilitarian gimmick than of psychological depth.

In Freud's quest for an understanding of human feelings he transcended liberalism and joined hands with thinkers usually associated with traditions alien to it. Along with Burke he recognized the intensity of destructive urges and the sense in which societal coercions can be psychologically necessary. With Marx he extended our appreciation of the extent of self-deception and self-alienation. And with both he could join the contemporary Augustinian complaint against classical liberalism:

. . . human ambitions, lusts and desires, are more inevitably inordinate . . . both human creativity and human evil reach greater heights, and . . . conflicts in the community between varying conceptions of the good and between competing expressions of vitality are of more tragic proportions than was anticipated in the basic philosophy which underlies democratic civilization.[3]

Unquestionably Freud challenges traditional liberal democratic theory. Alexander has summarized the nature of this confrontation:

Those who have advocated self-government and put their faith in the individual have sacrificed psychological insight and denied

[2] Reinhold Niebuhr: *Christian Realism and Practical Problems* (New York: Scribner's; 1953), p. 6.

[3] Reinhold Niebuhr: *The Children of Light and the Children of Darkness* (New York: Scribner's; 1944), p. 22.

or minimized the asocial forces in man, declaring him to be basically social, and exaggerating, as Locke did, the power of reason. The notion of a human nature in conflict with itself, disrupted by the opposition of social and asocial inclinations, the view that the social self develops from an asocial nucleus but that the social trends are also dynamic and emotional in nature, and finally the conception that reason's control can be extended by a detailed knowledge of the repressed asocial tendencies—all this was not known before Freud.[4]

Freud's shattering of rationalistic presuppositions is perhaps that aspect of his thought which has had the greatest effect on our political thinking. Freud demonstrated the degree to which the child lives within the adult, the extent to which psychological insecurities prevent men from ruling themselves. As Erikson has said, "in order to ban autocracy, exploitation, and inequality in the world, we must first realize that the first inequality in life is that of child and adult."[5] This intolerance of the distortion of human capacities is always just below the surface in psychoanalysis. Even when Freud sounds most like Burke, for example, it is the potentially liberating role of restraints that intrigues him.

Freud's thought, in other words, can be read as the liberal tradition turning on itself in self-inquiry. Yet while one can legitimately interpret Freud in these terms, this does not by any means imply that we have found the "real" Freud. Intellectual reality is richer than that; within scholarly limits there is a sense in which, as Nietzsche said,

Every great human being has a retroactive force: all history is again placed in the scales for his sake, and a thousand secrets of the past crawl out of their hideouts—into *his* sun. There is no

[4] Alexander: *Our Age of Unreason*, p. 39.

[5] Erik Erikson: *Identity and the Life Cycle* (New York: International Universities Press; 1960), p. 100.

way of telling what may yet become history some day. Perhaps the past is essentially undiscovered! So many retroactive forces are still required.[6]

If we remain suitably aware that the Freud we find is in good measure a projection of our own concerns, that psychoanalysis is itself neither inherently liberal nor conservative but contains strands from both, then we are less likely to mislead ourselves.

[6] Nietzsche: *The Portable Nietzsche*, p. 94.

*CHAPTER V*

# Civilization: Tragedy and Possibility

## Reform

From a broad point of view Freud stands out as one of history's great reformers; he waged a campaign for more than thirty years against conventional sexual morality. This aspect of his thought became widely popularized, and was easily misunderstood. Looking closely at Freud's own life, and at the standards of behavior he expected of people, one would conclude that he himself was very much a Victorian gentleman. But in terms of his own era, he was quite radical. In a letter to Putnam, Freud declared that he stood "for an infinitely freer sexual life. . . ."[1] Although he always distinguished between his reformism and his commitment to scientific understanding, there is a sense in which in social life scientific understanding is inherently radical. Societies live by myths; hence Freud's system inevitably

[1] Freud: *Letters*, p. 314.

conflicted with the standards of his society. "We cannot help observing with a critical eye and we have found it impossible to side with conventional sexual morality or to form a very high opinion of the manner in which society attempts the practical regulation of the problems of sexual life."[2]

Despite his insights into the positive values of social coercion, Freud reiterates, as late as his last, uncompleted book, the more generally familiar negative view. We must not forget, he wrote, "to include the influence of civilization among the determinants of neurosis. It is easy . . . for a barbarian to be healthy; for a civilized man the task is hard."[3] Because of the radical tendencies within his work, Freud became for some the Bohemian idol, and for others the feared subverter of all moral life. Although the subtleties of Freud's views on civilization are easy to miss, the liberating aspect of his ideas certainly get across. In 1907 he maintained that "a social reform allowing a certain amount of sexual freedom would be the best way to render sexual traumata harmless."[4] Freud stood on the side of the individual, and looked truculently at society; psychoanalysis, he wrote, "stands in opposition to everything that is conventionally restricted, well-established and generally accepted."[5]

Freud's social criticism appears extensively in an essay he published in 1908, "Civilized Sexual Morality and Modern Nervous Illness." It is a concrete plea for greater sexual freedom. Its premise is that if the sexual instincts are not gratified in the real world, they will provide the energy

[2] *Standard Edition*, Vol. 16, p. 434.

[3] Ibid., Vol. 23, p. 185.

[4] *The Minutes of the Vienna Psychoanalytic Society*, Vol. I, p. 273.

[5] *Standard Edition*, Vol. 18, p. 178.

for neurotic substitutes. Neuroses were in Freud's view partly a consequence of Victorian prudery. At this time Freud was particularly concerned with the problems of "neurasthenics," whose difficulties could be explained by inhibitions in their sexual lives. He questioned "whether our 'civilized' sexual morality is worth the sacrifice which it imposes on us. . . ."[6]

The sexual origin of neuroses had been uppermost in Freud's mind throughout the 1890's. He was always offended by the dishonesty of the social rules for sexual behavior; "there are very many more . . . hypocrites than truly civilized men. . . ."[7] If the increase in neurasthenia, which other observers had noted as well, was due to the excessive moral standards of modern society, then the first step in reform was a "higher degree of honesty about sexual things."[8] "Above all, a place must be created in public opinion for the discussion of the problems of sexual life. It will have to become possible to talk about these things without being stamped as a trouble-maker or as a person who makes capital out of the lower instincts."[9] Like Marx, Freud accused society—in terms of its own ideals—of deceiving itself. Freud invoked liberal values, such as individual self-fulfillment, in order to demonstrate that the *status quo* needed to be changed.

Freud's plea on behalf of the individual has been convincing because he always showed himself aware of the conflicting claims of moral values. He was eloquent about the injustice of civilized restrictions, and at the same time

[6] Ibid., Vol. 9, p. 204.
[7] Ibid., Vol. 14, p. 284.
[8] Ibid., Vol. 3, p. 266.
[9] Ibid., p. 278.

recognized the legitimacy of the "claims of civilization." He saw that the sexual drives can be incompatible with each other; pregenital and bisexual trends must be overcome, and the asocial impulses tamed. Renunciation is necessary if civilized life is to be possible at all.

We believe that civilization has been created under the pressure of the exigencies of life at the cost of satisfaction of the instincts; and we believe that civilization is to a large extent being constantly created anew, since each individual who makes a fresh entry into human society repeats this sacrifice of instinctual satisfaction for the benefit of the whole community.[1]

This polarity between the need for individual fulfillment and the necessity of social coercion was a central theme throughout Freud's social thinking. His ability to retain *both* poles within his framework separated him from romantic anarchism, just as his rationalism and scientific commitments saved him from conservatism.

Freud viewed culture as a defense system against anxiety. "The whole course of the history of civilization is no more than an account of the various methods adopted by mankind for 'binding' their unsatisfied wishes. . . ."[2] Precisely because of the passionate nature of his instincts, man needs defenses against them; the insatiability of man's drives produces insecurities so deep that only social coercions can provide relief. "The neuroses themselves have turned out to be attempts to find *individual* solutions for the problems of compensating for unsatisfied wishes, while the institutions seek to provide *social* solutions for these same problems."[3]

[1] Ibid., Vol. 15, pp. 22–3.
[2] Ibid., Vol. 13, p. 186.
[3] Ibid.

With the growth of ego psychology it became apparent that social institutions could help the individual not only by these negative, compensatory functions, but also by promoting ego adaptations. Social institutions do not mainly express men's destructive or irrational tendencies, but also lighten their conflicts by confirming identities. Rituals guide, and initiation rites promote inner integration. It would be mistaken to think that rules have only a psychologically inhibiting effect; they also provide men with the facilities to accomplish ends which would be impossible without social life. Culture is not just a deprivation, but a means of individual fulfillment.

Freud saw this Janus character of social life, the sense in which society both frustrates and fulfills men's needs. Depending on whether he is concentrating on the sexual or aggressive drives, he is more or less aware of the restrictive or the purposive aspects of social life. Freud held radical social views because he thought that "it is quite impossible to adjust the claims of the sexual instinct to the demands of civilization";[4] but he accepted the inevitability of the conflict between the individual and society and sought ways of maximizing individualism within a social context. Whatever Freud's insight into our dark needs, there is never any doubt as to his values—rationality and independence. Although by and large Freud brings ill tidings for traditional liberal theory, his theory of the ineluctability of human drives also lends empirical support to men's aspiration to freedom: "Experience teaches us that for most people there is a limit beyond which their constitution cannot comply with the demands of civilization."[5]

[4] Ibid., Vol. 11, p. 190.
[5] Ibid., Vol. 9, p. 191.

## 2  Cultural Differences

While Freud's views on the importance of liberating man's sexual energies, as well as on the origin of culture in instinctual renunciation, are well known, critics often accuse him of ignoring cultural forces. Although he was concerned throughout his work with balancing the claims of civilization against the needs of individualism, many commentators have found him blind to social factors and historical change.[1] Much revisionist psychologizing is founded on Freud's theories being reputedly culture-bound. This issue is important enough to warrant scrutiny.

One explanation of Freud's discoveries undoubtedly lies in the character of the Austro-Hungarian Empire. "The discrepancy between the official ideology and the facts of the political reality was apt to weaken anyone's confidence in the reality of words, slogans, authoritative statements, and was prone to foster the development of a critical mind."[2] The gulf between reality and official ideology stimulated a general intellectual revolt, a search for the actualities beneath the pious formulas of official truth. This revolt was led by those ideally placed to see the discrepancy because they had nothing to gain from accepting the official view, namely, the educated Jews. And mordant irony was their weapon for piercing the veil of the structure of formal beliefs.

There are really some strikingly specific comparisons be-

[1] For example, cf. Philip Rieff: "The Authority of the Past," *Social Research*, Vol. 21, No. 4 (Winter 1954), p. 441, and "History, Psychoanalysis, and the Social Sciences," *Ethics*, Vol. 63, No. 2 (January 1953), p. 112.

[2] Erich Fromm: *Sigmund Freud's Mission* (New York: Harper & Bros.; 1959), p. 4.

tween the Austrian political system and psychoanalytic doctrine:

> For [the Austrian] . . . ruling class the main question was not to know the real problems of their state and society in order to solve them, but to deflect them, to deceive the reality which was unmanageable and fearful in itself. . . . Knowing the task ascribed to the Ego, by Freudian psychoanalysis, the image of an astute politician comes almost inevitably to one's mind.[3]

The vigorous cultural conflict between East and West that had its vortex in Vienna's cosmopolitan intellectual life, the very intensity of the contending forces, as well as the sense that liberal culture was on the verge of being undermined, are reflected throughout Freud's thought. Many of his more lugubrious sentiments can be found in other Viennese *fin de siècle* writers.

Even if one conceded that Freud's particular social context makes some of his ideas obsolete, that need not be the end of the culture-bound line of argument. For it may well be that the historical parallels between his period and our own go far to explain the relevance of psychoanalysis for contemporary political thought. Cultural relativism is a double-edged sword; if the passage of historical time has rendered parts of Freud's theories antiquated, it may at the same time account for the greater relevance of those social realities which Freud's psychology did focus on. World War II "has in many aspects brought Western society nearer to the socio-cultural pattern characteristic of the Austro-Hungarian Empire during the last decades of its existence."[4] The Viennese intelligentsia were the first to face one of the central perplexities of twentieth-century political history

---

[3] Zevedei Barbu: "The Historical Pattern of Psychoanalysis," *British Journal of Sociology*, Vol. 3, No. 1 (March 1952), p. 74.

[4] Ibid., p. 65.

—the undermining of liberal beliefs. In fact pre-World War I Vienna exemplifies the collapse of all the traditional values of pre-industrial civilization. It was at that point that Victorian common-sense notions about human psychology underwent the most searching scrutiny.

Freud would have been the last person to raise any sort of cultural interpretations of his ideas. He did not have the multiple interests of a contemporary social scientist. As a psychologist Freud naturally emphasized inner psychic realities. His daughter Anna has said of the therapy of adults, "we assume that the patient suffers from a conflict, not with the environment but within the structure of his own personality. . . ."[5] A therapist focuses on intrapsychic tensions; although these inner conflicts are not all there is to the patient's life, they are most of what a therapist has to work with. Depth psychology is an addition, not an alternative, to common-sense reality explanations; it focuses on the individual's perception of his environment, on the way we each distort the external world.

Actually, in Freud's earliest writings he overestimated the importance of the environment as a cause of his patients' troubles. He thought then in terms of an actual trauma, like a childhood seduction—a deed, not a fantasy. When he realized that he had been mistaken about the reality of the seduction stories, he swung to the opposite conclusion of overemphasizing internal realities. Not until the growth of ego psychology did Freud achieve a balance between inner needs and outer actualities. With the widening social perspective of his old age, Freud was better able to describe the ego as the point of contact between the individual and his environment. The expanding scope of psy-

[5] A. Freud: "Problems of Technique in Adult Analysis," *Bulletin of the Philadelphia Association for Psychoanalysis*, Vol. 4, No. 3 (1954), p. 45.

choanalytic treatment, for example the psychoanalysis of children, has also facilitated the incorporation of environmental factors within psychoanalytic thinking. As Anna Freud has recently said, "the analyst of adults is a firm believer in psychic, as opposed to external, reality. . . . For the analyst of children, on the other hand, all the indications point in the opposite direction, bearing witness to the powerful influence of the environment."[6] It is nevertheless not easy to consider adaptive mechanisms for coping with reality without at the same time obscuring the interest in inner motivation which characterized early psychoanalysis.

Much of the debate over whether psychoanalysis has adequately considered the role of cultural factors has centered on a clinical phenomenon which members of all psychological schools have noticed. Neurotic symptomatology has changed during this century; cases "in which overt symptoms appear as the presenting problem"[7] have declined. A new concept of symptom-free neuroses, labeled "character neuroses," has arisen. The appearance of these character disorders has been accompanied by a drastic decline in the cases of conversion hysteria which so fascinated Freud in the 1890's. In Jones's experience,

conversion hysteria was far commoner in those days than after the First World War. Paralyses and anaesthesis were to be seen in every hospital, and most infirmaries could produce patients with astasia-abasia who had been bed-ridden for perhaps twenty or thirty years. Hysterical convulsions were similarly frequent, and apart from those seen in hospital I often enough had to minister to girls in convulsions met with on a stroll through the town.[8]

[6] A. Freud: *Normality and Pathology in Childhood*, p. 50.
[7] Brown: *Freud and the Post-Freudians*, p. 81.
[8] Ernest Jones: *Free Associations* (New York: Basic Books; 1959), pp. 124–5.

Old-fashioned cases of conversion hysteria now appear in technologically backward areas of the world, or in groups isolated in one way or another from modern society.

It may not have been perchance that after the first World War Freud turned his attention to narcissism and ego problems in the specific sense. The mechanisms and instinctual conflicts involved evidently play an increasingly important role in the present epoch whereas . . . the "classical" neuroses such as conversion hysteria . . . now occur less frequently.[9]

Erikson draws the general conclusion that "the patient of today suffers most under the problem of what he should believe in and who he should—or, indeed, might—be or become; while the patient of early psychoanalysis suffered most under inhibitions which prevented him from being what or who he thought he knew he was."[1]

These changes in the forms of neuroses in the West have suggested to many that, as Hartmann has put it, "the deep structure of the personality . . . [has been] modified by cultural conditions."[2] It is still somewhat uncertain which social forces have been most directly responsible for these clinical changes. Federn thought that the spread of psychoanalytic teachings was in part responsible for the decline of hysteria: "Because of the recognition of the connection between sexual repression and hysteria, and the more reasonable attitude on the part of society toward sexuality . . . hysteria has decreased."[3] Changes in sexual mores are not

9 Adorno: "Freudian Theory and the Pattern of Fascist Propaganda," p. 281.

1 Erikson: *Childhood and Society*, p. 239.

2 Heinz Hartmann: "Psychoanalysis and Sociology," in *Psychoanalysis Today*, ed. Sandor Lorand (New York: International Universities Press; 1944), p. 331.

3 Paul Federn: "Psychoanalysis As A Therapy of Society," *The American Imago*, Vol. 1, No. 4 (December 1940), p. 77.

due of course solely to psychoanalysis; the events inaugurated by World War I, along with the spread of the socialist movement and developments in birth control, have led, for example, to a radical difference in the general status of women. Whatever the nature of the causal forces at work, it is evident that

the children of our generation are brought up more leniently than before and, consequently, seem to take longer before they establish a firm ego structure. This may account for the fact that the less well-defined and fluctuating developmental disorders are on the increase at the expense of the real infantile neurosis which was more frequently recorded and treated by the analytic workers of the past.[4]

The problem of the disappearance of conversion hysteria has also been colored by new ways of classifying psychiatric cases. It is unlikely that many of Freud's early patients of *Studies on Hysteria* would now be diagnosed in the same way; a contemporary psychiatrist would more likely be struck by the deeper disturbances of a borderline or psychotic kind that might underlie a hysterical façade. In fact, one sometimes wonders which has changed the more in the last half century, the problems of patients or the conceptions of psychiatrists.

Skeptics of Freud's approach to the social environment have been concerned about more than the puzzling shifts in the frequency of clinical cases. Freud's biological language, as well as his preoccupation with inner realities, made it seem as if he conceived of the individual's development as entirely free from environmental pressures. Yet when Freud writes about child development, he is con-

---

[4] A. Freud: "The Mutual Influences in the Development of the Ego and the Id," p. 50.

cerned with the child's relation to its parents and siblings —that is, to the child's family. "In the individual's mental life someone else is invariably involved, as a model, as an object, as a helper, as an opponent; and so from the very first individual psychology . . . is at the same time social psychology as well."[5] As we have already seen, according to Freud's conception of the ego, it grows by the continual influence of the external world. And the superego embodies first the standards of parents and then those of society.

Freud's use of the concept of "instincts" was a very special one: "By an 'instinct' is provisionally to be understood the psychical representative of an endosomatic, continuously flowing source of stimulation. . . . The concept of instinct is thus one of those lying on the frontier between the mental and the physical."[6] As a concept, instinct was an attempt to unify the body and the mind; it had a special meaning in psychoanalysis, as Hendrick has pointed out, as "a biological need experienced mentally as emotion, and impelling the organism to tension-relieving behavior."[7] Freud was not interested in drive activity as such, but in drives as motivating forces, the "mental representatives"[8] of instincts. Freud's interest in instinctual life was that of a psychologist, and did not block an understanding of the importance of the social environment. "The mutual relations of men," he once wrote, "are profoundly influenced by the amount of instinctual satisfaction which the existing wealth makes possible. . . ."[9]

One need not underplay the importance which primary

[5] *Standard Edition*, Vol. 18, p. 69.

[6] Ibid., Vol. 7, p. 168.

[7] Ives Hendrick: "Instinct and Ego During Infancy," *The Psychoanalytic Quarterly*, Vol. 11 (1942), p. 40.

[8] *Standard Edition*, Vol. 20, p. 265.

[9] Ibid., Vol. 21, p. 6.

drives of a sexual and aggressive nature had for Freud. And he was much less clear than psychoanalysts would be now-adays about there being both "maturational" and "develop-mental" aspects of the child's psychic growth—in other words, a continuum of psychic needs relatively independ-ent, to a greater or less extent, of outside influence. Yet nothing in Freud's early work precluded this later theoreti-cal elaboration. His daughter Anna has tried to follow his teachings in her studies of children, and has pioneered in helping small children by working with their mothers.

I refuse to believe that mothers need to change their personalities before they can change the handling of their child . . . in rearing their children mothers are not only guided by instinct and misled by distorting personal influences, but they are to an even larger degree dependent on tradition and public opinion, both of which are open to change.[1]

Whatever one may think of Freud's own theories, his pupils have certainly paid attention to the child's interaction with its human environment.

Although Freud, as a psychologist, never systematized the relation of his patients to social life, there are certainly hints in his writings that he was not obtuse to differing social realities. The patients Freud treated came from numerous national backgrounds. Of his Russian patient, known as the Wolf-Man, Freud commented that "personal peculiarities in the patient and a national character that was foreign to ours made the task of feeling one's way into his mind a laborious one."[2] In writing about another of his patients,

---

[1] A. Freud: "The Child Guidance Clinic as a Center of Prophylaxis and En-lightenment," in *Recent Developments in Psychoanalytic Child Therapy*, ed. Joseph Weinreb (New York: International Universities Press; 1960), p. 37.

[2] *Standard Edition*, Vol. 17, p. 104.

Freud noted some behavior as customary for middle-class circles in Vienna.[3] The expense of his treatment naturally limited the variety of social classes from which his patients came. But when asked by Wortis whether he found "much difference in the form and frequency of neuroses in different social classes," Freud is reported to have replied, "to be sure, each group reacts differently."[4] In writing about female psychology, Freud cautioned that "we must beware . . . of underestimating the influence of social customs, which . . . force women into passive situations."[5] Even as early as his case of Dora, Freud stated that "it follows from the nature of the facts which form the material of psychoanalysis that we are obliged to pay as much attention in our case histories to the purely human and social circumstances of our patients as to the somatic data and the symptoms of the disorder."[6] Although Freud never developed these clinical asides in any way, they do demonstrate that he took the external realities of his patients into account. His commitment to psychological understanding presumably would have kept him from pursuing further this direction of thought.

Freud's interest in social life and his awareness of environmental factors extended to the different forms emotional conflicts could take under differing historical conditions. For example, he observed that

In the present state of our civilization self-injury which does not have total self-destruction as its aim has no other choice whatever than to hide itself behind something accidental or to mani-

---

[3] Ibid., Vol. 14, p. 160.
[4] Wortis: *Fragments of an Analysis with Freud*, p. 131.
[5] *Standard Edition*, Vol. 22, p. 116.
[6] Quoted in Jones: *Sigmund Freud*, Vol. III, p. 336.

fest itself by imitating the onset of a spontaneous illness. Formerly self-injury was a customary sign of mourning; at other periods it could express trends towards piety and renunciation of the world.[7]

Elsewhere Freud commented that "we need not be surprised to find that, whereas the neuroses of our unpsychological modern days take on a hypochondriacal aspect and appear disguised as organic illnesses, the neuroses of early times emerge in demonological trappings."[8] Freud thought that in his own time "neurosis takes the place of the monasteries which used to be the refuge of all whom life had disappointed or who felt too weak to face it."[9] All of these comments remained asides on Freud's part, and were never even partially synthesized. However, they do show that he was not as insensitive to historical change as some seem to assume.

While Freud certainly did not lack the historian's interest in growth, he was tempted to construct historical stages on scanty evidence; his sense of history was too grandiose and pretentious. Ultimately he was more interested in illustrating timeless truths than in learning about unique historical developments. For example, in *Totem and Taboo* Freud postulates three main stages in human history in an attempt to correlate these with the individual's three-stage libidinal development. As first one's libido is invested in oneself, then in one's parents, and finally in other adults, so too man's picture of the world had undergone a similar evolution, moving from the animistic (or mythological), to the religious, to the scientific, as man strove to cope with his magical feelings.

[7] *Standard Edition*, Vol. 6, p. 179.
[8] Ibid., Vol. 19, p. 72.
[9] Ibid., Vol. 11, p. 50.

At the animistic stage men ascribe omnipotence to *themselves*. At the religious stage they transfer it to the gods, but do not seriously abandon it themselves, for they reserve the power of influencing the gods in a variety of ways according to their wishes. The scientific view of the universe no longer affords any room for human omnipotence; men have acknowledged their smallness and submitted resignedly to death and the other necessities of nature.[1]

Although Freud's belief that the steps to civilization were chronologically arranged may sound naïve, it was quite a common notion during the Enlightenment.

The difficulty with such historical fables is that they may block the way to more fruitful studies of culture and personality. As a matter of principle Freud would have insisted on the psychological unity of men. In those days national character studies had racist connotations. Furthermore, as a Jew trying to escape from a religion which emphasized separateness, it is understandable that Freud would have difficulty appreciating the work of those who did not need to insist on psychological uniformities.[2] Now that the emphasis within psychoanalytic thinking has shifted from id mechanisms to those of the ego, it may be easier for psychoanalytic concepts to shed light on the ways in which environmental factors help individuals to master their inner conflicts. Hartmann has at least endorsed the psychoanalytic legitimacy of such concerns, declaring his interest

In what manner and to what degree does a given social structure bring to the surface, provoke or reinforce certain instinctual tendencies or certain sublimations. . . ? The way in which different social structures facilitate the solution of certain psychic conflicts

---

[1] Ibid., Vol. 13, p. 88.
[2] Geoffrey Gorer, in *Psychoanalysis Observed*, ed. Charles Rycroft (London: Constable; 1966), p. 41.

by a participation—by action or in phantasy—with the given
social realities, merits special investigation.[3]

Psychoanalysis should now present no conceptual blocks to
fruitful interdisciplinary cooperation.


## 3  *Man's Discomfort*

However one limits any claim that Freud neglected the
role of the environment, there is a sense in which the revisionists have rightly challenged his views on culture. It
is not so much that Freud ignored cultural factors, as that
he understood mainly the costs of civilization. The revisionist tendency is an intellectually amiable one. The post-Freudian literature has none of the disturbing quality of Freud's
own writings. Revisionism has a soothingly reassuring tone.
Instead of Freud's complex grasp of the way culture both
thwarts and fulfills human needs, the revisionist substitute
a less tragic view of the relation of man to society. Change
modern civilization, they advise, and man's naturally harmonious nature will be able to unfold itself. The notion that
neurosis is due to mental conflict tends to disappear; it is the
environment which needs changing.

Freud expressed his sense of the conflictedness of life
most eloquently in *Civilization and Its Discontents* (1929).
He was impressed by the pervasiveness of suffering in civilized society—coming from bodily infirmities, from other
human beings, and from nature itself. Although Freud
could sometimes, as in *The Future of an Illusion*, write like
an eighteenth-century libertarian, here his sense of the inevitable cruelties of life was uppermost in his mind.

[3] Hartmann: "Psychoanalysis and Sociology," p. 332.

Freud's feelings about civilized society were split. On the one hand social coercions frustrated man's most intense passions. "The feeling of happiness derived from the satisfaction of a wild instinctual impulse untamed by the ego is incomparably more intense than that derived from sating an instinct that has been tamed."[1] On the other hand, the possibility of such complete satisfaction opens the door to complete frustration. The abandon of love is a double-edged sword; one can be "abandoned" in the completion of instinctual release, and yet the commitment to a lover raises the possibility of "abandonment" in the sense of loss; "we are never so defenseless against suffering as when we love, never so helplessly unhappy as when we have lost our loved object."[2] Modifications of instincts and defenses against them are ways of avoiding the most terrible despairs. Social coercions, from the point of view of man's impulses, are compromises; they simultaneously evade complete happiness and utter dissatisfaction.

The premise of Freud's thesis was the analogy between individual development and the process of civilization. The individual's instinctual energy can be displaced from its primary aim; this is the mechanism Freud termed "sublimation." "The task here is that of shifting the instinctual aims in such a way that they cannot come up against frustration from the external world."[3] Work offers an excellent outlet; it also attaches the individual to the real world which exists independently of his desires. But the intensity of such sublimated satisfactions is mild "compared with that derived from the sating of crude and primary instinctual impulses; it does not convulse our physical being."[4]

[1] *Standard Edition*, Vol. 21, p. 79.
[2] Ibid., p. 82.
[3] Ibid., p. 79.
[4] Ibid., pp. 79–80.

Hence the "great majority of people only work under the stress of necessity. . . ."[5]

Another means of defense against the passionate urges of men is simply restriction. For civilization to be powerful enough to perform its function of protecting men against each other and against nature, it must be, according to Freud, empowered by equally intense energy. Throughout Freud's thought there is a sense of the limits of life, the truth behind the maxim that one cannot have one's cake and eat it too. As Helene Deutsch once put it in another context, "the law of conservation of energy seems to have its parallel in psychic events."[6] On a deep level, what one expends of psychic energy in any one direction must be at the cost of other possible alternatives. There are inescapable conflicts in life among one's talents. Human gain is almost always paid for by human loss.

Freud described the logic behind his view that renunciation is essential to civilized society:

Human life in common is only made possible when a majority comes together which is stronger than any separate individual and which remains united against all separate individuals. . . . This replacement of the power of the individual by the power of the community constitutes the decisive step of civilization. The essence of it lies in the fact that the members of the community restrict themselves in their possibilities of satisfaction, whereas the individual knew no such restrictions.[7]

This position should not be understood as a kind of social contract gimmick, whereby individual satisfaction is magically maximized through social controls. The parallel in

[5] Ibid., p. 80.
[6] Helene Deutsch: "Absence of Grief," *Psychoanalytic Quarterly*, Vol. 6 (1937), p. 22.
[7] *Standard Edition*, Vol. 21, p. 95.

Freud's mind is the way a child is socialized, through countless instinctual restrictions, into adulthood. Freud's theory has the virtue of its honesty: "the liberty of the individual is no gift of civilization."[8]

The central theme of all Freud's previous criticisms of civilized morality had been that civilization frustrates sexuality. Here Freud looks at sexual restraints from the social as well as the individual point of view. His concern with social unity leads him to speculate to what extent there are sources of frustration other than those which originate from culture. "Sometimes one seems to perceive that it is not only the pressure of civilization but something in the nature of the [sexual] function itself which denies us full satisfaction and urges us along other paths."[9]

If Freud feels torn between the claims of sexuality and those of civilized life, he feels no such ambivalence here about the aggressive drives. "In consequence of . . . [the] primary mutual hostility of human beings, civilized society is perpetually threatened with disintegration."[1]

As a rule this cruel aggressiveness waits for some provocation or puts itself at the service of some other purpose, whose goal might also have been reached by milder measures. In circumstances that are favourable to it, when the mental counter-forces which ordinarily inhibit it are out of action, it also manifests itself spontaneously and reveals man as a savage beast. . . .[2]

Freud explicitly rejects Marxian hopes for the melioristic consequences of alterations in property rights. "Aggressiveness was not created by property."[3]

Social unity then is achieved on the ruins of human de-

8 Ibid., p. 95.
9 Ibid., p. 105.
1 Ibid., p. 112.
2 Ibid., p. 111-12.
3 Ibid., p. 113.

sires. Men need the security of civilized life so deeply that they renounce the gratification of instincts in exchange for society. Frustration of sexual and aggressive drives is entailed by their very character. Men are hoisted in their own petards. Human passions require an equally powerful system of restraints.

In his account of social cohesion, Freud maintains the elitism of *Group Psychology and the Analysis of the Ego*; he continues to insist on the importance of ruling figures as common objects of identification. He fears that only a minority appreciates great men, and that in America especially there is a danger of "the psychological poverty of groups." "This danger is most threatening where the bonds of a society are chiefly constituted by the identification of its members with one another, while individuals of the leader type do not acquire the importance that should fall to them in the formation of a group."[4] Like Bagehot, Comte, Carlyle, Nietzsche, and other nineteenth-century thinkers, Freud felt that communal standards were the result of the "impression left behind by the personalities of great men."[5]

Only if society can successfully internalize human aggression can civilization be maintained. "Civilization . . . obtains mastery over the individual's . . . desire for aggression by weakening and disarming it and by setting up an agency within him to watch over it, like a garrison in a conquered city."[6] This agency is the superego. The power of the cultural superego is derived from the character of the aggressive drives. Even when they are renounced in reality, aggressive wishes persist. The tension between the superego's standards

[4] Ibid., pp. 115–16.
[5] Ibid., p. 141.
[6] Ibid., pp. 123–4.

and the persistence of aggressive impulses ensures an un-relieved sense of guilt.

Furthermore, the aggression that we fail to discharge outwardly (for fear of the superego's prohibition) is then taken up by the superego itself, and discharged inwardly against the ego, intensifying the sense of guilt. "Every renunciation of instinct . . . becomes a dynamic source of conscience and every fresh renunciation increases the latter's severity and intolerance."[7] Although its source has been the renunciation rather than the fulfillment of a forbidden instinct, this inevitable severity and intolerance is experienced by the individual as a sense of guilt. Thus, while fear of the superego ensures restraints on instinctual satisfactions, these restraints in turn can only result in heightened anxiety, the inevitable sense of guilt that determines civilized unhappiness. "A threatened external unhappiness—loss of love and punishment on the part of the external authority—has been exchanged for a permanent internal unhappiness, for the tension of a sense of guilt."[8]

## 4   Health

No matter how gloomy Freud's vision may seem, one should recall that his interests were drawn to these abstract formulations while he was still a practicing clinician. His theories were always connected with case material. He illustrated in *Moses and Monotheism* the way an inner aspiration can be self-defeating by the example of the patient who as a young man had defiantly striven to free himself

[7] Ibid., p. 128.
[8] Ibid.

from his father, but who had nevertheless eventually grown into "a faithful copy of his father."[1] Jones elaborated on the mechanism by which at the end of Sisyphean labors one has attained exactly what one set out to overcome: "The influence of the paternal figure may be so great that the boy, instead of developing something new and individual wherewith to express his own personality, often aims at simply displacing the father with the object of reigning in his stead in the same fashion as his father did and with his same attributes."[2] What on the surface appear as the most strenuous efforts to change can turn out to be the starkest repetitions.

The essentially neurotic nature of such problems can be illustrated by a defense mechanism which Fenichel called the "counter-phobic attitude." If one has a phobia, it means of course that one has to avoid certain situations which one considers, for whatever reason, dangerous; counterphobias, on the other hand, involve seeking out those danger situations, in order to prove that the threat is illusory.

It often happens that a person shows a preference for the very situations of which he is apparently afraid . . . a still present anxiety is warded off more effectively by *seeking* situations in which it usually appears than by *avoiding* them . . . [or] he seeks out what was once feared in the same way as a traumatic neurotic dreams of his trauma, or as a child experiences pleasurably in play what he is afraid of in reality.[3]

This defense against anxiety is essentially that of warding off danger by doing it first. Yet it is neurotic in the sense that one is bound to the very terrors one tries to overcome,

---

[1] Ibid., Vol. 23, p. 80.

[2] Ernest Jones: "Evolution and Revolution," *International Journal of Psychoanalysis,* Vol. 22, Parts 3 and 4 (1941), p. 198

[3] Otto Fenichel: "The Counter-Phobic Attitude," *The Collected Papers of Otto Fenichel,* 2nd Series (New York: W. W. Norton; 1954), pp. 164, 168.

that in the attempt to master anxieties, no matter how energetically, one is still tied to the same fears. So if on one level one seeks to overcome a conflict, on another level one seeks out that conflict itself. Freud called this "the fatal truth that has laid it down that flight is precisely an instrument that delivers one over to what one is fleeing from."[4]

Self-destructive behavior comprises the psychological material which Freud set out to explain. In a psychological sense, what a man most dreads, he also longs for. And, in fact, what someone fears can lead to what he fears coming true. Helene Deutsch has written of situations in which "the fear of pregnancy becomes a motive for it, just as the fear of death, the unbearable tension of expectation, can become a motive for suicide."[5] Psychologists here are describing what we all recognize as "the attraction of the forbidden." Artists have probably always understood these unconscious processes. Edgar Allan Poe, for example, used the notion of what he called the "Imp of the Perverse"; "through its promptings we act, for the reason that we should *not.*"

Who has not, a hundred times, found himself committing a vile or a silly action, for no other reason than because he knows he should *not*? . . . It was this unfathomable longing of the soul *to vex itself*—to offer violence to its own nature—to do wrong for the wrong's sake only—that urged me to continue. . . .[6]

The psychoanalytic explanation of this phenomenon would focus on the guilt which seeks suffering as a means of relief. Neurotic suffering can have the meaning of self-

[4] *Standard Edition*, Vol. 9, p. 42.

[5] Helene Deutsch: *The Psychology of Women*, Vol. II (New York: Grune & Stratton; 1945), p. 340.

[6] Edgar Allan Poe: *Selected Writings*, ed. E. H. Davidson (Boston: Houghton Mifflin; 1950), pp. 225–6, and p. 201.

inflicted punishment. And as discussed earlier, by appeasing unconscious guilt in exchange for suffering, one can perform those acts which our consciences forbid. We have here a vicious circle. Guilt produces the need to suffer; and the suffering permits the gratification of forbidden impulses as an exchange, which only reinforces the initial guilt.

Earlier we saw the extent to which these illustrations from depth psychology require alterations in traditional justifications of punishment. Here we can see that such examples also illustrate the sense in which psychoanalysis views man's fate as intrinsic in his own soul. This notion is a return to the Greek view that character is fate.[7] As Freud himself put it, "Fate and the oracle were no more than materializations of an internal necessity. . . ."[8]

Psychoanalytic therapy presupposes the contrast between self-destructive and self-fulfilling acts. The constructive forces of life are as much a part of human psychology as the "Imp of the Perverse." As Freud once put it, "tendencies toward progress and recovery . . . remain active even after the formation of neurotic symptoms."[9] As a whole, however, psychoanalysis has been much more interested in illness than in health, in pathological processes than in recuperative trends.

[7] George Eliot, however, would have us keep our feet on the ground over all this. "For the tragedy of our lives is not created entirely from within. 'Character,' says Novalis, in one of his questionable aphorisms, 'character is destiny.' But not the whole of our destiny. Hamlet, Prince of Denmark, was speculative and irresolute, and we have a great tragedy in consequence. But if his father had lived to a good old age, and his uncle had died an early death, we can conceive Hamlet's having married Ophelia and got through life with a reputation of sanity, notwithstanding many soliloquies and some moody sarcasms towards the fair daughter of Polonius, to say nothing of the frankest incivility to his father-in-law." *The Mill on the Floss* (New York: Collier Books; 1962), p. 440.

[8] *Standard Edition*, Vol. 20, p. 63.

[9] Ibid., Vol. 14, p. 272.

It should come as no surprise that psychoanalysis has been preoccupied with failures rather than successes. As a therapeutic agent, psychoanalytic treatment is called upon to treat the inner forces that interfere with the lives of patients, and to leave alone successful sublimations. The integrated aspects of a person operate silently. It is a well-known difficulty that contemporary "psychiatric vocabulary is not only smaller but less accurate when designating health than when designating illness."[1] One must be careful not to take the short cut of describing a normal process by a terminology which implies illness. Freud described the dilemma between "the Scylla of underestimating the importance of the repressed unconscious and the Charybdis of judging the normal entirely by the standards of the pathological."[2]

According to Freud, "analytic therapy . . . does not seek to add or to introduce anything new, but to take away something, to bring out something. . . ."[3] The feelings that psychoanalytic treatment strives to remove are all those inauthentic impulses which can be put under the rubric of alienation. Freud offered this hope to analytic patients: "We seek . . . to enrich him from his own internal sources, by putting at the disposal of his ego those energies which, owing to repression, are inaccessibly confined in his unconscious, as well as those which his ego is obliged to squander in the fruitless task of maintaining these repressions."[4] The analyst makes an alliance with the healthy part of the patient's ego; with the help of this outside strength, the patient can now face various parts of his personality which

[1] Peter Knapp, Sidney Levin, Robert McCarter, Henry Wermer, and Elizabeth Zetzel: "Suitability for Psychoanalysis," *The Psychoanalytic Quarterly*, Vol. 29, No. 4 (October 1954), p. 465.

[2] *Standard Edition*, Vol. 18, p. 138.

[3] Ibid., Vol., 7, p. 261.

[4] Ibid., Vol. 20, p. 256.

previously he had been forced to keep from awareness. The contract between the analyst and patient is made for the sake of the latter's individualism: as Freud put it, "the patient should be educated to liberate and fulfill his own nature, not to resemble ourselves."[5]

This treatment process need not involve any social conformism per se. Freud wanted his patients to become whole; he aimed "at making the individual capable of becoming a civilized and useful member of society with the least possible sacrifice of his own activity."[6] The charge that psychoanalytic treatment entails merely "adjustment" to the social *status quo* would seem more properly directed at some of the revisionists; it is they who tend to erase any distinction between social malaise and individual ill health. Fromm goes so far as to maintain that "whether or not the individual is healthy . . . is primarily not an individual matter, but depends on the structure of his society."[7] Fromm does, to be sure, advocate extensive social reforms. But he sometimes lacks the depth psychologist's perception of the gap between the individual's psychic efficiency and the demands of his society. As Kurt Eissler has pointed out, psychopathology may in certain circumstances lead "to performance constructive in terms of society's needs. Psychopathology, however, is always detrimental in terms of the individual microcosm."[8]

We can see from this, as well as from our earlier discussion of the psychoanalytic attitude toward behavior, that psychoanalytic treatment should involve much more than

[5] Ibid., Vol. 17, p. 165.

[6] Ibid., Vol. 10, p. 146.

[7] Erich Fromm: *The Sane Society* (London: Routledge & Kegan Paul; 1956), p. 72.

[8] Kurt Eissler: "The Efficient Soldier," *The Psychoanalytic Study of Society*, Vol. I, pp. 87–8.

successful "adjustment" to contemporary society. To quote Eissler again, "society only evaluates behavior and does not care about motivations. But psychoanalysts should never make themselves the puppets of society and accept superficial behavior patterns as indices of psychic reality."[9] After all, "adjustment and conformity have very little to do with reality acceptance."[1] Money-Kyrle defines optimum normality as simply "optimum freedom from distortion in unconscious phantasy."[2] According to Devereux, it is "the duty of the therapist to free the patient of his personal neurosis, without converting it into the prevailing social neurosis."[3] Eissler even maintains that "the resistance a person can put up against the onslaught of strong mass sentiments is an index of the degree of personality integration. . . ."[4]

Psychoanalytic treatment must be understood in terms of changes within the individual's psyche. Therapy involves, to put the matter broadly, a general psychological loosening up. By temporarily regressing to former fixation points, the patient can succeed in releasing his ties to his past. Analysis involves a partial moratorium from living in the real world; "the analytic situation is an artificial, tilted one . . . there is none other in life that it really reproduces."[5]

[9] Eissler: "The Chicago Institute of Psychoanalysis," p. 134.

[1] George Devereux: "Social Negativism and Criminal Psychopathology," *Journal of Criminal Psychopathology*, Vol. I, No. 4 (April 1940), p. 327.

[2] Roger Money-Kyrle: "Some Aspects of Political Ethics from the Psychoanalytic Point of View," *International Journal of Psychoanalysis*, Vol. 25 (1944), p. 168.

[3] George Devereux: "Maladjustment and Social Neurosis," *American Sociological Review*, Vol. 4, No. 6 (December 1939), p. 846.

[4] Kurt Eissler: "Objective (Behavioristic) Criteria of Recovery from Neuropsychiatric Disorders," *Journal of Nervous and Mental Disease*, Vol. 106, No. 5 (November 1947), p. 501.

[5] Phyllis Greenacre: "The Role of Transference," *Journal of the American Psychoanalytic Association*, Vol. 11, No. 4 (October 1954), p. 222.

As mental energy is liberated from past fixations, it is free to flow toward current reality.

The cure at which psychoanalytic therapy aims involves what Fenichel has called the "thawing out" of "frozen" conflicts "between instinct and defense, so that in place of an automatic way of acting a conflict is once more experienced. . . ."[6] Horney agreed that "there are two characteristics . . . which one may discern in all neuroses . . . a certain rigidity in reaction and a discrepancy between potentialities and accomplishments."[7] Overcoming a neurosis requires a loosening of defensive structures, an increase in emotional genuineness; yet there must remain an "optimal pressure by the repressed, which is an essential factor in the maintenance of vital feelings."[8] The net therapeutic result should be a general increase in psychic adaptiveness. Kubie has spoken about this measure of health as

flexibility, the freedom to learn through experience, the freedom to change with changing internal and external circumstances, to be influenced by reasonable argument, admonitions, exhortation, and the appeal to emotions; the freedom to respond appropriately to the stimulus of reward and punishment, and especially the freedom to cease when sated. The essence of normality is flexibility in all of these vital ways. The essence of illness is the freezing of behavior into unalterable and insatiable patterns.[9]

From this point of view mental health is not a matter of social adjustment, but rather the capacity for constant and creative inner readjustment.

[6] Otto Fenichel: *Problems of Psychoanalytic Technique* (New York: The Psychonanalytic Quarterly; 1941), p. 40.

[7] Karen Horney: *The Neurotic Personality of Our Time* (London: Routledge & Kegan Paul; 1937), p. 22.

[8] Eissler: *Medical Orthodoxy and the Future of Psychoanalysis*, p. 61.

[9] L. S. Kubie: *Neurotic Distortion of the Creative Process* (New York: The Noonday Press; 1961), pp. 20–1.

The psychic changes during psychoanalytic treatment are frequently expressed in terms of the strength of the ego. Freud wanted to "restore the ego, to free it from its restrictions, and to give it back the command over the id which it has lost owing to its early repressions."[1] This increased self-mastery is made possible because, as Jones put it, "conscious control is substituted for automatic expression, the significance of which was not realized. . . ."[2] "The [emotional] affect attached to an unconscious idea operates more strongly and, since it cannot be inhibited, more injuriously than the affect attached to a conscious one."[3] To achieve increased consciousness, psychoanalysis aims at the maximum verbalization of psychic phenomena.

The psychoanalytic notion of the mastery of an impulse means the ability "to keep the instinct in a state of tension."[4] Inner stress need not be simply a waste of mental energy:

The development and toleration of . . . anxiety is not only inevitable but also desirable both as a stimulus to early infantile development, and as an essential prerequisite for the construction of adequate defenses in all danger situations, whether they arise from within or from without . . . the capacity to develop and tolerate . . . anxiety is decisive for the achievement of mental stability and health.[5]

The aim of increasing the ego's mastery over the various unconscious psychic forces also entails the goal of modifying the harshness of the superego. A harsh superego, as

---

[1] *Standard Edition*, Vol. 20, p. 205.

[2] Jones: *Papers on Psychoanalysis*, p. 76.

[3] *Standard Edition*, Vol. 7, p. 49.

[4] Herman Nunberg: *Theory and Practice of Psychoanalysis*, Vol. I (New York: International Universities Press; 1948), p. 180.

[5] Elizabeth R. Zetzel: "Anxiety and the Capacity to Bear It," *International Journal of Psychoanalysis*, Vol. 30, Part I (1949), pp. 5, 10.

we have just seen again in discussing neurotic self-de-
structiveness, can all too easily be bribed by suffering into
permitting the gratification of forbidden wishes. The increased self-mastery gained through treatment involves
greater awareness of instinctual needs, less dependence on
earlier emotional positions, and a less harsh superego.

Although an understanding of psychoanalytic therapy is
essential in order to comprehend Freud's contribution to
individualism, one must not mistake the place of therapy
within the psychoanalytic system as a whole. While early
in his career Freud was very concerned with the therapeutic
removal of particular symptoms, by the end of his life he
considered symptomatic improvements a mere by-product
of a properly conducted psychoanalysis. Clinical success can
never be more than a dubious test of any theoretical view;
a great variety of psychiatric techniques have cures to their
credit. Freud repeatedly expressed his fears lest psychoanalysis as a therapeutic procedure swallow up psychoanalysis as
a science.

Freud's central claims always rested on the ability of his
theories to increase our understanding. It is sometimes easier to demonstrate mechanisms which psychoanalysis has
discovered on cases that are relatively difficult to cure. In
psychotic illnesses, for example, a break occurs between the
individual and external reality, as contrasted to the neurotic's lack of contact with his inner impulses; "so many
things that in the neuroses have to be laboriously fetched
up from the depths are found in the psychoses on the surface, visible to every eye."[6] No wonder that the study of
the psychotic, who is relatively difficult to cure by psychotherapy, has been viewed as "probably the best means of

[6] *Standard Edition*, Vol. 20, p. 60.

convincing the novitiate in psychiatry of the truth of psychoanalytic mechanisms."[7]

According to the experience of one psychoanalyst, "relatively few patients presenting themselves for psychotherapeutic help are suitable for orthodox psychoanalytic techniques, but all of them are entitled to the kind of dynamic assessment and appraisal which psychoanalytic knowledge provides."[8] The ultimate faith of psychoanalysts is that increased scientific knowledge will eventually increase the practical abilities of therapists and our preventive efforts as parents and social planners. Here again we see the extent to which Freud is in the rationalist tradition of the Enlightenment.

The notion of health inherent in Freud's concept of psychoanalytic treatment is of crucial importance for our purposes; his concept of psychological normality is one possible answer to the liberal quest for an elucidation of the value of self-fulfillment. Freud's notion of health was in good measure an ideal. No psychoanalyst would claim to have had much, if any, acquaintance with the completely normal mind. We need not be surprised that psychic health was for Freud in part a normative concept; to the extent that Freud was a therapist, as distinct from a scientist, he was demonstrating in practice the importance of health as a goal.

Yet no other concept illustrates more starkly the difficulties in relating the realm of the *ought* to the world of the *is*. Although psychological health and sickness are normative categories, they can with equal justice be considered empirical concepts. It was of course one of Freud's greatest achievements to demonstrate the psychopathology of every-

[7] Oberndorf: *A History of Psychoanalysis in America*, p. 87.
[8] Knight, in *Psychoanalytic Psychiatry and Psychology*, p. 67.

day life, to show the ways in which irrational forces are at work in many spheres of our existence. All of us, for example, have psychotic layers in us; we reveal our most primitive wishes in our dream life. Freud thought that by studying the abnormal one could see the everyday in exaggeration; "pathology, by making things larger and coarser, can draw our attention to normal conditions which would otherwise have escaped us."[9] All of us demonstrate in everyday slips of the tongue some of the mechanisms that Freud used to explain neurotic symptoms. Neurotics, according to Freud, "fall ill of the same complexes against which we healthy people struggle as well."[1]

One may well wonder how it is possible diagnostically to distinguish between health and illness. If irrational mechanisms are so widespread, are we not all equally sick? Is not psychic health some cloud-cuckoo-land concept? However, in real life we are not always at such a loss in distinguishing sickness from health. Justice Frankfurter has defined a "nervous" person as one "who makes other people nervous."[2] The distinction between health and illness is often a practical one.

In Freud's metapsychological terminology, the issue is an economic one; the difference between normal and pathological behavior is the relative strength of the conflicting forces. In other words, each of us has his unconscious; each of us dreams, commits slips, acts out, and even has symptoms. The question is one of the balance of strength between our sense of reality and our irrational tendencies. Again,

[9] *Standard Edition*, Vol. 22, p. 58.

[1] Ibid., Vol. 9, p. 210.

[2] Wallace Mendelson, ed.: *Felix Frankfurter: A Tribute* (New York: Reynal & Co.; 1964), p. 40.

from the economic point of view, sickness is a question of more or less, of the relative dominance of unconscious forces.

It is also helpful to look at psychic health from a developmental, or genetic, point of view. This was one of the first ways in which the issue was discussed in the early psychoanalytic literature. Abraham, for example, spoke of the growing person achieving "a steady conquest of his narcissism."[3] The "genital personality" was the ideal, understandable in part as a negatively defined concept; from the analyst's perspective, the individual overcomes by growing up the ambivalences of the pre-genital stages. In achieving object-love, he can escape all the irrationalities of narcissistic mechanisms; "the ability to tolerate difference from oneself is a good test of maturity."[4]

Narcissism can be viewed as similar to the Christian notion of pride; self-love consists in the inability to overcome that self-preoccupation which interprets every failure as a personal humiliation, and which also stymies any attempt to interact with other people in terms other than one's own. The term "genitality" is associated with the ideal of normality since the "aim of analysis is the development of a personality with powerful instinctual trends but at the same time with great capacity for controlling them."[5] Yet even here it is very much a matter of degree; "no developmental stage . . . is ever entirely surmounted or completely obliterated."[6]

Psychoanalysts have been very restrained in their writings on this developmental ideal. Doctors after all begin

[3] Abraham: *Selected Papers*, p. 416.

[4] Storr: *The Integrity of the Personality*, p. 85.

[5] Ferenczi: *Further Contributions to the Theory and Technique of Psychoanalysis*, p. 292.

[6] Abraham: *Selected Papers*, p. 416.

with disease; when the symptoms and underlying causes
are removed, that is the end of the matter. From a doctor's
point of view, a state of health is one of which the patient
usually is not consciously aware. It is the faith healers who
have traditionally begun their analysis with the concept of
health in the foreground.[7] There is, furthermore, a special
reason for the suspiciousness of psychoanalysts when the
subject of normality arises. From a clinician's point of view,
normality is likely to indicate merely that the person "went
around without much trouble because . . . [his] complexi-
ties were stored away out of reach."[8] Such an individual
would be cut off from some of his most important emotions, as well as from the feelings of other people. It is possible to be too well defended. "There is," Winnicott thinks,
"much sanity that has a symptomatic quality. . . ."[9]

The metapsychological point of view on health which
has been most well developed in our own day is given in
structural terms. Contemporary ego psychology does lend
a different twist to the psychoanalytic conception of health,
emphasizing its qualitative aspect. Hartmann has raised the
question, for example, of the degree to which there are
spheres of the ego which are conflict-free, autonomous, and
reasonably safe from regression. In order to ascertain mental health, one must inquire "how secure is the autonomy
of the non-defensive functions of the ego, and how well are
they protected against being weakened by the energic demands of the defensive structures."[1] In addition, therefore,

[7] Shklar: *Legalism*, p. 232.

[8] Wortis: *Fragments of an Analysis with Freud*, p. 77.

[9] Donald Winnicott: *Collected Papers* (London: Tavistock Publications; 1958),
p. 150.

[1] Heinz Hartmann: "Towards A Concept of Mental Health," *British Journal
of Medical Psychology*, Vol. 33, No. 4 (1960), p. 247.

to the plasticity of the ego which Kubie emphasizes, the ego must be capable of resisting regression. In other words, the original instincts must be adequately neutralized before there can be a healthy ego.

This structural point of view is an improvement, at least as far as describing the question of health goes, over the historically earlier topographical perspective, which simply emphasized making an unconscious wish conscious. The earlier standpoint can err on the side of excessive rationalism. It can, for one thing, overlook the question of whether the ego has the capacity to deal with the wish that comes into consciousness, either by accepting or condemning it. For example, if the therapist neglects to take account of the integrative capacities of the patient's ego, he might be worse off thanks to his increase in pure knowledge. Furthermore, the conscious-unconscious dichotomy, when applied to the concept of health, tends to oppose the rational to the sick; this would neglect that we all have irrational trends in us which are entirely healthy. No conception of psychological normality will ever make sense which does not emphasize the importance of our access to primary emotional processes, our capacity for experiencing emotions in their full poignancy. Health must involve "increased closeness to reality together with capability of achieving distance from reality."[2]

The psychoanalytic picture of mental health is a far cry from its popularizations. It does not involve a utopian vision of personal happiness; anxiety and despair do not disappear. After all, only infants and psychotics are dominated by the pleasure principle. The largest number "of happy

[2] Eissler: "Notes Upon the Emotionality of a Schizophrenic Patient and Its Relation to Problems of Technique," p. 220.

and contented people are either in mental hospitals or in institutions for the mentally defective."[3] "Freud once made the remark in a small circle of his pupils that absolute happiness falls to the lot only of an absolute Narcissus, free from all dependencies."[4] Hartmann refers to a syndrome as "health-neuroses": "those afflicted by them cannot allow themselves to suffer or to feel ill or depressed." He goes on to insist that "a healthy person must have the capacity to suffer and be depressed."[5]

What psychoanalytic treatment can "conquer are only parts of psychogenesis: expressions of conflicts, developmental failures. We do not eliminate the original source of neurosis; we only help to achieve better ability to change neurotic frustrations into valid compensations."[6] Analysis can teach us where to compromise. As Freud put it in a letter, "One should not try to eradicate one's complexes, but come to terms with them. . . ."[7] Psychoanalytic treatment constitutes an intervention in the development of one's personality, but it can only help one to cure oneself. There is no mold toward which analytic patients should be pushed. In the end mental health is based on a harmonious equilibrium of mental forces.

Normality consists in the capacity to endure—to tolerate frustration, delay, ambiguity, separation, depression. This tough-minded stoicism comes close to the cosmic resignation of the ancients. "The beginning of all mental morbidity is cowardice before, and fear of, mental pain. . . .

[3] Brown: *Freud and the Post-Freudians*, p. 212.

[4] Deutsch: "Freud and His Pupils," p. 186.

[5] Heinz Hartmann: "Psychoanalysis and the Concept of Health," *International Journal of Psychoanalysis*, Vol. 20 (1939), p. 311.

[6] Helene Deutsch: "Psychoanalytic Therapy in the Light of Follow-Up," *Journal of the American Psychoanalytic Association*, Vol. 7, No. 3 (July 1959), p. 458.

[7] Quoted in Jones: *Sigmund Freud*, Vol. II, p. 452.

Whoever wants to remain mentally sound should stand a good deal of the pain of frustration, and of the despair created through the loss of an object, before he can begin to compensate for the loss and to master the pain."[8] These qualities of endurance become in Freud's terminology "reality acceptance." One of Freud's favorite sayings was "One must learn to bear some portion of uncertainty."[9] When once asked what he thought a normal person ought to be able to accomplish, Freud replied with the maxim: "to love and to work."[1]

## 5 Freedom as a Value

The main problem with the psychoanalytic concept of health is the difficulty in determining its logical status. Ever since the collapse of the medieval world view, there have been philosophers who have pointed out that all true propositions need not be logically harmonious.[1] The statements "X is a just course of action" and "X is an unjust course of action" do not contradict each other in the same way that the statements "X is a red cloth" and "X is a black cloth" do. In the latter case it is possible to set up standard procedures for determining the color of the cloth. In fact we reserve the category "color-blind" for those few who are systematically unable to determine differentiations in colors. In the former case, however, where the disagreement involves a question of value, there is in principle no similar

---

[8] Paul Federn: *Ego Psychology and the Psychoses* (New York: Basic Books; 1952), p. 278.

[9] Sachs: *Freud*, p. 145.

[1] Erikson: *Identity and the Life Cycle*, p. 96.

[1] Sir Isaiah Berlin: "Equality," *Proceedings of the Aristotelian Society, New Series*, Vol. 56 (1956), pp. 318–19.

way of settling the issue; "if one person says a thing is good and another person says the same thing is not good, then they are not contradicting each other."[2]

There are, to be sure, ways of engaging in moral arguments; it is possible to explore the facts of a course of action, as well as to make sure that each side is aware of the implications of his position. And it is possible to refer the issue to a general principle agreed upon by all sides. Yet it is still conceivable that at the end of the discussion each side will come away with a contrasting judgment. Although we may decide that one side is morally more correct than the other, and even better argued than the other, logically we cannot conclude that the disagreement has the same status as the question of the color of the cloth. In a moral argument each side can hold that its judgment is true for itself; there is in principle no independent way of resolving the dispute.

The distinction between the logic of questions of fact and value has engaged philosophers for centuries. This traditional preoccupation is relevant in this context because of the importance of the concept of health within psychoanalysis. To say that an act is immature or neurotic is to imply a standard of maturity or health. Yet both the latter concepts are obviously morally loaded; maturity or health seem desirable almost by definition, just as the category "murder" evokes a negative response within us. Whether or not positive or negative feelings are *universally* aroused by the invocation of such concepts, the danger is ever-present that we will smuggle a moral judgment into a discussion through the use of a logically ambiguous concept like health. It is always logically proper to ask whether health, or a healthy act, is also good. G. E. Moore was insistent on this point:

[2] A. H. Basson: *David Hume* (London: Penguin Books; 1958), p. 103.

"Is it so obvious that the normal must be good? Is it really obvious that health . . . is good? . . . It is . . . always an open question whether anything that is natural is good."[3] Margaret Macdonald expresses this tradition within English philosophy:

> . . . nature provides no standards or ideals. All that exists . . . is of the same logical type. There are not, by nature, prize roses, works of art, oppressed or unoppressed citizens. Standards are determined by human choice, not set by nature independently of men. Natural events cannot tell us what we ought to do until we have made certain decisions. . . .[4]

Even if we agree to the worthiness of developing human capacities, we are still left with the problem of choosing which potentialities to foster.

Fromm, however, takes a different view; he believes that "psychology . . . can . . . be the basis for building objective and valid norms of conduct."[5] Nor is there any ambiguity in what he means by "objective"; "what is good or bad for man is not a metaphysical question, but an empirical one that can be answered on the basis of an analysis of man's nature and the effect which certain conditions have on him."[6] Fromm sweeps aside the post-medieval in-

---

[3] G. E. Moore: *Principia Ethica* (Cambridge: The University Press; 1959), pp. 43–4.

[4] Laslett, ed.: *Philosophy, Politics, and Society*, p. 45. Hartmann has offered an explanation of the human source of the naturalistic fallacy. He points to "the psychological roots of the frequent incapacity to distinguish statements of fact from problems of moral validity. . . . In the early years . . . these demands are brought to bear on the child in a way that makes them incontrovertible and absolute . . . moral value judgments . . . are presented to the child in the form of statements of facts, as 'This is good' or 'This is bad,' 'You are good' or 'You are bad.'" *Psychoanalysis and Moral Values* (New York: International Universities Press; 1960), pp. 63–4.

[5] Erich Fromm: *Man for Himself* (New York: Holt; 1947), p. vii.

[6] Fromm: *The Sane Society*, p. 266.

sistence on the logical gulf between factual and normative statements, adopting a pre-modern position about the definitive hierarchy of values. He finds "an amazing agreement among all thinkers whose aim was the growth and happiness of man."[7] By amalgamating "the great teachings of all cultures,"[8] Fromm finds no incompatibility among morally true statements.

Freud was philosophically more sophisticated. Within his system, healthiness was

a purely conventional practical concept and has no real scientific meaning. It simply means that a person gets on well: it doesn't mean that the person is particularly worthy. There are "healthy" people who are not worth anything, and on the other hand "unhealthy" neurotic people who are very worthy individuals indeed.[9]

Not only did Freud not hold that all moral conflicts could be resolved by repairing to the standard of health; he specifically commented that the analytic process did not automatically provide the answers to moral conundrums.

Analysis makes for *unity*, but not necessarily for *goodness*. I do not agree with Socrates and Putnam that all our faults arise from confusion and ignorance. I think that too heavy a burden is laid on analysis when one asks of it that it should be able to realize every precious ideal.[1]

Among Freud's pupils the trend has been to emphasize that "there are many mutually contradictory values in the world, that the realization of one goes at the expense of another one, and that there is a point where the price paid for the

---

[7] Fromm: *Man for Himself*, p. 172.
[8] Fromm: *The Sane Society*, p. 69.
[9] Wortis: *Fragments of an Analysis with Freud*, p. 80.
[1] Quoted in Jones: *Sigmund Freud*, Vol. II, p. 182.

realization of one value is too great. . . ."[2] "We can urge health as one consideration, but certainly not as the only one, if we wish to prescribe for society."[3] And when prescribing, it is better to do so openly; Hartmann has warned against the "hidden preachers"[4] who smuggle in ethical prescriptions under the guise of scientific understanding.

While Freud was aware of the potential conflict between moral values, it is doubtful if he was fully conscious of the nature of his commitment to psychoanalysis. One can question whether the ideal of "unity" itself is the absolute positive value that Freud apparently assumes it is. Hermann Hesse's *Steppenwolf*, for example, has satirized the ideal as belonging to the narrow perspective of the bourgeois:

His ideal is not to give up but to maintain his identity. He strives neither for the saintly nor its opposite. The absolute is his abhorrence . . . his aim is to make a home for himself between two extremes in a temperate zone without violent storms and tempests. . . . A man can not live intensely except at the cost of the self. Now the bourgeois treasures nothing more highly than the self (rudimentary as this may be). And so at the cost of intensity he achieves his own preservation and security.[5]

Self-mastery can have restricting and narrowing results, as well as liberating ones.

One of Fromm's merits is that he has at least tried to develop the vision of human freedom that is implicit in psychoanalytic therapy. Characteristically, Freud merely alluded to the problem of freedom and psychoanalysis in a

[2] Waelder: "Characteristics of Totalitarianism," *The Psychoanalytic Study of Society*, Vol. 1, p. 20.

[3] Ernest van den Haag: "Psychoanalysis and the Social Sciences," in *Psychoanalysis and Social Science*, p. 184.

[4] Hartmann: *Psychoanalysis and Moral Values*, p. 23.

[5] H. Hesse: *Steppenwolf* (New York: Holt; 1963), p. 52.

footnote: "after all, analysis does not set out to make pathological reactions impossible, but to give the patient's ego
*freedom* to decide one way or the other."[6] It is not too unusual, within traditional political theory, to speak of hinder-
ing hindrances; usually, though, this refers to hindrances
external to the human personality. Freud, as we have already seen, focused on the problem of removing inner compulsions rather than external restraints. Although "man has
rid himself from old enemies of freedom," as Fromm has
expressed it, "new enemies of a different nature have arisen;
enemies which are not essentially external restraints, but
internal factors blocking the full realization of his personality."[7]

Linking freedom to self-development is bound to have
some disturbing overtones to any friend of liberty. Would
not such a concept of freedom justify authoritarian interferences in human privacy? Does it not entitle the psychoanalyst to meddle in almost any way for the sake of the
patient's own good? And how is the patient to determine
when his dependencies are being properly cultivated by the
therapist, and where his own judgment is being unfairly
violated? Although in fact the lines are very hard to draw,
theoretically, at least, whatever a therapist does is for the
sake of human autonomy; the ideal itself can set some limits
to what is done in practice.

A genuine interpretation is an act whereby the *quality of intel-
ligibility* is added to the patient's own statements and acts. *Sub-
stantive* additions are not interpretations, but an attack on the
patient's autonomy as a person. This view is compatible with
. . . [the] apt specification that the analyst must add no bricks

6 *Standard Edition*, Vol. 19, p. 50.
7 Fromm: *Escape From Freedom*, p. 104.

to the patient's psyche, but must merely rearrange those already present in an egosyntonic and functional manner.[8]

The role of therapeutic help should be familiar to us simply on the model of everyday life; each of us, as friend or spouse, helps and is helped in such ways. Before expecting a person to make an autonomous choice, we must consider whether he has the psychic capacity to exercise whatever external options he may have. The ability to choose rationally presupposes a high degree of psychological development; inner conflicts and regressive slides can leave anyone blocked and confused.

Self-mastery is an essential part of human freedom. This insight, along with the confidence that self-understanding leads to self-overcoming, has a lineage in intellectual history at least as ancient as Plato, and is best represented among modern thinkers by Rousseau.

Freedom . . . was for Rousseau not a matter of doing as one pleases, but of not being compelled, either from within or from without, to do what one does *not* wish to do. Inner compulsion is thus a most severe form of enslavement. . . . The history of man so far has been one of unrelenting self-deformation, and thus of inner conflict, insecurity, insincerity and disordered passions. Freedom lies precisely in avoiding these injuries to the self. Independence and inner strength mean the preservation of one's integral character.[9]

To the extent that authority could help prevent a person from injuring himself, Rousseau thought that men could

---

[8] George Devereux: "Some Criteria for the Timing of Confrontations and Interpretations," *International Journal of Psychoanalysis*, Vol. 32 (1951), pp. 20–1.

[9] Judith N. Shklar: "Rousseau's Images of Authority," *American Political Science Review*, Vol. 58 (December 1964), pp. 919–32.

be "forced" to be free. Likewise, unfulfilled inner possibilities create a feeling of oppression. As one psychoanalyst has recently put it, "the True Self is the theoretical position from which come the spontaneous gesture and the personal idea. . . . Only the True Self can be creative and only the True Self can feel real."[1]

As we have seen, in the analytic context the patient's increased self-knowledge "frees" him by releasing him from inner tyrannies and disharmonies. Self-knowledge also frees in another way; acceptance of one's own limitations is an important prerequisite for self-realization. A frequent callow reaction to Freud is dismay at the limits on human action implied by his findings—whether limits set by early childhood experiences or those imposed by the extent of our self-deceptions. For Americans, raised with the expectation of boundless possibilities, this has been an especially difficult problem. But surely it becomes possible for our spontaneity to flower only once we have recognized our limits, only once we are willing to accept certain boundaries. All limitations are not equally coercive; *some* rules are necessary to structure life in order to make self-realization possible.

It would be a mistake, however, not to confront directly the consequences of what Freud does have to say about determinism. When faced with the doctrine of "free will," Freud can only reply that "you nourish the illusion of there being such a thing as psychical freedom, and you will not give it up."[2] One of the curiosities of this "illusion" is that we feel it much more strongly about the trivial aspects of

[1] Donald Winnicott: *The Maturational Processes and the Facilitating Environment* (London: Hogarth Press; 1965), p. 148.
[2] *Standard Edition*, Vol. 15, p. 49.

life than the weighty; we are more likely to defend a slip or a joke as being without causal meaning than we would the choice of a career or a marriage partner. Freud promoted the search for causal meaning in all mental life, by means of the technique of free associations, and this emphasis lifted psychiatry out of its purely descriptive phase of the late nineteenth century.

Freud's determinism does not conflict, as some have thought, with his therapeutic goals. "To discover the cause of something is not to prove that it is inevitable. On the contrary the discovery of the cause of a disease is often the first step towards preventing it."[3] Causality, in the context of psychoanalysis, is a logical principle, not an empirical generalization. "The principle of causality is not, of course, strictly speaking a scientific law but rather a necessary assumption without which no science would be possible."[4]

A voluntary action does not mean an action without a cause. "When we say that . . . [a man] could have chosen not to perform a certain action, we mean that the man would have chosen not to perform it if certain conditions had been different."[5] Psychoanalytic therapy is founded on the notion that a person's awareness of the motives behind a potential action can influence the action itself; neurotic symptoms can in theory be dissolved once their component motives have been worked through.

Determinism does not say that causal factors of the distant past, nor even of the recent past, compel a certain neurotic course in an individual for the rest of his life . . . new forces and influences

---

[3] P. H. Nowell-Smith: *Ethics* (London: Penguin Books; 1954), p. 297.

[4] Brown: *Freud and the Post-Freudians*, p. 3.

[5] Mary Warnock: *Ethics Since 1900* (London: Oxford University Press; 1960), p. 145.

are always being added which have the possibility of altering the end product, and a scientific psychotherapy . . . becomes a new causal factor brought to bear on the sick patient.[6]

Behind all Freud's awareness of men's inner coercions, of the extent to which the conscious ego is merely the visible part of the iceberg, is an Enlightenment dream of freedom. Human freedom is superlatively a question of degree; it is not so much something that is there or not there, but that is present or absent to varying extents.

Still, if every psychic event has a cause, whether conscious, unconscious, or both, then one can legitimately raise the question of prediction. As Hartmann has pointed out, "prediction, or predictability, is in analysis not accidental but belongs to its essence . . . our technique is constantly based on such tentative predictions."[7] Freud thought that the fundamental obstacle to psychoanalytic prediction was the economic or quantitative factor. "Even supposing that we have a complete knowledge of the aetiological factors that decide a given result, nevertheless what we know about them is only their quality, and not their relative strength."[8] In fact, clinically the question of prediction remains a disturbing one.

Of course no prediction can be made in a vacuum; the initial conditions must be specified first. "The analyst can reasonably be asked to predict only a person's future behavior not as it will actually materialize under unknown conditions, but as it will be under *specific conditions*."[9] Assuming the initial conditions can be specified,

[6] Knight, in *Psychoanalytic Psychiatry and Psychology*, p. 378.

[7] Heinz Hartmann: "Discussion of Anna Freud's 'Child Observation and Prediction of Development' ", *Psychoanalytic Study of the Child*, Vol. 13, p. 121.

[8] *Standard Edition*, Vol. 18, p. 168.

[9] Robert Waelder: "Psychic Determinism and the Possibility of Predictions," *The Psychoanalytic Quarterly*, Vol. 32, No. 1 (January 1963), p. 30.

behavior can be predicted in either of the following extreme conditions: if it is wholly or predominantly determined by unconscious drives and primitive mechanisms, with little or no influence from reality factors . . . or, on the contrary, if behavior is wholly or predominantly determined by the requirements of the situation with little or no influence from other sources.[1]

Since most of life falls between those two extremes, psychoanalytic predictions have not been too successful.

For Freud, neither the assumed causality of events nor the possibilities of retrodiction or prediction denies the psychological ideal of the responsible human being. Any textbook on psychoanalytic technique could demonstrate the extent to which, far from absolving patients of responsibility for their acts, psychoanalysis entails an ever-widening sphere of accountability to oneself. "The patient must learn to renounce guidance and to settle his conflicts by himself."[2] Freud did not offer psychoanalytic doctrine as an alibi: according to Fenichel, analysts "demonstrate, whenever it is possible, that the patient in reality brings about things which he seems to experience passively."[3] Although "every human being's responsibility is limited, because no human act is performed under the full control of the conscious ego,"[4] Freud's central therapeutic intention was to extend the realm of that control, to make men more genuine masters of themselves.

[1] Waelder: "Psychoanalysis, Scientific Method, and Philosophy," p. 628.
[2] Fenichel: *Problems of Psychoanalytic Technique*, p. 93.
[3] Ibid., p. 35.
[4] Alexander and Staub: *The Criminal, the Judge, and the Public*, p. 85.

# Woodrow Wilson

One might have expected that in turning his great psychological and literary skills to writing the life of a contemporary, particularly in collaboration with a statesman who knew Wilson personally, Freud would have produced a model biography. If a man ever influenced modern history it was Wilson at Versailles. Yet the Freud-Bullitt biography is a disappointingly bad one, so much so that our task should be to seek out some of the sources of Freud's mistakes, in the hope that we can learn more about the pitfalls of such undertakings. To study past errors in order better to master the future is after all in the best tradition of Freud himself.

The publication of the book in 1967 created the literary sensation that the event deserved. The Wilson biography has had over the years an underground reputation. A handful of Freud's pupils who were close to him in the early thirties knew of the book's existence; and the rest of us with an interest in personality theory and social science read about it in Jones's brief references in the third volume of his biography of Freud. This study of Wilson has always been a ghostly presence hovering over anyone working in the field. The main problem, now that it has finally come to life, is to determine what lessons it can teach us about the use of psychoanalysis in history.

One might think that the publicity over the Wilson book would ensure that it could never suffer the fate of Freud's study of Moses. One would like to think that this was so startlingly bad a book that critics would have to sit down and find out why it was such a mechanistic application of psychoanalytic concepts to the life of one of America's great men. Yet by a curious twist of circumstances, the book seems about to be consigned to a limbo not unlike that surrounding *Moses and Monotheism*. Whereas psychoanalysts have generally ignored all the problems that lay behind Freud's treatment of the Moses theme, they feel justified in dismissing the Wilson book altogether by maintaining that Freud had very little hand in it at all.[1] As one perceptive writer has pointed out, the anguished psychoanalysts have "greeted this posthumous work of the Master as if it were something between a forged First Folio and the Protocols of Zion."[2]

It is true that the facts surrounding the publication of this book by Freud and Bullitt have cast a cloud over the authenticity of the text. Before proceeding to discuss the book we must first settle whether it was partly written by

[1] Erik Erikson: "The Strange Case of Freud, Bullitt, and Woodrow Wilson: A Dubious Collaboration," *The New York Review of Books* (Ferbuary 9, 1967), p. 4.

[2] Barbara Tuchman: "Can History Use Freud?" *The Atlantic* (February 1967), p. 40.

Freud at all. All the reasons for the long delay in the appearance of this volume have not been explained, and with Bullitt's subsequent death we may never be certain of the story. It seems at least possible that Bullitt set about publishing this manuscript because of his declining health; he could have known that the text would be edited by someone for the Freud family if it came out after his own death. One published reason for the long delay was the second Mrs. Wilson's longevity. But one might have thought that her death in 1961, if she was the bar to publication, would have moved Bullitt to permit the book's appearance then. It would be surprising, but perhaps contradictory enough to be psychologically plausible, for a man of Bullitt's dubious reputation to be so straight-laced as to worry about Mrs. Wilson's feelings for her dead husband.

There were certainly at least several other reasons in the 1930's for not publishing the book then and there. Bullitt had his political career, Wilson was still a hero to his party, and the issue of the League of Nations still survived if only in the rhetoric of public men. It is also likely that Bullitt might have objected to making publicly known his collaboration with Freud. Every patient has a right to the privacy of his relationship to his analyst, and one can respect any impulse on Bullitt's part to restrict the knowledge of his own involvement in therapy, as well as that of his immediate family.

In addition to these difficulties surrounding the publication of the book when it was first written, Bullitt reported that the co-authors were for a time in disagreement over some parts of the manuscript. Bullitt himself did a great disservice to the cause of the book's authenticity by his secrecy regarding exactly which points Freud and he were at odds over. Furthermore, Bullitt claimed to have lost the original manuscripts in Freud's own hand, and to have forgotten the name of the old private secretary in Vienna who translated the book from Freud's difficult handwriting. None of the drafts seems to have survived. Since anything Freud wrote had great emotional meaning to those around him, and a historical if not yet a monetary value, it is a bit hard to believe that so much should have disappeared so completely. The changes Bullitt exacted from Freud, and which Bullitt refused to discuss publicly afterwards, were made not only in the last months of Freud's life, but also after Freud was immensely indebted to Bullitt for his help in rescuing the Freud family from the Nazis.

The style of the book is indeed appalling, and to the extent that style makes the man, this is not a work of Freud's. Freud's sentences were always packed with meaning and colored by many shades of significance. Above all the brutal quality of the Wilson book, the monotonous and cold treatment of a human life, leaves one with the conviction that it did not come from Freud's own hand. According to Freud's daughter Anna, the ideas were given by her father to Bullitt, but the manner of application and the style were Bullitt's own.

But Freud cannot be absolved of any responsibility for this work. We must ask which of Freud's ideas proved so misleading to Bullitt, what there was in the psychoanalytic thinking of that time to lend support to such a study. It must be said on Bullitt's behalf that many of the themes in the study of Wilson were very important in Freud's own life. It is possible in fact that a very clumsy translation might be partly responsible for the questionable-looking manuscript we now see. Freud's own command of written English was at best imperfect. Although Bullitt claimed[3]

---

[3] Letter from Bullitt to Jones, July 22, 1955 (Jones Archives).

that the two of them debated the book sentence by sentence, one wonders how interested Freud would have been in checking over the translations that Bullitt had prepared for him. But no collaborative effort by any two writers can be expected to retain the distinctive style of one of them.

When Ernest Jones first read the manuscript in the United States in the spring of 1956, although he considered it a poor book he never contested the authenticity of Freud's collaboration with Bullitt.[4] As he wrote somewhat later, "Although a joint work, it is not hard to distinguish the analytic contributions of the one author from the political contributions of the other."[5] In July of 1965, as soon as Bullitt had consented to the publication of the manuscript, Dr. Kurt Eissler—as head of the Freud Archives—brought the good news to the International Congress of psychoanalysts: "Due to the activities of Dr. Schur . . . one manuscript which has been missing from the Standard Edition—namely, Freud's manuscript which was written in cooperation with Mr. Bullen [sic] about President Wilson—has now been given free and has been studied. I hear that it is a very exciting manuscript and probably will be published within a year or so."[6] At that time the Freud family hoped that Bullitt would permit the manuscript to be edited. Even though Bullitt would not permit any changes in the manuscript, the Freud family did not refuse to accept its share of the royalties.

Freud's own view of his part in writing the book should go far to settle the matter. With the exception of the digest of data on Wilson's childhood and youth, which Bullitt prepared by himself, Freud acknowledged his full responsibil-

---

[4] Letter from Jones to Bullitt, June 7, 1956 (Jones Archives).

[5] Jones: *Sigmund Freud*, Vol. III, p. 151.

[6] *International Journal of Psychoanalysis*, Vol. 47, Part I (1966), p. 98.

ity: "For the analytic part we are both equally responsible; it has been written by us working together."[7] Freud's generosity in letting Bullitt decide the time of publication seems entirely in character. It can, however, be guessed that Freud resented the secretiveness which Bullitt imposed on the whole enterprise. Freud once wanted to speak with one of his favorite pupils about the book; Ernst Kris explained later to Jones that

when the final typescript of the Wilson manuscript was submitted to Freud, he wanted me to read it and I was to come, as usually, on a Sunday afternoon and to read the paper in his waiting room. When I arrived Freud said that Mr. Bullitt had a few hours ago requested the return of the "volume" and Freud could not think of a valid reason for retaining it. He commented on this occasion on Bullitt's secretiveness, mentioned that the material was not to be published as long as a Democratic administration was in office, and made a few, very general remarks on the content of his own contribution.[8]

While one might have expected that Freud would have turned to one of the members of his own family for advice, his daughter Anna for example, in this instance at any rate he felt closest to his pupils.[9] Bullitt, on his part, showed the manuscript in 1930 and 1932 to relatives of his; the manuscript was apparently completed at that stage, with the exception of an additional chapter which Freud wanted to add, but which Bullitt was finally able to persuade Freud to drop during a trip to London shortly before Freud's death.

It may seem a bit hard to understand that Freud should

[7] Sigmund Freud and William C. Bullitt: *Thomas Woodrow Wilson* (Boston: Houghton Mifflin; 1967), p. xiv.

[8] Letter from Ernst Kris to Ernest Jones, September 24, 1955 (Jones Archives).

[9] Freud gave or sent a few pages of the manuscript to Ruth Mack Brunswick, another of his favorite pupils.

have relied on Bullitt so heavily, both to provide the basic
research for the book and to dispose of the final manuscript. Yet it is easy to document just how naïve Freud
could be about contemporary political events. He never
seems to have understood the rise of Nazism and the threat
it posed to himself, his family, and his students; he is reported to have said before Hitler came to power, "A nation that produced Goethe could not possibly go to the
bad."[1] Like many others he resorted to wishful thinking in
order to convince himself that it was unnecessary to leave
Vienna.

It is perfectly true that in his state of health it was
no rosy prospect to think of leaving what had been for so
many years his home, to go to a land where the doctors
would be unfamiliar with his case. And those of us who
merely have the task of guessing the outcome of the next
election can underestimate the problem of speculating about
as revolutionary a development as the rise of Hitler. Nevertheless, Freud's gullibility about political life needs no elaborate supporting evidence. There is all the more reason,
therefore, to suspect that Freud's aversion to Wilson had
mainly emotional causes, and was not the conviction of a
seasoned student of world affairs. Nor was Freud cautious
as a historian; in a letter to Thomas Mann, he explained
Napoleon's expedition to Egypt in terms of his identification with his brother Joseph.[2] It is fortunate that this poetic
fancy was never blown up into a book.

It is easy to understand why Bullitt would be an attractive figure to Freud. Bullitt was a success in the world of
public affairs in which Freud was such an innocent, and
Freud might have admired him excessively because of this

[1] Jones: *Sigmund Freud*, Vol. III, p. 151.
[2] Freud: *Letters*, pp. 428–30.

gulf between their respective talents. Freud was frequently attracted to people who were brilliant and adventurous but unstable. He often let himself be taken in by fascinating personalities who were less well-organized and upright than himself. Bullitt came to Vienna, moreover, at a period when Freud was treating a number of other very rich Americans. Bullitt had social status and international political connections. While Freud scorned to pursue his own life for worldly purposes, he had a certain admiration for such success.

What Bullitt has recounted of Freud's self-doubts about his own work, and his reason for collaborating on the Wilson study in the first place, fit the rest of the evidence about Freud at this point in his life. Bullitt says that Freud was "depressed" about his work, "because he had written everything he wished to write and his mind was emptied. . . . To collaborate with me would compel him to start writing again. That would give him new life."[3] We have seen earlier that Freud's last years were not his most creative as a psychologist, and that his human capacities were being eroded by his illness and age. As Freud wrote in 1929 in a letter about his study of Dostoevsky, "I always write reluctantly nowadays."[4]

Turning to the book itself, it is all too easy to summarize the argument, since the central points are repeated with so little variation. Wilson suffered from a passive relationship to his father, and spent most of his life trying to cope with this early tie. In some instances Wilson overcompensated his dependent need for a strong father by excessive verbal combativeness; in other instances he retreated much too readily in the face of external pressure. An interesting ex-

[3] Freud and Bullitt: *Thomas Woodrow Wilson*, pp. v–vi.
[4] *Standard Edition*, Vol. 21, p. 195.

planation for Wilson's conduct which emerges from this analysis, although it is reiterated a bit woodenly, is the suggestion that one means of Wilson's handling his passivity to his father was to have young men unquestioningly dependent on him. Thus, for example, "by identifying himself with his father and House with himself, he was able to recreate in his unconscious his own relationship to his own 'incomparable father,' and, in the person of House, to receive from himself the love he wanted and could no longer get from his own father."[5]

With some such exceptions, the book rings with such a curiously old-fashioned language that it has the air of a genuine psychoanalytic antique. There is Freud's own literalistic belief in the existence of fixed quantities of libido to be disposed of. The starkness of the argument and the cheap quality of the interpretations offered have disturbed many readers. What are suggested as explanations of human motivation may be in part true, yet the actions they are supposed to explain can often also be traced to something else entirely. Different situations can mobilize very different qualities in a person. Wilson emerges as a robot, divided up into neat little spheres, with his masculinity in one place and his femininity in another. The true psychologist knows that such sharp lines of demarcation are a ridiculous approach to understanding a person; a human being cannot be described as if he were composed of a set of boxes, with each of his complexes securely isolated. In psychology it is the inbetweens which are important.

Whatever Freud says in his Introduction about the category of normal-pathological being inadequate, in the book itself almost no attempt is made to place the pathological

---

[5] Freud and Bullitt: *Thomas Woodrow Wilson*, p. 214.

material in the perspective of a personality which was functional. The authors write as if psychoanalysis were only about other people. Wilson is scarcely the only one of us to believe in his own immortality; psychoanalysis has taught us that at some level of our unconscious we all believe we are God. The book claims to have uncovered "the neurosis which controlled . . . [Wilson's] life,"[6] and is so reckless as to describe Wilson near his death as "very close to psychosis."[7] What has been omitted, of course, are all Wilson's achievements, either as a great teacher, a legislative and administrative leader, or a molder of world opinion. The whole man is not discussed here.

Equally damaging is the lack of research into the social context in which Wilson grew up. One would have to establish very securely what the social conventions of the Reconstruction South were before one could claim to have understood what was idiosyncratic in what Wilson said or wrote. On the other hand, we should resist the temptation to judge this book in terms of current knowledge about Wilson's life. It is hard, for example, to put out of mind all the recent evidence about Wilson's boyhood. To make matters more complicated, this study relied on sources which are no longer considered trustworthy. Historical perspective is necessary to the understanding of Wilson's life, as well as psychological studies about that life.

This particular study, though, seems too crude in relating hypotheses about inner psychic states to political events themselves. For example, the book argues that the "*Lusitania* note gave release to his hostility to his father, the supplementary instruction to his passivity to his father."[8]

[6] Ibid., p. 285.
[7] Ibid., p. 289.
[8] Ibid., p. 169.

While it may be legitimate to speculate about the positive
and negative elements of the oedipal tie in a political leader,
and the place these feelings might have in the structure of
his personality as a whole, it is obviously improper to trace
specific political acts so grossly to such relatively inaccessi-
ble and deeply imbedded portions of a character structure.
Moreover, there were more sources of Wilson's public failures than his own private limitations.

Although this book does not paint a picture as internally
consistent and convincing as Freud's own study of Leonardo (which though it errs at least does so with artistry),
it would be mistaken to underplay Freud's own involvement in the figure of Wilson as well as in specific interpretations of his life. It was axiomatic among Freud's pupils
that he hated Wilson. According to Jones, when he visited
Freud after World War I Freud had "hard things to say
about President Wilson. . . ."[9] When Keynes' book on the
peace treaty came out, Freud's feelings about Wilson were
well enough known among his students for James Strachey
to have lent him a copy. In *Group Psychology and the
Analysis of the Ego,* Freud referred to the "fantastic promises of the American President's Fourteen Points."[1] In the
Wilson book Freud himself acknowledged the "antipathy"
he felt for Wilson. As a patient close to Freud and his family remarked, "Bullitt and Freud fell in love at first sight
on the basis of their hatred of Wilson."[2] Allen Dulles perceptively pointed out that each of the authors "appears . . .
to be a man bitter towards Woodrow Wilson and, as over
long years they worked together on this book . . . un-

[9] Jones: *Sigmund Freud,* Vol. III, p. 16.
[1] *Standard Edition,* Vol. 18, p. 95.
[2] Interview with Mark Brunswick, January 25, 1966.

doubtedly the bitterness of the one played on that of the other. . . ."[3]

Now Freud was of course an Austrian, and Wilson had helped break up the Empire. It was not so much Freud's patriotism, which did not go very deep, that was affronted, as his image of himself as above all national ties; Wilson, as the apostle of nationalism, clashed with Freud's own attempt to surmount his Jewish identity. It may also be significant that after Versailles Vienna was wrecked economically. Moreover, Wilson had stood for the hope of all liberals, and his failure at Versailles demonstrated the inadequacy of liberal moralism in international relations. A whole generation of liberals, and not just Freud, hated Wilson as the political leader who proved the hollowness of some of their own most cherished ideals.

But there were yet more personal reasons for Freud's emotional involvement in Wilson, and even if some large-scale socio-economic causes might support Freud's hatred of Wilson, it should be worth while to trace out their effects in Freud's thought. Bullitt has provided us with a crucial clue: Freud "had been interested in Wilson ever since he had discovered that they were both born in 1856."[4] Anyone who has studied Freud's life with care would spot such an identification as characteristic. In *The Interpretations of Dreams*, Freud recalls

sticking labels on the flat backs of my wooden soldiers with the names of Napoleon's marshals written on them. And at that time my declared favourite was already Masséna (or to give the name its Jewish form, Manasseh). (No doubt this preference was also

---

3 Allen Dulles: "A Foreign Affairs Scholar Views the Real Woodrow Wilson," *Look* (December 13, 1966), p. 50.

4 Freud and Bullitt: *Thomas Woodrow Wilson*, p. vi.

partly to be explained by the fact that my birthday fell on the same day as his, exactly a hundred years later.)[5]

It need not be surprising that there was an identificatory tie between Freud and Wilson if we assume that there must be some such explanation for the empathy which any psychological study presupposes. Indeed, one's own personality should enter into a psychological study. Yet self-awareness checks the confidence with which one advances propositions. In the case of Moses, Freud used him as a projective screen, and although Freud was only partially aware of the meaning the figure Moses had for him, he recognized the study as so much his own creation that he spoke about it as a novel. In the instance of the Wilson study, however, Bullitt's whole interest in Wilson may have given Freud too much support for the notion that their study was an objective one. Apparently neither Bullitt nor Freud ever guessed that this study was in any way autobiographical on Freud's part.[6]

We can take, for example, the book's emphasis on Wilson's pleasures connected with his mouth, especially his talent for rhetoric. Freud himself smoked constantly, and, perhaps more relevant here, he too had once been a great orator. But it was no longer possible for him to speak easily in public—not after his cancer of the jaw. We found this same link, Freud's difficulties in speaking in his last years, behind his identification with the Moses legend. Furthermore, what Freud and Bullitt say of Wilson's relationships to women sounds very much like Freud's own experience. Freud had trouble holding on to his best male pupils, and found the inferior ones boring; so increasingly he used women around him as an audience for his ideas. One of

[5] *Standard Edition*, Vol. IV, pp. 197–8.
[6] Telephone conversation with Bullitt, October 15, 1966.

Freud's pupils once counted seven women surrounding Freud at a concert in Vienna; they were the ladies in waiting in Freud's court. In addition to these bases for identification which Freud found in Wilson's life, there is the obvious fact that Freud too had once had ambitions to be a political leader. It had also been one of his mother's dreams for him. Freud was a man with a mission, like Wilson; when the Nazis drove him from Vienna, he was feeble and ill, yet during the night journey from Paris to London he dreamed that he was landing at Pevensey. As Freud explained to one of his sons, Pevensey was the place where William the Conqueror had landed in 1066.[7]

There are other themes about Wilson in the Freud-Bullitt book which remind one of Freud's own experience and personality. Both had one-track minds, both grew up surrounded by sisters, both worked without a secretary, both were invalids, and both lived in relative isolation. But the point made about Wilson which is most strikingly relevant to Freud himself is the whole treatment of the theme of betrayal and persecution. It was Freud himself, and not just Wilson, who was among the world's great haters. Both Wilson and Freud were fighters who never forgave their opponents. The Freud-Bullitt book reports that Wilson would not speak with one of his associates after breaking with him, and that when another of his former friends, Hibben, came to pay his respects after their falling out, "Wilson looked at him, turned on his heel and walked away."[8] In Freud's life, he had once had great admiration for Breuer, but for a variety of reasons this developed into an intense loathing. Years after their quarrel, when Breuer was an old man walking in Vienna with his daughter-in-law, he spotted

7 Jones: *Sigmund Freud*, Vol. III, p. 228.
8 Freud and Bullitt: *Thomas Woodrow Wilson*, p. 124.

Freud "coming head on towards him. Instinctively, he
opened his arms. Freud passed professing not to see him."[9]
Others have reported this same experience with Freud.[1]

The controversies in Freud's life centered so often on the
father-son theme. Freud had to become a father, to escape
being a son; to be bested always meant to be put back into
the role of a son. The motivation that Freud and Bullitt see
in Wilson's need for younger disciples fits Freud's own life
perfectly. It was Freud who felt he had all those defecting
pupils; it was he whose high expectations and hopes ended
so often in disappointment. As Freud and Bullitt say in the
Wilson book, "He who disappoints a hope betrays a hope."[2]

The student of Freud's life, once he begins to look in
Freud's studies of Moses and Leonardo for autobiographical
hints, is bound to conclude that the Wilson study also is cut
to fit Freud himself. Allen Dulles sees Bullitt in the book,
so it may well be a matter of knowledgeability whose hand
one can spot first. "Bullitt is a man who espoused causes
and individuals and then turned from them abruptly and
with real passion. In fact, he had certain of the characteristics that he imputes to Wilson."[3] Certainly Bullitt double-
crossed people to gain his own ends. He had once idolized
Wilson, and after their disagreement at Versailles he returned to America and betrayed Wilson; he went before
the Senate Foreign Relations Committee and aired all the
skepticism that Wilson's Secretary of State had felt about
the Treaty of Versailles, as well as the hesitations of other
members of Wilson's administration.

---

[9] Letter from Hanna Breuer to Jones, April 21, 1954 (Jones Archives).

[1] For example, in exactly this same way Freud never forgave Paul Klemperer
for leaving the Vienna Psychoanalytic Society at the time of Adler.

[2] Freud and Bullitt: *Thomas Woodrow Wilson*, p. 215.

[3] Dulles: "A Foreign Affairs Scholar Views the Real Woodrow Wilson," p. 50.

We will probably never know very much about what went on between Freud and Bullitt, or whether or not the emotions that were awakened and utilized in treatment became distorting influences on the Wilson book itself. It seems to have been welcome to Freud to have such a projection of his worst self in Wilson, without being identified. And what Bullitt saw in Wilson may have been what Freud meant to Bullitt. It must have been partly Bullitt who unconsciously saw identities between Wilson and Freud. Through a heavy-handed use of Freud's ideas, by cooperating in projecting some of Freud's least attractive features on the man Wilson, Bullitt may have been settling some scores against Freud himself. As in the discussion of *Moses and Monotheism*, unraveling the sources of these themes can lead to dark and murky territory.

Freud's hatred of Wilson can be further traced to quite an obvious source, which is that Wilson was an American. The issue of Freud's feelings toward America has come up already; we alluded earlier to his set of negative opinions about America. Wilson stood for all that pious provincialism which Freud saw in America, "God's own country." It may be a long time before we know the worst of what Freud had to say about America, since for the sake of the psychoanalytic movement in America some of his comments have been deliberately censored from his letters.[4]

Although he tolerated individual Americans, he expected that American psychoanalysts would someday repudiate his work.[5] In retaliation, he had some devastating wishes for America. As he is reported to have said of Americans, "This race is sentenced to disappear from the face of the earth. They can no longer open their mouths to speak; soon they

4 Letter from Anna Freud to Jones, March 4, 1957 (Jones Archives).
5 Interview with Dr. Irmarita Putnam, June 30, 1966.

will also not be able to do so to eat, and they will die of starvation." Whatever the normal irritations of a psycho-analyst forced to listen to his patients mumbling in a foreign tongue, when we know how Freud suffered from his cancer, how it interfered with his speaking, and how endangered by starvation from his illness he really was, then we must conclude that there was a good deal of projection behind his whole animosity toward America in the first place.

One of the most psychologically crude judgments to be found in this book is the very arbitrary distinction between masculinity and femininity. It is reiterated *ad nauseum* that Wilson never had a fist fight in his life. This is almost as if Freud were parodying Americans, who in popular mythology have amalgamated cowboyism and manliness. Freud's attitude toward women, despite the fact that he was surrounded by them toward the end of his life, was slightly patronizing. He was a loyal and devoted admirer of his female pupils, yet showed more than an undercurrent of devaluation toward their sex. Perhaps it was his shyness with women which held him back from understanding them; but he had disdain for dependencies and passivity, qualities associated in our culture with femininity. On the one hand he was sufficiently at ease with his "femininity" to be able to be preoccupied with the inner life. Yet one always wonders whether he could be at peace with the disorganized, the maternal, or the infantile.

Freud was a stranger to music, the food of love. As he once wrote, "with music . . . I am almost incapable of obtaining any pleasure. Some rationalistic, or perhaps analytic, turn of mind in me rebels against being moved by a thing without knowing why I am thus affected and what it is that affects me thus."[6] Interestingly enough, Freud could be fond of operas, where there are words (and dramatic interest). Throughout his psychology Freud was always more interested in the magic of words than in the magic of nonverbal means of communication. The very method of treatment he evolved clearly demonstrates his rationalistic trend. None of this should be taken as a denial that Freud's self-analysis went very far; if he had been able to go further with it, he would not have been the same man who was able to make the original discoveries.

We have already seen the degree to which Freud was baffled by religion as a positive phenomenon; its fearful, and not its loving aspects, were uppermost in his mind. Wilson's religiosity, his involvement with what Freud considered the worst of the "illusions of religion," contributed to Freud's aversion. Beside all his struggling with the notion of God, there was in Freud an intense need to believe in something beyond himself. What we find in the Wilson book is, as Erikson has pointed out, a "Moses-like indignation at all false 'Christian' prophecy."[7]

Once we authenticate certain themes within the Wilson book as Freud's own, we have the obligation to consider more fully the ways in which the book fails so. We have in the Wilson study—particularly when viewed in the light of his other biographical reconstructions—another opportunity to see some of the limitations of Freud's psychology. Freud is great enough to withstand the closest scrutiny. These books are important for us precisely because they are not Freud at his best; as long as one understands that Freud

---

[6] *Standard Edition*, Vol. 13, p. 211.

[7] Erikson: "The Strange Case of Freud, Bullitt, and Woodrow Wilson," p. 3.

is at his worst here, and then proceeds in that spirit, one
can learn to avoid his particular mistakes, and those which
his formulations might lead one to commit.

When using the older psychoanalytic propositions, there
is always the danger that no one will end up looking very
good under a psychoanalytic microscope. Freud studied the
Moses legend as if it were a patient. Once Freud was a
historical legend himself, the patients who could help him
in self-understanding had to be historical figures as well.
Freud's tendency in his Leonardo study was to treat the
master's paintings as if they were the fantasies of a patient. Psychoanalytic dissection of this kind will tend to
expose the repressed and the infantile, and it is not surprising if it results in the depreciation of its subjects.

For patients in treatment, there is at least the justification
that their pathological difficulties are quite properly the
focus of attention. But there is less justification for looking
at the abnormal in studying historical figures. With an integrated and functioning person, furthermore, pathological
interferences can be stored away and hard to get at. But
even with patients there was a danger of negativism in the
earlier psychoanalytic approach. One can learn things in a
fractional way, but the trouble with the pre-ego psychological approach was that the synthetic aspect of the psychoanalytic task was too often overlooked. And this artistry
of course is exactly what is missing from this study of Wilson. There is no discussion of what his strengths were like,
what the qualities were that got him to the Presidency in
the first place. Bullitt's researches seem to have been confined only to those people who had nothing good to say
for Wilson at all.

But one does see in the Wilson study, and this is worth
remembering, evidence of how radical and revolutionary

Freud was. The tendency has been to try to house-break Freud, to fit him into conventional wisdom; yet he keeps defying every attempt to conservatize his work. What is so annoying about the use of Freud in contemporary psychiatry is the way in which he is invoked to justify the *status quo*. No one seems very eager to identify with the Freud who ignored everything that had been said and written before, who dared to try to understand what had previously been considered utterly meaningless. Freud wrote and thought shocking things; it is well to remember that he was anti-establishment to the last.

There are some specific points in the Wilson book which can teach us what to avoid. First of all, there are too many psychological "formulas." No human being can be frozen into a formula, or at least this is possible only on a very deep level of personality; but in this instance not enough material was available to Freud and Bullitt to justify the kind of conclusions they drew. Furthermore, the notion that empathy for others is based on self-understanding is true, but not quite enough; this analysis of Wilson in absentia is based on the premise that if one understands oneself one can understand other people. But when it comes to trying to understand people whose characters seem incomprehensible or repugnant to us, then this whole notion can encourage brutality and ruthlessness; such people seem so strange to us, and yet none of the usual restraints of scholarship are there to contain what one feels entitled to maintain.

Finally, the Wilson book exemplifies all the dangers of artificial collaboration between students of different disciplines; to be used in social research, psychoanalysis has to be thoroughly digested. The kind of psychiatric name-calling we see in the Wilson book is still going on. Above all,

perhaps the greatest danger in using psychodynamic knowledge of any kind is the illusion of grandiosity. And this
book on Wilson reminds us that Freud himself was not
immune to the temptations of others. As Freud wrote
grandly a few years before his death:

I perceived ever more clearly that the events of human history,
the interactions between human nature, cultural development
and the precipitates of premaeval experience (the most prominent
of which is religion) are no more than a reflection of the dynamic
conflicts between the ego, the id and the super-ego, which psychoanalysis studies in the individual—are the very same processes repeated upon a wider stage.[8]

Had Freud shown greater humility in the face of mass phenomena, had he acknowledged that they cannot be understood on the simple analogies of mental conflict, the Wilson
fiasco would have been impossible.

It seems unfortunate to have to end with a discussion of
Freud's treatment of Wilson, yet it is perhaps appropriate.
This book has been as much about what the relation between Freud and political and social thought should not
be, as about what that relation can be. We are still at a fairly
early stage of understanding the implications of unconscious
mental forces. What has been attempted here is a clarification of Freud's contribution to our understanding of man
in society, in order to leave the way open for the future.

One of the central themes of this book has been the
distinction between the manifest and the latent contributions which Freud's ideas can offer. Whatever Freud's own
applications of psychoanalytic concepts to social theory,
clinical psychoanalysis has had a life of its own. While

[8] *Standard Edition*, Vol. 20, p. 72.

there is a haphazard quality to the social subjects Freud chose to write about, even though we have tried to trace their roots in his personal make-up, his clinical works have greater objective coherence. In terms of the historical development of Freud's ideas, there was a significant difference between his systematic elaboration of clinical theories and his casual social applications of psychoanalysis. One of the most striking aspects of the evolution of his strictly psychoanalytic thought is that it possessed a self-generating quality; the growth of the structural point of view, for example, was related in an integral way to Freud's previous doctrines. There was an inner coherence as Freud introduced each new set of concepts. He would move from his earlier position in order to arrive at a more elaborate explanation of clinical material. It is this inner connection within Freud's clinical thought which makes it possible, in retrospect, to structure psychoanalysis into a coherent system.

This distinction between Freud's clinical contributions and his social theory, between the inner momentum of his great discoveries and the *ad hoc* quality of his social applications, helps to explain why it has been possible for psychiatry since Freud to move ahead. Freud left a body of work which was sufficiently outside his own personality for others to work with and improve on. Although contemporary American psychiatry would be inconceivable without Freud, there are certain aspects of Freud's own interpretations which now seem obviously out of date scientifically. It need not be a criticism of Freud to point out that psychoanalysis has developed since his death; he was great enough to have set going a process which was capable of many self-corrections.

The Georges' book on Wilson and House[9] has merits which the master's own study lacks; and the explanation for this is not that the genius of Freud has been over-rated, but rather that Freud's own impetus to clinical understanding has permitted others to go beyond him. To read the Ray Stannard Baker biography of Wilson (which came out in the 1920's) is to realize how far away is the era when one could treat the childhood and youth of a man without some notion of depth psychology. If biographies are now inevitably more subtle on such issues, the credit belongs largely to Freud, even though in the short run he did little himself to extend the psychological understanding of historical figures.

To the extent that the study of the relation between Freud and political and social thought is helpful, it should be liberating. A great model can free our energies and aspirations, which is no doubt one reason why greatness is so fascinating. The study of a great figure in intellectual history inevitably raises many issues which it would be very easy to side-step when discussing a minor thinker. Genius has the aura of limitlessness, it is like a crystal which refracts at different angles, offering us an unlimited mirror for self-understanding. The study of genius can come close to being the study of man.

[9] Alexander L. and Juliette L. George: *President Wilson and Colonel House* (New York: Dover; 1956).

*Index*

*A NOTE ABOUT THE AUTHOR*

✳

*PAUL ROAZEN was born in Boston, Massachusetts, in 1936. He attended the Brookline public schools and Harvard University, from which he received his A.B. in 1958 and his Ph.D. in 1965. He also did graduate work at the University of Chicago and Magdalen College, Oxford. Since 1961 he has been teaching political theory at Harvard, in the Government Department, and is also the author of* Brother Animal: The Story of Freud and Tausk *(1969). Mr. Roazen is married and lives in Cambridge, Massachusetts.*

# VINTAGE WORKS OF SCIENCE
## AND PSYCHOLOGY

*A free catalogue of* VINTAGE BOOKS *will be sent at your request. Write to* Vintage Books, 457 Madison Avenue, New York, New York 10022.

# VINTAGE HISTORY AND CRITICISM OF
## LITERATURE, MUSIC, AND ART

*A free catalogue of* VINTAGE BOOKS *will be sent at your request. Write to* Vintage Books, 457 Madison Avenue, New York, New York 10022.